The History of Rutherglen
and East Kilbride

The History of Rutherglen and East Kilbride, 1793

Published with a view to promote the Study of Antiquity and Natural History

by

David Ure, A.M.,

Preacher of the Gospel,
Corresponding Member of the Natural History
Society of Edinburgh

Glasgow
The Grimsay Press
2003

The Grimsay Press
an imprint of
Zeticula
57 St Vincent Crescent
Glasgow
G3 8NQ

http://www.thegrimsaypress.co.uk
admin@thegrimsaypress.co.uk

Transferred to digital printing in 2003

Copyright © Zeticula 2003

First published in Great Britain in 1793

ISBN 0 902664 76 X

Reproduced from the copy in the Library of the University of Paisley, Scotland

All rights reserved. No part of this publication may be reproduced, stored in a retrieval system, or transmitted in any form or by any means, electronic, mechanical, photocopying, recording or otherwise, without the prior permission of the publishers.

PREFACE.

THE progress of the arts and sciences is greatly accelerated by the history of antiquity and of nature. An extensive acquaintance with the customs and manners of ancient times is of the same advantage to useful improvements, as the instructions dictated by a judicious experience are to the art of conducting our lives with wisdom and prudence. A retrospective view, in both cases, furnishes the means of preventing many hurtful mistakes that would otherwise be committed. The history of nature, equally with that of antiquity, lends her assistance to the useful arts. The better we are acquainted with the objects of natural history, the more able we shall be to apply these objects, with success, to the various pursuits of life. Besides, by accurate researches into what is past, and by candid inquiries into the nature and properties of present objects, a wide field of useful contemplation is opened to the mind.

SENSIBLE of these advantages, not a few of mankind are keenly engaged in the pleasing study of nature. A sufficient knowledge of that extensive science cannot easily be obtained, without the assistance of a considerable collection of the various objects of which it treats. To procure these, every part of the world is diligently searched by the inquisitive eye of the antiquarian and natural historian. Our own country has not been wanting in furnishing a considerable number of excellent materials for these collections. More might still be done, were the natural history of Scotland better known. We have in our possession many remains of antiquity, and not a few of the more uncommon productions of nature, which have drawn the attention of learned philosophers in the neighbouring nations. Nor have they been overlooked by our own countrymen. Several worthy and distinguished persons have, at different periods, laudably employed themselves in carefully inquiring into antiquity, nature and art.

WILLING to do every thing in my power to elucidate the history of my native country, I wrote, in the year 1789, an account of East-Kilbride, and subjoined to it a considerable number of draughts of animal and vegetable petrifactions, that were found in the parish. I borrowed the outlines of my plan from the Rt. Hon. the Earl of Buchan's prospectus for a parochial history of Scotland. What I had written I intended to communicate to the Society, of which the Earl was the founder. Having finished the manuscript and drawings, it was thought proper to publish them. The only reason was, that the draughts of the fossils, being put into the hands of the public, might be the means of exciting in some a spirit of investigation into that part of natural history,

PREFACE. v

hiftory, to which they more particularly had a refpect, and to the ftudy of which, this part of the country afforded not a few opportunities. I had no fooner begun to prepare the manufcript for the prefs, than the Rev. D. Connell of Kilbride, whom I ferved as an affiftant, was carried away by death. My connection with that parifh being then at an end, I went to England, where I ftayed a few months. In the mean-while, Sir John Sinclair's profpectus for a parochial hiftory of Scotland made its appearance. The fame reafon that induced me not to give the manufcript to the Society of Antiquaries, induced me not to give it to Sir John. I fent him, however, a compend, which he was pleafed to infert in his very excellent work. Whilft I was preparing for the prefs, my attention was accidentally directed to the Borough and Parifh of Rutherglen, as affording materials for a pretty extenfive hiftory. I foon found, that the place contained many things, refpecting antiquity and natural hiftory, that were by no means unworthy the attention of the public. Without lofs of time I began to arrange, into a regular form, whatever I thought conducive to elucidate the hiftory of that ancient Borough. In this I was greatly affifted, by having accefs to all the public records poffeffed by the community.

AFTER the profpectus for the publication was difperfed, feveral things, in both parifhes, were
accidentally

accidentally discovered, which I thought would be highly improper to omit. Owing to this, I was forced to go beyond the bounds I had prescribed to myself; and to make several alterations in the arrangement of the Plates, which occasions, among them, a confusion, easily observed. I hope, however, that in this respect, I shall meet with the indulgence of the candid reader.

With regard to the language, I have this only to observe, that I studied perspicuity and brevity. The draughts of the fossils are from specimens in my possession. The execution of them, though not very fine, is, in general, pretty accurate; and better suited to represent these fossil bodies, than could be done by the most embellished engravings. The Plates are thrown off with an excellent *Ink*, lately invented by Sir John Dalrymple, Bart. one of the Barons of the Exchequer.

I have not indulged myself in making theories; and have but seldom referred to the theories already made. Facts, however, I have related, simply and without disguise, as they made their appearance. If any thing rests upon tradition or report, I generally mention tradition or report as my authority.

Glasgow, 28th Jan. 1793.

CONTENTS.

                                                                      Page

CHAP. I. *Of the Borough of Rutherglen, its Charters, Set, Antiquities, Commissioners and Provosts Names,* -   1

CHAP. II. *Of the Parish of Rutherglen, its Extent, Agriculture, Antiquities, Trade, Proper Names,* - - 107

CHAP. III. *Of the Parish of East-Kilbride, its Extent, Population, Places of Note, Proper Names.* 141

CHAP. IV. *Of Agriculture, Trade, Diseases, Poor, State of Religion, Church, Sepulchral Monuments,* - 180

CHAP. V. *Of the Natural History of Rutherglen and Kilbride, containing an Account of Indigenous Animals, Plants and Fossils,* - - - 229

CHAP. VI. *Of Extraneous Fossils, containing an Account of Vegetable Impressions, Petrified Wood, Shells, Entrochi, Coralloides, and Fishes Teeth,* - 295

The following mistakes will, it is hoped, be corrected by the reader.

Page 2, line 15, for *fifth*, read sixth.
120, l. 26, for 33, r. 26.
121, l. 5, for 41, r. 34½.

THE HISTORY OF RUTHERGLEN.

CHAP. I.

OF THE BOROUGH OF RUTHERGLEN, ITS CHARTERS, SET, ANTIQUITIES, &c.

THE Royal Borough of RUTHERGLEN is situated in the lower ward of the county of Lanark, and within the bounds of the presbytery of Glasgow, and synod of Glasgow and Ayr. It stands on the south bank of the river Clyde, in North Lat. 55° 51′ and West Long. 4° 13′. It is two miles and a half to the south-east of Glasgow, and about nine miles to the west of Hamilton.

THE origin of Rutherglen, if we believe the traditional account of the name, must be placed at a very distant period.

The origin and antiquity of nations and families are often difcovered by their names. By thefe we are carried back to fome remote period, which prefents to our view certain perfons and actions, the remembrance of which, many fucceffive ages have not been able to obliterate. Proper names, not unfrequently, remain unaltered during the obfcurity of barbarifm, and amidft the devaftations of war; they often furvive the greateft changes that take place in the cuftoms and manners of nations; and retain their original meaning, though fometimes obfcured by the wildeft fables, and moft gloomy fuperftition.

The name of Rutherglen, or by contraction Ruglen, is commonly faid to be derived from king *Reuther*, or *Reutherus*, the fifth, in the genealogy of the Kings of Scotland, from Fergus the firft. This King, according to the Scottifh hiftorians, was the fon of Dornadilla, whofe memory is ftill preferved in the name of Dun-Dornadilla, a venerable ruin, in Strathmore.

From Reuther, or Reuda, as Bede calls him, the Scots were, for a long time, called *Dalreudini*. He began to reign about the year 213, before the chriftian æra. Having experienced the various changes of a war, by which his army was greatly exhaufted, he retired to the mountainous country of Argyle, where he remained in peace for feveral years.

years. Finding, at length, that his forces, now greatly increased, were inflamed with the love of war, he left his retirements, and, by many successful attacks upon the Britons, regained the ancient boundaries of his kingdom.*

From the above account it appears that the Dalreudini, or Scots, possessed, both in the beginning and end of Reuda's reign, a more extensive tract of land than the county of Argyle.

The truth of this observation will still farther appear by considering the literal meaning of the expression *Dalreudini*. It properly signifies the inhabitants of the valley or plain of Reuda. No place, perhaps, in Scotland corresponds to the etymology of this name so well as Rutherglen: the termination *glen* in the one word is synonymous with *dal* in the other; the word dal signifying a plain or valley, as Crom-dal, the crooked plain,† Dalray, the King's vale, &c.

Is it not, therefore, highly probable that Rutherglen was the capital of the district inhabited, at some time or other, by the Scots or Dalreudini?

Some modern historians, who seem to be much better acquainted with the antiquities of Scotland than

* *Buchanan*, Life of *Reutherus*.   † Shaw's History of Moray.

than its ancient inhabitants were, have denied the existence either of king Dornadilla, or Reutherus. But it surely requires a much greater degree of implicit faith to believe their ideal system of negatives, than to believe the accounts which the earliest historians of our country have left on record concerning the Kings of Scotland.

It is probable that some of these accounts may have originated from tradition: but tradition, when it refers to the great events of a nation, is, not unfrequently, a faithful historian; especially amongst a people like the Scots, whose sagacious Bards, were, for time immemorial, employed in celebrating these events, and perpetuating their memory. Some fables, and not a few errors, may have been interwoven with their narrations; but these fables, or what, to us now, may seem to deserve that appellation, were, in many instances, we have reason to believe, founded on fact. Shall the wildest fables and romances of Greek and Roman historians be, with almost a sacred care, faithfully transmitted to posterity, and be made to refer to events which actually took place, and shall the history of our own nation, for several complete centuries, be wholly rejected, as having no foundation on truth, because there may be some things mentioned in that history for which we cannot easily account?

BUT,

BUT, exclusive of all conjectures, founded on tradition, or etymology of names, we are sure, from authentic records, that Rutherglen is a very ancient town. From the following charters it is evident that it was erected a Royal Borough in the reign of king David I.

Carta Roberti, Regis Scottorum. anno Dom. 1324.

ROBERTUS. Dei gratia, Rex Scottorum, Omnibus probis hominibus totius terre sue, salutem, Sciatis Nos. inspexisse, ac veracit intellexisse, Cartam. venande. memorie. Dm Willim Dei gra. illustris Regis Scottorum, pdecessoris nri, factam. Burgensibus. de Rutherglen, non abolitam, non Cancellatam, nec in aliqua sui pte Viciatam: set vero Sigillo, ipius Regis Signatam, in hec verba. Wills. Dei gra Rex Scott Epis, Abbib Comitib, Baronib. Justis. Vicecom ppositis, ministris. et omib probis homib. totius tre sue. Clericis, et Laiois Saltm. Sciant pfentes et futi. me concessisse. et dedisse. et hac Carta, mea confirmasse. Burgo. meo de Ruthglen, et Burgensib. meis. eiusdem ville, omes Consuetudines, & Rectitudines quas huerunt tempore Reg Dauid Aui mei et illas Diuisas. quas eis concessit. Scilicet. de Neithan, Vsq Polmacde. Et de Garin Vsq keluin. et de Loudn, vsq prenteineth. Et de karnebuth. ad karn. Et quicuq detulit Tholmem. vel alia iura. que pdct ville, tempore Reg dauid, ptinuerunt. Vbicuq. ppositus pfate ville, vel Seruiens eius, illu Attinge possit. in Cuicuq tra attingat. Dns tre illius, inueniat. pposito de Ruthglen. vel Seriuenti Suo, Auxilm, vt Disturbet. don heant. iura Reg. Et n Dns Ville, hoc fecit; Volo. vt ipe sit. in forisfacto meo. de decem libris, Et phibeo fimit. ne aliqs educat

aliquid.

aliquid. ad vendendu. infrà iftas diuifas pnotatas; nifi prius fuerit ad Burgu de Ruthglen. Teft Ern Abbe. de melros, Jocel. Arch. de Dunkeldin. Robto de London. Walto Corbet. Willo Comyn. Walto de Berclai. Camario. Johe. de Lond apud Jeddeburch. Quam quidem. ǫceſſionem, & donatonem. in omib punctis & articulis suis, pdtis Burgenſib de Ruthglen. & eor Succeſſorib, pro nobis & hedib nris. approbam. Ratificam. et hac pſenti Carta nra. inppetuu. Confirmamus, Conceſſimus etiam. eiſdem. Burgenſibus de Ruthglen & eor Succeſſorib. & hac pſenti Carta nra Conſmauimus eiſdem. q̄ de Tholneio. & Conſuitudine. de. dominicis Catallis. ſuis. p totum. Regnu nrm Liberi ſint. et quieti inppetuu. prout Carta bone memorie. dm Alexr Scdi. dei gra. illuſtris Reg Scott. pdeceſſoris nri Sup eadem Libertate eiſdem confecta. plem iuſte. pportat & teſtat. In cuius Rei teſtemoniu pſenti Carte nre Sigillu nrm ſecim apponi. Teſtib Ven in. Xto patb. Willo & Willo Sct Andr & Dunkelden eccliar dei gra Epis. Bernard. Abbe de Abirbroth. Cancellar nro. Walter Sen Scot. Jacobo Dno. de Duglas. & Alexo Fraz Cam nro. militib apd BerWicu Sup TWedam. Viceſimo Die Aprilis. Anno Reg Noſtri Octauodecimo.

Eadem, ſine Contractionibus.

ROBERTUS, Dei gratia Rex Scottorum,* Omnibus probis hominibus, totius terræ ſuæ; ſalutem. Sciatis, Nos inſpexiſſe, ac veraciter intellexiſſe, Cartam, venerandæ memoriæ Domini Willielmi, Dei gratia illuſtris Regis Scottorum, predeceſſoris noſtri, factam Burgenſibus de Rutherglen, non abolitam,

non

---

* The people of Scotland were ſo jealous of their ancient rights, and of the freedom of their nation, that they would not permit their Kings to ſtyle themſelves Kings of Scotland, as being ſole proprietors of the land, but Kings of the Scots; choſen originally by the free voice of the people, and ſupported by their arms. This mode of expreſſion is now adopted in France.

non Cancellatam, nec in aliqua sui parte, viciatam, fed vero Sigillo ipfius Regis Signatam; in hæc verba. Willielmus, Dei gratia Rex Scottorum, Epifcopis, Abbatibus, Comitibus, Baronibus, Juftitiariis, Vicecomitibus, Præpofitis, Miniftris, et omnibus probis hominibus, totius terræ fuæ, Clericis, et Laicis; Salutem. Sciant, præfentes et futuri, me conffeffe, et dediffe, et, hac Carta mea, confirmaviffe, Burgo meo de Rutherglen, et Burgenfibus meis ejufdem villæ, omnes Confuetudines, et Rectitudines, quas habuerunt tempore Regis Davidis, Avi mei; et illas Divifas, quas eis conceffit; Scilicet, de Neithan, ufque ad Polmacde: Et, de Garin, ufque ad kelvin: et, de Loudun, ufque ad prenteineth: Et, de karnebuth, ad karun. Et quicunque detulerit Tholneum, vel alia jura, quæ, prædictæ villæ, tempore Regis davidis, pertinuerunt, Ubicunque præpofitus præfatæ villæ, vel Serviens ejus, illum Attingere poffit; in Cujuscunque terra attingat, Dominus terræ illius inveniat præpofito de Rutherglen, vel Servienti Suo, Auxilium, ut Difturbetur, donec habeant jura Regalia. Et nifi Dominus Villæ hoc fecerit, Volo, ut ipfe fit, in forisfacto meo, de decem libris. Et prohibeo firmiter, ne aliquis educat aliquid ad vendendum, infra iftas divifas prænominatas, nifi prius fuerit ad Burgum de Rutherglen. Teftibus, Ernefto, Abbate de melros; Jocelino, Archidiacono de Dunkeldin; Roberto de London; Waltero Corbet; Willielmo Comyn; Waltero de Berelai, Camerario; Johanne de Lond, apud Jeddeburch. Quam quidem conceffionem, et donationem, in omnibus punctis, et articulis fuis, prædictis Burgenfibus de Rutherglen, et eorum Succefforibus, pro nobis, et hæredibus noftris, Approbamus, Ratificamus; et, hac præfenti Carta noftra, inperpetuum Confirmamus. Conceffimus etiam eifdem Burgenfibus de Rutherglen, et eorum Succefforibus, et hac præfenti Carta noftra, Confirmavimus eifdem, quod de Tholneio, et Confuetudine, de dominicis Catallis fuis, per totum Regnum noftrum Liberi fint, et quieti, inperpetuum; prout Carta, bonæ memoriæ Domini Alexandri Secundi, Dei gratia, illuftris Regis Scottorum,

rum, prædecefforis noftri, Super eadem Libertate eifdem, confecta plerumque jufte præportat, et teftat. In cujus Rei teftimonium, præfenti Cartæ noftræ Sigillum noftrum fecimus apponi. Teftibus. Venerandis in Chrifto patribus, Willielmo, et Willielmo Sancti Andreæ, et Dunkelden ecclefiarum, Dei gratia Epifcopis. Bernardo, Abbate de Abirbroth, Cancellario noftro. Waltero, Senefcallo Scotiæ: Jacobo, Domino de Duglas: Et Alexandro Frazer, Camerario noftro, militibus. apud BerWicum fuper TWedam. Vicefimo Die Aprilis. Anno, Regni Noftri, Octavodecimo.

CARTA JACOBI V. *Regis Scotorum.* ann. Dom. 1542.

JACOBUS, Dei gratia Rex Scotorum, Omnibus probis hominibus, Totius terre fue, Clericis, et Laicis; falutem. Sciatis, Quia poft noftram, legitimam, et perfectam vigintiquinq etatem completam, Revocationemq generalem, approbauimus, ratificauimus, et confirmauimus: Et, hac pnti Carta nra, approbamus, ratificamus, et, pro nobis, et nrs fucceforibus, confirmamus omnes cartas, et infeofamenta, fact, per quondam dauidem, willelmum, alexrm, Robertum Scotorum reges, et alios nros nobiliffimos predeceffores, bone memorie, quorum animabus propicietur deus, pro creatione ville de ruthirglen, in liberum burgum regalem; cum omnibus priuilegiis, libertatibus, per ipfos, eidem, ac prepofito, baliuis, burgenfibus, et comitati eiufdem, pntibus et affuturis, infra omnes limites; a nethan, ad polmacdy: et, a garin, a keluin: et, a loudun, ad prenteineth: et, le carnebuth, ad karun: et omnia alia loca, in dictis infeofamentis, fpecificat. Ordinan q. nemo capiat cuftumas, nec alia iura, que ad dictam Villam, tempore prefati quondam dauidis Regis, pertinuernt. Et Vbicunq dictus prepofitus, aut feriandus, dicti burgi

nri,

tri, Illum apprehendere poterit; q. dominus huius terre, in qua
apprehensus fuerit, predictos, prepositum, balliuos, et eorum
feriandos, adiuuet; donec eorum custumas, et iura, acquitant.
Et si dns Illius ville, aut terrarum, in hoc defecerit, q idem sit
in vno amerciamento decem librarum. Acetiam, inhibendo omnibus nrs liegiis; q nullus eorum, aliqua bona, extra predictos
limites, vendenda sumat, nisi prius, ad prefatum nrm burgum
apportentur. Necnon, concedendo dictis preposito, balliuis, et
comitati eiusdem burgi, ac eorum successoribus; q ipi, de omnibus tholoneis, custumis, et consuetudine, suorum catallorum, et
bonorum, in omnibus partibus regni nri, sint pro perpetuo liberi:
Tenend, de nobis, et nris successoribus, prout in prefatis cartis, et
infeofamentis, desuper confectis, latius continetur. Soluendo
Inde, annuatim, prefati prepositus, balliui, comitas, et eorum
successores; summam tresdecem librarum monete, regni nri; ad
duos anni terminos consuetos; festa, Videlicet, penthecostes; et
sancti martini, in hieme; per equales portiones, Videlicet; qua-
dragita solidos, nobis, et nris successoribus; et Vndecim libras,
annuatim, vicariis chori eccle cathedralis glasguen, ad eosdem
terminos; per equales portiones tantum.* In cuius Rei testi-
monim; huic pnti Carte nostre confirmationis, Magnm Sigillum
nrm Apponi precepimus. Testibus: Reuendissimo, et Reu-
endo in Christo patribus, gawino, Archiepo glasguen; et cancellario nro: georgio, Epo Dunkelden, dilectis nris: fratre Natu-
rali, et consanguineis, Jacobo morauie, comite: et Archibaldo,
comite ergadie, dno campbell, et lorne: et Malcolmo, dno flemy-
ing; Magno camerario nro: Dilectis nris familiaribus, Thoma
erskyn, de brechyn, milite; secretario nro: Jacobo kyrkcaldy,
de grange, thesaurario nro: David Wood, de crag, compotorum
nrorm rotulatore: Magris Jacobo foulis, de colintoun, nrorum

B   rotulorum

---

* *That sum of money, as we find from Extracts, in possession of the town of Rutherglen, was given to the Cathedral "pro sustentatione Diaconi, et Sub-*
"*diaconi ministrant. in choro dict. eccle. et ad luminar. ibidem, ex con-*
"*cessione D. regis Roberti primi, in puram, et perpetuam elimosinam.*"

rotulorum regni ac confilii: Et thoma Bellenden, de auchinoule, nrorum Jufticiarie, et cancellarie clerico, et directore. Apud edinburgh, Vndecimo die Menfis Junii, Anno Dm, Milleſimo, Quingentefimo, quadragefimofecundo. Et Regni noftri vicefimonono.

It appears from the following note, on the back of each of thefe charters, that they were produced in Edinburgh, in the year 1656, and received as authentic.

Edinburgh. ye. 15 Martij 1656.

PRODUCIT be Walter Riddel, baillie of Rutherglen; and ane Minut, takine, & Recordit in the books of Exchequer. Conforme to the act granent. By me

(Signed)   *W. Purvies Clk.*

The charter of king Robert Bruce is remarkably well written: the letters are fmall but well fhaped, and the ftrokes fine. A *fac fimile* of this ancient record would be a valuable addition to the Diplomata Scotiæ. The writing of king James' charter is not fo delicate as the other, but the letters are far from being bad; they are more of a modern fhape, and the ftrokes much coarfer.

The following copies of two charters granted in the years 1617, and 1640, contain the fubftance of the above Latin charters, and may therefore ferve in place of a tranflation.

Charter of king James VI. in favour of the burgh of Rutherglen. 1617.

JAMES, By the grace of God, &c. We Confidering The fingullar ftudy, and fedulous care, which our Moft noble progenitors Kings of Scotland, of bleffed Memory, did undergo, in erecting Burghs within the faid Kingdom of Scotland; by whofs encreafs, civility, profit, and ornament, does moft exift, and is daily augmented. Among the number of which burghs, our moft illuftrious Progenitors, efpecially King David, King William, Alexander, Robert, and James the fifth of that name, Kings of Scotland; now by the fpace of five hundred years and above, did erect the Burgh of Rutherglen, fitwat in the weft pairt of this our kingdom of Scotland, in ane free Burgh Royall; and gave and granted to the faid Burgh, and the Inhabitants therof, and ther fucceffors for ever, fundry Lands, and Rents; and with all the priviledges, Liberties, and Immunities, belonging, or known to belong, to any Burgh Royall within our faid Kingdom of Scotland. And we being moft willing not only to ratifie, confirme, and approve all and fundry Rights, Infeftments, Liberties, priviledges, and Immunities, formerly granted to the faid Burgh, by our Moft noble progenitors. But alfo to grant to them new Infeftments, and Difpofitions therof, and to our pith, and powr to amplifie and extend ther Liberties, priviledges and Immunities. Therfor, and for diverfs other great Refpects, and good Confiderations, moving us: and of our certain knowledge, and proper motive, with fpeciall advice and confent of our Moft trufty Cowfin and Counfelour, John, Earle of Marr, Lord Erfkin, Lord high Treffurer, Comptroller, and Generall recever of our faid kingdom of Scotland; and of Sir Gideon Murray of Elibank, Knight, Treffurer, Comptroler, and Recever deputie of the faid kingdom; We have Ratified, approven, and for us and our fucceffors,

ceffors, perpetwallie confirmed; and be the tenor of this our charter, we doe ratifie, approve, and for us and our fucceffors perpetwallie confirm, all and fundry Charters and Infeftments, Precepts, and Inftruments of feafling, confirmation, acts, decretts, and fentances, with all Gifts, priviledges, and Immunities therin Contained, made, given, and granted, and confirmed be our moft noble progenitors, to our faid Burgh of Rutherglen, and Inhabitants therof, of whatfomever Tenor, or Tenors; Content, or Contents; dait, or daits the fame be: and especialie, but prejudice of the faid generality, and particular charter of Confirmatione granted be our moft Noble progenitor King James the fifth, be which he ratified, and approved all and fundrie Charters and Infeftments made and granted be the faids, David, William, Alexander, and Robert, Kings of Scotland, and others his Moft Noble predeceffors, of worthy memory, for creating and erecting our faid Burgh of Rutherglen, in ane free Burgh Royall, with all priviledges, liberties, and immunities granted be them therto, and to the Proveft, Baillies, Burgeffes and Communitie therof, then prefent and to come, within all its Bounds and Limits, from Netham to Polmadie; and from Garen to Kelvin; and from Lowdoun to Prenteineth; and from Carnburgh to Carron, and in all the other places fpecified and contained in the faids Infeftments. Ordaining alfo, be the faid Charter, That none uplift the cuftoms, or other teinds pertaining to the faid Burgh, in the lifetime of the faid King David. And wherever the Proveft, and Baillies of our faid Burgh, or ther officers, or ferjands fhould apprehend any fuch, that the Heiritor of that land, in which he there were found, fhould helpe and affift the forfaid Proveft, Baillies, and ther ferjands, till they fhould redover ther cuftoms, rights, and teinds: and if the Heiritors of any Toun, or Lands, fhould be deficient in this, that he fhould be fined in Ten punds Scots; and alfo inhibiting all our Leidges, That none of them bring ther goods to be fold beyond any of the forfaid Limits, till firft, they be brought, and

offered

offered to our faid Burgh; as alfo giving, and granting to the Proveft, Baillies, and communitie of our faid Burgh, and to ther fucceffors, that they fhall be, for ever, free of all Tolls, Cuftoms, and Impofitions of ther Cattall and goods, in all the pairts of this our kingdom; as in the faid charter of Confirmation, ratifieing, and approving, the forfaids charters, and infeftments, to our faid Burgh of Rutherglen, and ther fucceffors, in form above written; of the dait the eleven day of June, the year of God, fifteen hundred and fourtie two, At more length is contained. With all and fundrie other Charters, Infeftments, Gifts, Priviledges, Immunities, Sentences, Decreets, and other Rights, and Evidences whatfomever, made, given, and granted, be us, or our Moft Noble progenitors; or be any other perfon, or perfons, to our faid Burgh of Rutherglen: or in favours of the Proveft, Baillies, Counfell, and Communitie therof; or ther predeceffors, or fucceffors, concerning the erection of the faid Burgh, in ane free Burgh of Royalty; and with all rights, titles, and priviledges pertaining therto, or which, be the Laws and Cuftoms of our kingdom, are known to pertain therto. And of all and fundrie lands, tenements, howfes, biggings, yards, rents, few farms, ground dues, and teinds, Orchards, crofts, milns, woods, fifhing, coals, coalhewghs, moores, mofs, fields, ways, paffages, ferms, or teinds Whatfomever; and of all and whatfomever other tenements, howfes, biggings, chappels, chappelyeards, and annual rents whatfomever, pertaining to the faid chapels, and altarages of kirks, founded with, and lying within the territorie, liberty, and Jurisdictione of our faid Burgh, and pertaining and belonging therto, and of which our faid Burgh was formerlie in poffeffion. and we will, and grant, and for us, and our fucceffors, decern, and ordain, that the forfaid generalitie, fhall not be prejudice of the fpecialitie forfaid; nor the forfaid fpecialitie, the faid generalitie: but that this prefent charter of Confirmation, and Approbation of the premiffes, in all time coming, fhall be of alfe great vallow, ftrength, and

efficafie

efficasie, and effect, in all respects to the said Burgh of Rutherglen, Provest, Baillies, Counsell, Communitie, and inhabitants therof, and ther successors, as of all and sundrie ther said Inseftments, Charters, Donations, Conversions, Sentences, rights, titles, and immunities, and every on therof, with the liberties, priviledges, and Immunities, specialie and generallie therin mentioned over, word by word, herin exprest and insert theranent; and all the Inconveniences which could follow theron; and all other objections, defects, and imperfections, if any be, which could be propossed, or aledged against the validitie of the same, or any on therof, or this our present Charter of Confirmation, we, for us and our successors, have disponed, and by the tenor of this our charter dispones for ever. Morover, will, but hurt, or prejudice of the saids Charters, Infeftments, Decrets, Donations, Commissions, rights, liberties and priviledges therin contained. And in farder corroboration therof, accumulating rights to rights, for the good and faithful service done, and to be done, to us, be the Provest, Baillies, Counsell and Inhabitants of the said Burgh of Rutherglen, ther predecessors, and successors; and that we may give them the better occasion of persevering in the samen, with advice and consent forsaid, of new have given, granted and disponed, and perpetwallie, and be the tenor herof, give, grant and dispone from us and our successors, perpetwallie confirm to the Provest, Baillies, Counsell, Communitie and Inhabitants of the said Burgh of Rutherglen, and ther successors for ever, all and haill the said Burgh of Rutherglen, territorie and communitie therof, with all sundrie cawswalities, howses, biggings, tenaments, yeards, orchards, churches, chappels, chappelries, tofts, crofts, outsetts, wayes, passadges, Milns, Multeries and seqwalls therof, coalls, Coallhewghs, rocks, Quarries, burns, dams, incarries, Laids and watergangs, fishing, moores, marshes, Greens, Commons, Loans, an. rents, few-ferm dewties, manses, fruits, profits, emoluments; and with all other priviledges, liberties and immunities whatsomever,

RUTHERGLEN.

ever, as well   as secular,
pertaining therto, lying within the said Burgh, libertie, Territorie and Jurisdiction therof; with special and full power and libertie to them, Yearlie to creat, elect, change and dispose the Provest, Baillies, Counsellors, Dean of gild, Tressurer, and all other Magistrats reqwisit and used in ane free Burgh royall; with Clarks, Serjands, Dempsters, and all other officers and members of Court; and with all other Liberties and Priviledges pertaining therto; and the Burgesses and inhabitants to use, freqwant and exerce the Liberties of free Burgesses alse freely, in all respects, as any other free Burgesses within any other free Burgh of our Kingdom of Scotland: as also with powr, libertie and licence to the said Provest, Baillies, Counsellors, Burgesses and Communitie of the said Burgh, and ther successors, in all time coming, to have, use and exerce the trade and traffiqwie of Merchants; and to bwy, sell, brok, coup all kind of merchantdice of our kingdom of Scotland, as the goods of other nations, not only within the said Burgh-lands, territorie jurisdiction and priviledges therof, but also within all other bownds and lands after mentioned: and to Intromit with, and uplift all the Customs and other dewties within all the bownds respectivelie forsaid: and to have use, and possess, within the said Burgh, ane Merchand Gildrie, with ane Dean of Guild, court, members and jurisdictions pertaining therto, liberties and priviledges therof, and alse freely, in all respects, as is granted to any other Burgh royall within this kingdom: and to have use, and enjoy, within the said Burgh, weeklie, ane Mercat day upon Saturday, with two fairs yearlie, Viz. the first to be Holden yearlie upon the eighteinth day of October, called Lukes day, to continow for fowr days; and the second the   day of
yearlie, of old called the Trinitie Sunday, to continow two days, according to the old and ancient custom of the said Burgh: and in like manner, with powr to the Provest, Baillies and Counsell of the said Burgh, and ther successors, and ther factors, customers
                                                                and

and servands, in ther names, to uplift all the Tolls, Customs, sies, Impositions, exactions and other dewties whatsomever, used and wont during the whole time of the said Mercat: and to exercise all other Liberties as freelie as any other Burgh within the said kingdom do enjoy, and possess fairs and mercats, or as they themselves, or ther predecessors, in any time bygone, did enjoy or possess. As also we, with advice and consent forsaid, have given and granted, & by the tenor of this our charter, give and grant to the said Provest, Baillies, Counsell, and Communitie of the said Burgh, and ther successors, full powr, libertie and commission, to make and publish acts, statuts, and ordinances, for the common good of the said Burgh; and for the maintaining, and observing of the liberties, and priviledges therof, be all the Burgesses and Inhabitants of the same; and be all other persons repairing therto, to be observed & obeyed, under such pains, as, to them, shall seem most expedient; according to the acts of Parliament, laws and practice of other Burghs; giving and granting to them to put to finall execution ther own ordinances, decrets and sentences; and all acts of Parliament, or secret Counsell, constitutions of Burghs, and all decrees, acts and sentences, made, and to be made, and preserved, in favours of ther own liberties; and that within the territorie of our said Burgh, and bounds, above specified; and to fitt, constitute and decerne them for the better executione therof, making and constituting themselves, and ther successors, Provest, Baillies and Counsellors, of the said Burgh, Judges in that pairt of the said Burgh, within the boundrie therof, With full powr to them, to conveen, prosecute, arrest and incarcerat the persons, contraveening ther said liberties, acts, decrets, ordinances and others forsaid, and the said persones to punish as . . . . of the law. With powr also to the said Provest, Baillies and Counsellors, of the said Burgh, and ther successors, to observe and defend, all and sundrie, the Gates and passages leading to, and from, the said Burgh, and all other pairts of this kingdom,

that

that they be not broken, or infringed by any perfon, but that they may be preferved, in all pairts of the famen paffages, in lenth, and breadth, and meafur, ufed and wont, that our fubjects may have eaffie accefs, and regrefs to and from our faid Burgh. Moreover, it being abundantly known to us that the faid Lands, tenaments, howffes, biggings, yeards, orchards, churches, chappels, chappelries, tofts, crofts, outfets, ways, paffages, milns, multeries and feqwalls therof, Coals, Coalhewghs, rocks, dams, qwarries, incarries, watergangs, fifhings, moores, marfhes, Greens, Commons, and Loans, and others particularlie and generalie above mentioned; with the offices, liberties, priviledges, and other above reherfed, to have been formerlie, and now to be Incorporat, decreted, unit, and annexed in ane free Burgh royall; and confidering alfo the faid Proveft, Baillies, Counfell, and Communitie of our faid Burgh to be ane univerfity, which, by its own nature, does continue, having no fpecial, nor particular fucceffor. Therfor we will and grant, and for us, and our fucceffors, decern, and ordain that ane feifin now be taken at the faid mercat crofs of Rutherglen, be vertue of this prefent infeftment, be the Proveft, or any ane of the Baillies of the faid Burgh, in name of all the Burgeffes, Counfellors, and Communitie therof, and ther fucceffors, be Deliverance of earth and ftone, ftaff or Batton, fhall ftand, and be ane fufficient feifin to the faid Burgh, and ther fucceffors for ever; for all and haill the faid Burghs territorie, and communitie therof; and for all and fundrie lands, tenements, howfes, biggings, &c. as above; with there liberties, priviledges, Immunities, and pertinents whatfomever, but any Rovocation, Retraction, taking, or recovering of any new feifin in any time coming, to be holden, and to be had, all and haill our faid Burgh of Rutherglen, territorie, and communitie therof; with all and fundrie lands, tenements, howfes, biggings, yeards, orchards, kirks, chappels, chappelries, tofts, crofts, outfets, ways, paffages, milns, multeries and feqwalls therof, Coals, Coalhewghs, rocks, dams, qwarries, incarries, leads

C and

and watergangs, fishings, moores, marshes, Greens, commons or loans, annual-rents, few-ferm dewties, mansion-howses, ferms, profits, emoluments, pairts, pendicles and pertinents forsaid, pertaining, and belonging therto; and with the haill offices, custtomes, dewties, and priviledges, above reherfed, to the faids Proveft, Baillies, Counfellors, and Communitie of our said Burgh of Rutherglen, and ther fucceffors, of us, and our fucceffors, in few-ferm and heritage, and free Burgh royall for ever, be all the rights, meiths, and marches therof, old and divided, as the fame ly, in lenth, and breadth, in howses, biggings, plains, moors, marshes, ways, Paffages, waters, ftanks, burns, Meadows, pafturages, Milns, multeries and feqwalls therof, hawking, hunting, fifhing, peats, turfs, coals, coalhewghs, cunnins, cunningers, doves, dovecoats, fmiddies, &c. woods, groves, &c. ftone and lime, &c. with Court, plaint, herrezell,* Bluidueit,† &c. Commonties,

---

* Herrezelda, is the beft aucht, ox or kow, or uther beaft quhilk ane husbandman poffeffour of the aucht pairt of ane dauach of land: (foure oxen gang) dwalland and deceasand theirupon, hes in his poffeffion, the the time of his deceafe, quhilk aucht fuld be given to his Landislord, or maister of the faid land. For Her in dutch, in latine herus, dominus, fignifies ane Lord or maister; and zeild is called ane gift, tribute or taxation, as in the auld acts of Parliament maid be king James the firft, it is written, that ane zeilde was gaddered, for the reliefe of him out of England. And ane uther zeilde was collected for refifting the rebelles in the north. Swa Herrezelda is ane gift given be onie man to his maister with the beft thing he hes. Swa it is manifeft that the Herrezelda is given, be reason of the tennants deceis, to his maister, as ane gift, for acknawledging and honouring of him, and theirfor in the civil law is called Laudemium and laudendo domino. Skene, in verbum.

† Bludueit. Uyte in Englifh is called Injuria, vel mifericordia. Ane un-law for wrang or injurie, fik as bloud: For they quha ar infeft with Bludueit hes free libertie to take up all unlawes or amerciaments of Court, for effufion of bloud: and to hald courtes theirupon, and to apply the famin to their awin utilitie and profite. Skene, in verbum.

monties, common paſſages, free iſh and entrie therto, &c. pitt and Gallous, and with all and ſundrie other liberties, commodities, profits, and eaſements, and juſt pertinents therof whatſumever, as well not named as named, as well under as beneath the ground, farr and near, belonging, or that juſtly are known to belong to the ſaid Burgh, territorie and priviledges therof anie manner of way, in all time coming, freelie, queitlie, fullie, weel and in peace, But anie Revocation, Contradiction, Impediment, or Obſtacle whatſumever. Giving therfor, yearly, the ſaids Proveſt, and Baillies, Counſell, and Communitie of the ſaid Burgh of Rutherglen, all and haill the ſume of Thretein Punds uſewall money of Scotland, at two uſewall termes in the year, Whitſunday and Martimeſs in winter, be eqwall portiones; Viz. the ſume of fourtie ſhilling Money forſaid to us and our ſucceſſors, and eleven punds Money forſaid yearlie to the Vicars of the Quire of the Cathedrall Kirk of Glaſgow, at the termes forſaid, be eqwall portiones, in name of few-ferm. Together with the ſervice of Burgh, uſed and wont, allenerlie. In wittneſs wherof, &c. Witneſſes. James Marqueſs of Hamilton, Earle of Arran, Lord Evan and Ardbrooty. George, Earle of Marcſchall. Lord Leith, Marriſchall of Scotland. Alexander, Earle of Dumfermling. Lord Fyvie, and regiſtar Chancellor. Thomas, Lord Binning, Secretary. Sir Richard Cockburn younger of Clarkington, Lord privie Seall. George Hay of Netherlyff, Clerk Regiſter. John Cockburn of Ormiſton, Juſtice Clerk. Mr. John Scott, of Scotts Tarbatt, director of the Chancelarie. At Edinburgh the twintie on of March, 1617; and of the Kings Reign the fiftieth year in Scotland, and fourtenth in England. Sealed the twintie ſeventh of March the ſaid year.

The following paragraph is written on the back of the charter.

PRODUCED thrice in the Exchequer, to be seen and Received, and ane Minute therof taken there. First, the seventh of July, 1619; George Hay, Clerk Register. Next the twelth of July, 1636, John Hay, Clerk Register. And last, the fysteenth of March, 1656, William Purves, Clerk.

As I had not an opportunity of seeing the above charter in the original, I cannot say much for the orthography of the copy: it seems to have been greatly modernized by the transcriber.

CHARTAR in favour of Rutherglen, granted by the King and Parliament, ann. 1640.

IN the Parliament, halden at Edinburgh, the sevintene day of november, the yeir of God Jaj vi & fourtie yeirs. Our Soverane Lord, and estates of Parliament, Ratefies, approves, and perpetualie confermis, The Charter of Confirmune, grantit be his ma^ies umq^le· darrest say^r·, of worthy memorie, under his heines great seall, conteining ane novo damus In favor of the Provest, Bailleis, counsall, and Comunitie of the burgh of Rutherglen, of ye dait, at Edinburgh, the tuenty ane day of march, the yeir of God, Jaj vi & sevintene yeiris: Quhairby his heines Umq^le· darrest fay^r·, w^t· advyse of his heines Thesaurer, prin^le· and deputie for the tyme yrin noiat, Ratefiet, approvit, and for his heines, and his successors, perpetuallie confirmit, All and q'sumever Chartars, and Infestmentis, Preceptis, Instru^ts· of

Saisines,

Saifines, Confirmaunes, actis, decreitis, and fentences, With all
donaunes, priviledges, and Imunities, conteinet y^rin, maid,
grantit, and confermit, be his ma^ties moft noble progenitors,
To the faid burgh of Rutherglen, and Induellars y^rof, of q'fumever tennor, or tennors; dait, or daitis; the famene be of. And
fpeciallie, & w^tout prejudice to ye foirfaid generalitie, &c. &c.
Ane particular Chartar of Confirmaune, grantit be his ma^ties
moft noble progenitor king James the fyift, Be vertew q^rof, he
Ratefiet, and approvit, All and fundrie Chartars, and Infeft-
mentis, maid and grantit, be umq^{le}. David, W^m., alex^r., and
Robert, kingis of Scotland, and uy^r. y^r. moft noble prediceffors,
of moft worthie memorie, for creaune, and erectioune, of the
faid burgh of Rutherglen, In ane frie burgh Royall, with all
priviledges, Liberties, and Imunities, grantit be thame to the
famene. And to the Proveft, baillies, burgeffes, and comunitie
y^rof, than pnt and to cum, Within the haill boundis, and mer-
ches, from Netham, to Polmadie; and from Garin to Kelvin;
and from Lowdoun, to prenteineth; And from Carneburgh, to
Carroune; And in all uy^r. places fpeit, and conteint in the
faidis infeftmentis; ordaining alfo, be the faid chartar, That na
perfone tak cuftomes, or uy^r. dewteis, belonging to the faid
burgh, qlk thairunto pertenit, in King Davids dayis. And
whairever the faidis Proveft, and bailleis of ye faid burgh, or
y^r. officiars, and ferjandis, could apprehend the fame perfone,
That the Lord of that land, q^rin the faid perfone fall be appre-
hendit, fall helpe the faidis proveft, and bailleis, and y^r. ferjandis,
Whill they acquire y^r. richtis, and dewteis. And if the faid
Lord or mafter of the faid toun, and Land, failzie y^rintill, That
he fall be in ane Unlaw; or amerchiament of Ten pundis. And
alfo Inhibiting all, and fundrie, oure foverane Lordis Lieges,
That na perfone tak any goodis to be fauld outw^t. the foirfaidis
boundis, Except they be firft brocht, and offerit, to the faid
burgh. And ficlyck Geiving, and granting to the faidis proveft,
bailleis, and comitie, of ye faid burgh, and y^r. fucceffors, That
they

they falbe perpetualie frie in all pairts of this kingdome, of all toillis, cuftomes, and Impofitions, of y^{r.} cattell, and goodis: As the faid chartar of Confirmaune Ratifieing, and approving, the foirfaids chartar, and Infeftmentis, To the faid burgh of Rutherglen, and y^{r.} fucceffors: In forme and maner abone wrin, of ye dait, the tuelf day of Junij, the yeir of God, Jaj v & fourtie tua yeirs, at mair lenth bears. Togidder w^{t.} all, and fundrie uy^{r.}, chartars, infeftments, donaunes, priviledges, Imunities, fentences, decreitis, and uy^{r.} richtis, and evidentis q^tfumevir; maid, gevin, and grantit, be oure faid foverane Lordis Umq^{le.} Darreft fay^{r.} and his moft noble progenitors; or any uy^{r.} perfone, or perfones, To the faid burgh of Rutherglen: Or in favor of the proveft, bailleis, counfall, and comunitie y^rof, or y^{r.} prediceffors; or fucceffors, concerning the erectioune of ye faid burgh, In ane frie burgh royall: And with all richtis, titles, and priviledges, perteining y^rto; or qlk, be the lawis, and confuetude of this kingdome, are known to perteine y^rto: And of all, and fundrie, Landis, tenementis, houffes, biggengiis, Zairdis, orcheardis, croftis, mylnis, wodis, fifhingis, coillis, coilheuchis, mwres, moffes, wayis, paffages, fermes, or dewteis q^tfumevir: And of all, and q^tfumevir, uy^{r.} tenements, houffes, biggengis, chappels, chappel Zairdis, and anuelrentis, q^tfumevir, perteining to the faidis chappels, and kirk altar, foundit and Lyand w^tin the territorie, Libertie, and Juridictioune, of the faid burgh; and perteining and belonging y^rto: And whairof the faid burgh was in ufe, and poffeffioune of before; As in the faid chartar of Confirmaune grantit be his ma^ties Umq^{le.} darreft fay^{r.} y^ranent; Ratifieing, and approving, the foirfaid chartar, and Infeftmentis, particularlie and generallie abone wrin, To the faid burgh of Rutherglen; And to the faidis proveft, bailleis, counfall, and comunitie y^rof, and y^{r.} fucceffors: Conteining the faid claus of novo damus, and certane uy^{r.} priviledges, Liberties, and Imunities, at mair lenth is conteinit. In all, and fundrie, heidis, articles, clauffes, provifiounes, conditiounes, and

circumftances

circumstances q'sumevir; speit, and conteinit, y'in: With all that here followis, or may follow, y'upon. Attoure, oure said soverane Lord, and estates of parliament, Willis, and grantis, That this pnt Confirmaune, and generalitie y'of, sall be alse valeid, and of alse great strenth, force, and effect; As gif the said chartar of Confirmaune, grantit be his ma'ies said Umq'· Darrest say'·, conteining the said novo Damus, had bene, word for word, insert heirintill. Extractum, de Libris actorum parliamenti, per me Dominum Alexandrum gibsone Juniorem de Durie, militem; clericum rotulorum regni, ac consilii, S D N regis; sub meis signo et subscriptione manualibus: &c.

(Signatur) Alex'· Gibsone, Cl. Regri.

Mr. Wight, in his enquiry into the rise and progress of Parliament, supposes that we have no evidence of any charters, granted to boroughs, older than the days of William the Lyon. He observes, however, " that in an unprinted Statute, in 1661, " in favour of the borough of Rutherglen, men- " tion is made, in a supplication by that borough, " that it had been erected a free borough by king " David, in the year 1126; but upon what autho- " rity, says he, that averment was made does not " appear." From the above charters it is evident that the town was erected into a free borough by king David, if not long before his time; for, from what appears in the charters, he might only have confirmed, and enlarged, its ancient rights and privileges.

It

It is impossible for us precisely to ascertain in what the importance of Rutherglen, at that time, consisted, which entitled its inhabitants to so many privileges and immunities, and induced the legislator to lay such an extensive tract of country under their jurisdiction.

When considered as a place of strength it was by no means contemptible. The castle of Rutherglen was ranked among the ancient fortresses of Scotland, and might on that account give the town a claim to more than ordinary attention from the King. This castle, which is said to have been at first built by the Monarch that gave name to the town, was considered as a place of importance so late as the year 1309.

At that unhappy period, Scotland was thrown into the greatest disorder, by powerful parties contending for the crown. An application had, by mutual consent, been made to Edward, King of England, to settle, by way of arbitration, the differences that had arisen among them. That ambitious Prince accepted the offer, but with a view to annex the kingdom of Scotland to the crown of England. To accomplish his design, he perfidiously fomented the differences he had undertaken amicably to compose. Improving the advantages that were thrown in his way, he reduced, by the assistance of Baliol's interest,

intereſt, a great part of Scotland under his power. The caſtle of Rutherglen, with many others, fell into the hands of the Engliſh; or rather into the hands of the antibrucean party, aided by the Engliſh. King Robert Bruce, who had to combat not only the forces of Edward, but Baliol's party in Scotland, laid ſiege to the caſtle of Rutherglen, as a place of too great importance to remain in the poſſeſſion of the enemy. Of this ſiege Sir David Dalrymple, in his annals of Scotland gives the following account.

"ANNO, 1309. Bruce laid ſiege to the caſtle of
"Rutherglen in Clydeſdale; Edward ſent his ne-
"phew the young Earl of Gloucester to raiſe the
"ſiege 3d December, 1309.*

SIR David adds, that, "Hiſtorians are ſilent
"as to this event, but it is probable that the ſiege

was

---

* The following is a copy of the Commiſſion given to the Earl of Glouceſter on that occaſion.

Anno, 1309. Gilbertus Comes Glouceſtriæ Capitaneus pro Expeditione Scotiæ.

Rex omnibus ad quos &c. Salutem. Sciatis quod cùm mittamus quoſdam Nobiles, et Magnates, et Fideles de Regno noſtro, cum equis et armis, in expeditionem noſtram, ad partes Scotiæ ad obſidionem Caſtri noſtri de Rotherglea, amovendam et ad Rebellionem et Proterviam Inimicorum et Rebellionum noſtrorum illuc, cum Dei adjutorio, reprimendas.

Nos

" was raised, for according to our writers, Edward
" the 2d in the following year penetrated to Ren-
" frew. Had Rutherglen been in the possession of
" the Scots it is not to be supposed that Renfrew
" would have remained under the English dominion,
" or that Edward would have directed his march
" thither. Rutherglen appears to have been won
" from the English in the year 1313. For (as he
" quotes from Barbour, page 220.) mean while the
" Scottish

Nos de circumspectione, probitate, et industria dilecti Nepotis et Fidelis nostri, Gilberti de Clare Comitis Glouceſtriæ et Hertfordiæ, plenam fiduciam optinentes*, ipsum Capitaneum nostrum expeditionis prædictæ & munitionum nostrarum in partibus illis constituimus per presentes.

In cujus, &c. quamdiu Regi placuerit duraturas.
Teste Rege apud Westm. tertio die Decembris.
Rym. Fœd. Angl. tom. iii. p. 193.

The King of England at that time claimed a right to the sovereignty of Scotland. The cowardly submission of Baliol laid a foundation for that claim, a claim which not only the Nobles of England, but all Europe knew to be unjust. Edward, like a bad politician, was premature in making his designs public. His insolent language, with respect to the Scots, and his too hasty attacks upon the indisputable independency of their nation, excited against him the resentment of the contending parties in Scotland. He was soon taught that his power was inadequate for supporting his ill-founded pretensions.

* Probably for *obtinentes*.

" Scottish arms prospered, Edward Bruce made
" himself master of the castles of Rutherglen and
" Dundee, and laid siege to the castle of Stirling."

Guthrie, in his History of Scotland, seems to insinuate that the siege was not raised. " For," says that historian, " Robert laid siege to the castle of
" Rutherglen, which the Earl of Gloucester was
" ordered to relieve. Before that could be done,
" the English nobility had obliged Edward to agree
" to an act, by which in fact he put the executive
" power of government into their hands, on pretence
" of his being left thereby more at liberty to pro-
" secute the war against the Scots. It appears that
" next year Robert had so much the better of the
" English, that he made a powerful descent into
" England, and carried fire and sword into that
" kingdom."

Robert, in one of his excursions, laid siege to the town of Durham. The principal inhabitants of the adjacent country had, with their best effects, taken shelter in the cathedral, which Bruce was about to destroy, had not a capitulation been made for its preservation. Soon after that he brought back his army, loaded with plunder, into Scotland, without being able to bring the English to battle.*

* Buchan. Hist. Sco. Lib. 8.

From these circumstances it is not probable that the siege of the castle of Rutherglen was raised, by the Earl of Gloucester, at the time above referred to. It might, however, have fallen into the hands of the English sometime afterwards, and be retaken by Edward Bruce, in the year 1313.

But in whatever point of light that matter is viewed, it appears that this place of strength was, both by Scots and English, thought to have been of considerable importance.

The castle was kept in good repair till a short time after the battle of Langside, when it was burnt by orders of the Regent out of revenge on the family of Hamilton, in whose custody it then was. One of the principal towers was, however, soon repaired, and, being enlarged by some modern improvements, became the seat of the Hamiltons of Eliftoun, Lairds of Shawfield, &c. At length, on the decline of that family, it was, about a century ago, left to fall into ruins, and, by frequent dilapidations, was soon levelled with the ground. The walls of this ancient tower were very thick and extremely solid. Each corner rested upon an uncommonly large foundation-stone that measured 5 feet in length, 4¼ in breadth, and 4 in thickness. These corner-stones, being very massy, were allowed to remain till about 34 years ago, when they were

quarried

quarried out as being cumberfome to a kitchen-garden, into which the fite of the fortrefs of Rutherglen is now converted. Some carved ftones belonging to the caftle are built in the dykes adjoining to the town. Thofe that made a part of the cornice, which was of that kind commonly known by the name of the block-cornice, are well cut and remarkably beautiful.

The final ruin of that ftately edifice has, like many others, been afcribed to the uncommon wickednefs and perfecuting fpirit of its proprietors. The following extract from Woddrow's Church Hiftory may be mentioned as a proof of this.

" Oct. 13th, 1660. Mr. John Dickfon, minifter
" of the gofpel at Rutherglen, was brought before
" the committee of eftates, and was imprifoned in
" Edinburgh tolbooth. Information had been given
" by Sir James Hamilton of Eliftoun, and fome of
" his parifhioners, of fome expreffions he had ufed
" in a fermon alledged to reflect upon the govern-
" ment and committee, and tending to fedition and
" divifion. This good man was kept in prifon till
" the parliament fat: his church vacated, and he
" was brought to much trouble. We fhall after-
" wards find him prifoner in the Bafs for near feven
" years, and yet he got through his troubles, and
" returned to his charge at Rutherglen, and for
" feveral

"several years after the Revolution served his Mas-
"ter there, till his death in a good old age. While
"that family who pursued him is a good while ago
"extinct, and their house, as Mr. Dickson very
"publicly foretold in the hearing of some yet alive,
"after it had been a habitation for owls, the foun-
"dation stones of it were digged up. The inhabi-
"tants there cannot but observe that the informers,
"accusers, and witnesses against Mr. Dickson, some
"of them then Magistrates of the town, are brought
"so low that they are supported by the charity of
"the parish."

RUTHERGLEN, besides being a place of considerable strength, appears to have been, at the time of its
erection into a Royal Borough, the only trading and
commercial town in this part of the country; which
circumstance must have added not a little to its
importance.

GLASGOW consisted, at that time, of a few clergy-
mens houses, and was consequently confined to the
neighbourhood of the cathedral.* The few inhabitants

---

* The existence of Rutherglen, as a considerable town, prior to the building of the cathedral itself, appears from the following traditional account universally known in this part of the country. It is told, that, when the high church was beginning to be built, a passage below ground was made between it and the

bitants it contained, looking on themſelves as the chief members of a richly endowed eccleſiaſtical community, lived upon the incomes of the church. From the ſpirit of the times it is highly probable that a people living in eaſe, affluence and dignity, would rather incline to ſerve at the altar than engage in the leſs lucrative, and more laborious purſuits of life. Theſe buſy ſcenes were, in a great meaſure, left to the inhabitants of Rutherglen, who, for ſeveral centuries, ſeem to have been wholly devoted to civil and commercial employments; and of conſequence were entitled to the particular attention of the legiſlator.

IF the church of Rutherglen, and that the *Piɞs*, or *Pechs*, as they are vulgarly, but perhaps more properly, called, came from Rutherglen through this hidden way every morning, and returned at night, all the time the church was building. Although the ſubterraneous paſſage is, like Dædalus' wings, undoubtedly fabulous, yet the ſtory is, like his, not deſtitute of meaning. It ſhews that Rutherglen was the only place in the neighbourhood where the workmen could find, at that time, proper victuals and accommodations for themſelves. Every thing uncommon, as the building of the high church was, and the crowds of artiſts employed in the work, raiſed the aſtoniſhment of the ignorant vulgar. Inchantments and miracles were very plenty in that ſuperſtitious age; hence the ſtory of the underground paſſage, and many other wonders which then appeared, and which are, to this day, handed down by tradition from father to ſon.

If Glasgow stood within the bounds over which the jurisdiction of Rutherglen originally extended, as appears by the above quoted charters to have been the case, it is but natural to suppose that the community of Rutherglen would continue to exact from Glasgow those customs and duties to which, by their charters, they believed themselves entitled. And this we find they actually did. But in these demands they perhaps went too great a length; at least it was thought they did by the inhabitants of Glasgow. The consequence was that a petition was laid before the throne, about the year 1226, and was so fortunate as to procure the following prohibitary act.

CARTA ALEXANDRI, R. II.

De tolneo non capiendo in Burgo de Glasgu.[*]

ALEXANDER, Dei gratia Rex Scottorum, omnibus probis hominibus totius terræ suæ, Clericis et Laicis, salutem. Sciant, præsentes et futuri, nos concessisse, et hac Carta, confirmasse Domino et Eccl^{ae}· St. Kentigerni de Glasgu, et Waltero Ep^{o}· ejusdem loci, et successoribus suis Epis. Ne Præpositi,

[*] The original charter was in the possession of Mr. Gibson author of the History of Glasgow; but as I never had an opportunity of consulting it I can say nothing about the orthography or writing.

Præpoſiti, vel Ballivi, vel ſervientes Noſtri de Rutherglen, Tolneum aut conſuetudinem capiant in Villa de Glaſgu. Sed illa capiant ad crucem de Schedeniſton, ſicut illa antiquitus † capi ſolebant. Quare prohibemus firmiter ne Præpoſiti, vel Ballivi, vel Servientes Noſtri de Rutherglen, tolneum aut conſuetudinem capiant in Villa de Glaſgu. Teſti: Thoma de Strivelin, Cancellario. Henr: de Raitt, Camerario. Rog: de Quince. John de Maccuſwelli. Davide Marſcalli. Waltero Biſſet. Apud Jedd: 29 die Octobris. Anno Regni Noſtri 12.

Afterwards, however, the privileges of Rutherglen were conſiderably abridged, as Glaſgow emerged from under eccleſiaſtical influence, and by trade and commerce became an active and induſtrious city. This abridgment of the powers of the borough did, as might be expected, materially affect its markets and fairs.

All the efforts conſiſtent with the powers of a Royal Borough, and agreeable to the narrow ſpirit of the times, were, upon this reverſe of circumſtances, called forth by the community of Rutherglen, to ſupport their credit, and regain, if poſſible, their once extenſive influence.

Finding

---

† From this expreſſion it appears probable, that the community of Rutherglen had, for a long time paſt, been in uſe of taking cuſtom for articles of ſale brought into Glaſgow: nor were they prohibited by this act from continuing the practice, but only not to collect their uſual cuſtom, within the town of Glaſgow, but at the croſs of Schedeniſton. Where that place was, is not now, perhaps, known. It is probable that it was in the vicinity of Glaſgow, and has long ſince changed its name.

FINDING that the weekly market was not frequented as usual, several compulsory acts of council were made, of which the following, in the year 1667, is an example.

" THE Magistrats orders that as the weekly mercat on the
" tewsdays was neglected every inhabitant and tradesman shall
" bring his goods to the mercat. Such as Lint, yarne, webs,
" cloathe lining and woollen, yron worke, seives, riddels, shooes,
" meill, beir, oattes and other graine, butter, cheise, fowlles,
" eggs, fleshe, and other victwalls and all other merchandiss;
" to be sold as occasione shall offer: and to stay in the said
" mercat for that effect from ten to twa a clock in the after-
" noone. Ilke persone under the paine of Fyve punds money
" *toties quoties* as they shall contravene theirin. And they doe
" heirby also requyre and command all the inhabitants of this
" burgh wha hes any such commodities and victwalls to buy
" for the use of their howse and familie That they buy the
" samyn heir at this mercat, and not to goe to other mercats."

THE good effects, if there were any, of this arbitrary decree of council were but of short duration. The market soon became as little frequented as formerly, and at length gradually decreased into non-existence; whilst, in the mean time, the market in Glasgow rose upon its ruins.

THE fairs of Rutherglen seem to have been equally on the decline with the market about the same period.

FEW

Few things are calculated to afford us better information, concerning the cuftoms and manners of any people, than their markets and fairs. As they were the chief and almoft only places of mercantile refort, they exhibit to our view the marketable commodities of the country; the cuftoms and duties impofed upon them; and, confequently, the principal fources of wealth and influence in all thofe places where they were held. From them we may alfo learn, what were the chief articles of provifion, of drefs and of luxury in former times; and what alterations have fince taken place in thefe refpects. Particular attention fhould therefore be paid, in the hiftory of any country, to the ftate of thefe public places of refort; to the different kinds of merchandife expofed to fale; to the laws by which they were regulated; and the peculiar cuftoms and forms that were obferved on thefe occafions.

There were anciently four fairs annually held in Rutherglen. To thefe were added two more, in the year 1685. Even thefe not being fufficient, two more were added, in the year 1693, each to continue for the fpace of four days.

It is hoped, that as royal charters for the eftablifhment of fairs are not in every perfon's poffeffion, the following copy of the charter, granted for the two laft mentioned fairs, will not be unacceptable to the public.

Warrand

Warrand of Parliament ffor two free fairs in favour of the Burgh of Rutherglen.

ATT Edinburgh, The Fifeteenth day of June, Jai. vi. & Nyntle three yeares. Our Soveraigne Lord and Ladie The King and Queens Majesties, Takeing to their Consideration, The Great conveniencie and advantage that will accress to their ma$^{ts.}$ Liedges, By haveing the two free faires underwritten att the Burgh Royall of Rutherglen. Therfore their Majesties, with advice, and consent of the Estates of Parliament, Doe heirby Give and Grant To the Magistrates of the said Burgh of Rutherglen present and to come ffull Power, Right, Liberrtie, and Priviledge of holding two free faires there; the one upon the eighteenth day of July; the other upon the eighteenth day of November yeirly. Each to stand and continue for the space of ffour days, ffor Buying and Selling of all kynd of country Manufactories, and small waire; And all kynd of Bestiall, as horse, nolt, sheep, and all other Merchandice; as use is, in that country. With Power to the saids Magistrates, present and to come, as said is, or such as they shall appoint, to Collect, Intromitt with, and uplift the Tolls, Customes and Duties belonging to the saids faires. And to enjoy all other Jurisdictiones, freedomes, priviledges, liberties and immunities pertaineing therto. Sicklyke, and as freely, as any other hes done, or may doe in the like case. Extracted furth of the Records of Parliament By George Viscount of Tarbat, Lord Macleod and Castlehaven, Clerk to the parliament and to their ma$^{ts.}$ Council, Exchequer, Registers and Rolls, &c.

(Signed)   Tarbat. Cl. Regr.

THE beſt frequented and, probably, the moſt ancient of all the fairs in Rutherglen, is the one called *St. Luke's;* it begins on the 3d Monday of October, old ſtyle, and continues the whole week.

FROM an old ballad publiſhed in Pinkerton's collection of Scotch Poems, 1786, author unknown, it appears that this fair was once held in great reputation, but was conſiderably on the decline when the poem was written. As the ballad is poſſeſſed of no ſmall merit, and contains ſome curious facts relative to the fair and the manners of the times, I have thought proper to give it a place in this part of the hiſtory.

TO yow, my lordis of renoun,
 The haill pepill of Rugling toun;
Burges, merchants, and indwellaris;
Craftſmen, officers, and meit-ſellaris;
Ryche men, puiranes, and gud yemen;
Wydows, maidins, and hyre-women;
Honeſt matrons, and guid wyfis;
Young men, and younkers that findil ſtrifis,
Magiſtratis, and men of degrie;
Servands, and ſic as luifis on fie:
Schortlie of the toun the haill menzie,
Maiſt humblie to yow now dois plenzie,
That our traffique dois clene decay;
Our ſchift and gaine is quyte away.

We

We haif na change within our burgh;
The grient girs growis our ftreithis through.
Our baxifteris of breid hes no faill;
The brofteris hes na change for aill.
The flefchers' fkamblis ar gane dry;
The heiland men bringis in na ky.
The merchands hes na change of wair;
The hoftellaris gettis na repair;
The craftismen ar not regardit;
The prentes boyis ar not rewardit;
The ftableris gettis na ftabil fies;
The hyre-women gettis na balbeis;
The hors-boyis ar hurt of thair waige.
There is no proffeit for a paige.

Schortlie, thair is na change within,
The court of ftrangeris is fa thin.
And all this forow, and mifcheif,
Is nouther cum of huir nor theif;
Nor be the force of enimeis;
Nor be privat confpiracieis.
Bot becaus men hes lattin doun
The fair, and market of our toun.
I mean the mercat of our hors;
Quhilk nather cumis to port, nor cors,
Nor to the croft our toun befyde;*
Quhar mony ane was wont to ryde.

At

* " *Nor to the croft our toun befyde.*" The Horfe Croft, containing a few acres of land, is fituated at the weft end of the town, and, with the main ftreet, was occupied by horfes brought to the Fair, when at its greateft fame. Afterwards, upon the decreafe complained of in the Poem, the horfes were confined to the ftreet only, and the Croft was fet apart for other purpofes. It was inclofed about 50 years ago, but ftill continues to be called the Horfe Croft. This circumftance, being known to very few ftrangers, affords a great probability that the Poem is authentic.

RUTHERGLEN.

At guit Sanct Lukis nobill fair
Quhair mony nobills did repair;
And for the wery wynter tyd
For ryddin hors did thame provyde,
For thame and all thair company;
That it was plefour thame to fe.
Bot now the nobillis takis na fors;
And cairis not for ryddin hors.
On hors thai will no mony fpend,
But fpairs it till ane uthair end.
Sua nevir is fene intill our toun
Lord, laird, burges, or baroun.
And quhair that mony gay gelding
Befoir did in our mercat ling,
Now fkantlie in it may be fene
Tuelf gait glydis, deir of a preine.

This cummis not, as we confidder,
That men to travel now ar flidder;
For mony now fo biffie ar,
Quhidder ye travell neir or far.
Go befoir, or byde behind,
Ye fall thame aye in your gat find:
Thoch nothing to thame thair perteine,
Yit thai will ay be biffie fene.

Nor yit tak thai this cair and paine,
On fute travellan on the plaine,
Bot rydes rycht foftlie on a * MEIR,
Well montit in thair ryding geir.
The richt reffoun thane till efpy,
Quhy rydin hors men will not by,

---

* The MEIR, feems to mean *pride*, as we fay a man is on 'his high horfe.'
PINK.

Is that thai get ane MEIR unbocht;
And fua thai think thai ryd for nocht.
And thinks it war ane fulifche act
On ryding hors to fpend the pact;
Haifand ane yaid at thair command,
To ryd on baith in burgh, and land.
This wikit MEIR fa weill thame ftaikis,
And ambillis with them in the glaikis,
That quha to hir dois anes him hant,
Thairefter he can not her want.
For fcho fo gloriouflie dois ryd,
That thame puffis up with pryd:
Be thai anes montit on hir bak,
Thai think in thame there is na lak.

Thair meit doublet dois them rejoys;
Thay fpred abrod thair ruffet hois;
Thay tak delyt in nedil wark,
Thay gloir in thair weill ruffit fark.
Thair litil bonet, or bred hat,
Sumtyme heiche, and fumtyme plat,
Waites not how on thair heid to ftand;
Thair glufis perfumit, in thair hand,
Helpis meikill thair countenance:
Et tout eft a la mode de France.
Thair dry fcarpenis, baythe tryme and meit;
Thair mullis glitteran on thair feit;
Thair gartans, knottet with a roys,
Putis all the laffis in thair chois.
They fnyte, thoch thair na mifter be,
That ye may thair trim napkyne fee;
And, gif ye richtly it confidder,
The goldin knappis fhall hing the gidder.

Quhaneas

Quhaneas thay talk of ony thing,
All tendis to thair awn loving;
Wald ye esteme thame be thair crakis,
Thay wald be Cesaris in thair actis:
For lordlie liberalitie,
Thay gone bot kingis for to be.
Thair ryches, as thairselfs dois count,
King Cresus' thresour may surmount.
Onto thair talis quha list attend,
Thay knaw all to the warkds end:
Gif ye will trew all that thay tell,
In everie thing thai do excell,
Tha ar the fassiouns, as I heir,
Of men that rydis on the MEIR.

The wemen als, that on HIR rydis,
Thay man be buskit up lyk brydis.
Thair heides heifit with fickin faillis;
With clarty * silk about thair taillis;
Thair gounis schant to schaw thair skin,
Suppois it be right oft full din.
To mak thame sma the waist is bound;
A buist to mak thair bellie round:
Thair buttokis bosterit up behind;
A fartigal to gathair wind.
Thair hois made of sum wantoun hew;
And quhene thai gang, as thai nocht knew,

F   Thay

---

* See Lindsay on *side* (i. e. *long*) *tails*, among his poems. Chaucer, in the Persones Tale, railing at extravagant dress, mentions " the coste of the embroiding; the disguising, endenting, or barring; ounding; paling; winding, or bending; and semblable wast of cloth in vanitee: but ther is also the costlewe furring in hir goune, so much pounsoning of chesel to maken holes; so much dagging of sheres; with the superfluitee in length of the foresaide gounes trailing in the dong, and in the myre, on hors, and eke on foot; as wel of man as of woman,' &c.   PINK.

Thay lift thair goun abone thair fchank:
Syne lyk ane brydlit cat thai brank.
Sum taunting wordes thai haif per * queir,
That fervice thame in all mateir.

THE decreafe of Luke's fair no doubt confiderably affected the town's revenues, arifing from the cuftoms levied from almoft every article expofed to fale. A remedy, however, for this evil was at hand: but it was fuch as might naturally be fuppofed rather to increafe than diminifh the caufe of complaint. Additional duties were impofed on goods brought to market. The following cuftom was, in the year 1658, exacted from wool and cloth brought to the fair.

"IT is ordered by Provoft, Baillies and Counfall that the "Cuftomer fhall exact of cuftome in tymecomming, for eache "pack, four fchilling; for a fardell † twa fchilling, and for "other things, that cometh to the mercat, as formerly, and no "farder."

ADDITIONAL

---

* *Per queir*, that is *by book, with formal exactnefs. Quair* is *book*, whence our *quire* of paper. 'Go thou litil *quayer*,' Caxton. Proverbs of Chreftine, 1478. He alfo often ufes *quaires* for *books* in his profe.

Go, litil quaire, unto my livis quene.
Chaucer, Complaint of Black Knight.

The blak bybill pronounce I fall *per queir*.
LINDSAY.

The word *Quair*, in this acceptation, is rendered immortal by *the Kings Quair* of James I.
PINK.

† Or three webs. The word *fardel* is derived from the Italian *fardello* a bundle or packet. *Bailey's Dict.*

ADDITIONAL duties were afterwards greatly enlarged, as appears from the following Table.

October 1st, 1670. *A Table of the rates and pryces of cuftome to be exacted by the Cuftomers at this nixt faire and in tymecomming for the goodes and merchandice following.*

Firft, for ane pack of walked woollen cloathe, or farges or other ftuffes at the importing to be fold within this burgh, Sex fchilling.

Item, at the exporting of a pack of cloathe woollen or Sarges &c, to be payed be the bwyer, fex fchilling Scotts.

Item, for a fardell of woollen cloathe, thrie webs, thrie fchilling.

Item, for twa walked webs, twa fchilling.

Item, for ane fingle walked web, twelff penneyes.

Item, for ane pack of playding, at the importing, fowr fchilling.

Item, for the exporting of a pack of playding, fowr fchilling,

Item, for a fingle web of playding or drogat, if it be above fextein ell, twelff penneyes; and if it be under feven, eight penneyes.

Item, for ilke paire of playdes imported, eight penneyes.

Item, for ilke peice or cutt of whyte lining cloathe, caryed upon a man or womans backe or arme, being above fex cutt, twa penneyes Scotts.

Item, for ane fardell of lyning cloathe imported on horfbacke, belonging to ane perfone, fowr fchilling.

Item, for ane pack of lyning cloathe bowght and exported, eight fchilling.

Item, for ane pack of bannets belonging to ane perfone, at the importing, thrie fchilling, and alfsmeikle at the exporting.

Item, for ilke chapman Creemer that caryes his pack on his back, twelff penneyes, and for thefe that hes thrie packs caryed on horfback, or on flaides, at twa fchilling.

Item, for ilke kow or young ftirk bull or oxen, and fwyne that is browght to the mercat, twelff penneyes, and alfsmeikle for ilke ane that is bowght, at the exporting.

Item, for ilke fardell of bannets belonging to ane perfone at the importing, ane fchilling fex penneyes, and alfsmeikle at the exporting be the bwyer.

Item, for ilke loade of frwit, fowr fchilling.

The Proveft, Bailleis and Counfell ratifies and approves the foirfaid table. And ordaines the faids rates and pryces to be exacted be the Cuftomers Intyme comming, and no farder, " And if any perfone or perfones Collectors of the cuftome or " there fervands fhall be fund or tryed to exact any more nor " according to the rates conteined in the befoirwrytin table, " they fhall be lyable, ilke ane of them, contra ebeeing the " premifs, In ane fyne and valow of twentie punds money, " *toties quoties*, to be payed to the profifsal for the publict ufe " of the court."

THESE cuftoms, having afterwards undergone many alterations and improvements, are now reduced to the following Table, according to which they are, at prefent, exacted.

CUSTOMS

CUSTOMS

OF THE

BURGH OF RUTHERGLEN.

	l.	s.	d.
For each Horse or Mare imported for sale	0	0	$1\frac{1}{2}$
Each Cow or Bull	0	0	$1\frac{2}{3}$
Each Pack of Linen Cloth	0	0	8
Each Load of Fruit	0	0	4
Each Slieck of Fruit	0	0	$0\frac{1}{2}$
Each Chapman's Pack with a Horse	0	0	2
Each Chapman bearing his Pack	0	0	1
Each Pack of Woolen Cloth	0	0	6
Each half Load of Cloth	0	0	3
Each single Web of Cloth	0	0	1
Each Sheep	0	0	$0\frac{1}{2}$
Each Horse sold or nieffered, and exported	0	0	$1\frac{1}{2}$

THE customs exacted at Luke's fair are, by way of distinction, called the *penny-custom*, because, at first, a penny Scots was demanded for each article exposed to sale at the market.

BUT the revenues of the town were concerned in other exactions than that of the penny-custom. The profits arising from the *Ellwand-Stock*, the *Ladles* and *Trone*, increased considerably the pecuniary product of these public markets.

THE

The *Ellwand-Stock* confisted of a great number of ellwands, marked by authority, to afcertain their juft length. Thefe were given out, for a certain fmall fum, to the fellers of cloth, during the fair, and the profits arifing from them were fold, by public roup, along with the penny-cuftom, to which they were frequently annexed.

Few things could have a better tendency to prevent deceit in the feller, and fufpicion in the buyer of cloth, than thefe properly adjufted meafures. The ftock was fometimes pretty confiderable, for we find that an addition of 80 ellwands was made to it in the year 1682. They were made by a wright in Glafgow, and coft four pund Scots.

The *Ladles* was a duty impofed upon grain, or meal, brought into the market for fale. It is faid to have been introduced into the weft of Scotland, when a great plague raged in the country, probably about the end of the fourteenth century. It was generally believed that money of every kind, but efpecially copper, readily catched and as readily communicated the infection. Owing to this opinion, country people, being ftrictly on their guard againft fo dreadful an evil, would not touch money from any perfon in a town where the plague was thought to be, until the money was held, for a confiderable time, in boiling water. It was believed,

and

RUTHERGLEN. 47

and perhaps not without reason, that this operation would entirely destroy the infection, if there were any. To humour this prevailing opinion of the people, and to prevent, if possible, the spread of the plague, a caldron, with boiling water, was kept always in readiness, in market places, on the market days. The money intended to be laid out, was put into an iron-ladle, and held for a certain time in the water. The ladle full of meal, in order to defray the necessary expences, was exacted from every load of meal brought to the market; and hence the origin of the name of the custom or duty.

PUBLIC taxes, however triffling or temporary their original causes may have been, are very seldom removed, and the unwary community is made to groan, for ages, under their increasing weight. The Ladles continued to be rigorously exacted, although the plague was at an end, the fire extinguished, and the caldron broken to pieces.

THE capacity of the *ladle* was appointed to be equal to the *fourth part* of a peck, as appears from an act passed in the year 1661. " The *ladle* is to " contain a *fourth part* of a peck, and is to be " taken out of each Sake of beir, malt, meil, peis, " beines, wheat, that comes from the country to " the town, for common sale." The following act, being

being more extensive than the former, was made in the year 1662.

"THE Provost, Baillies and Counsell, for the better de-
" fraying of the publict debts and burdings of this incorpora-
" tione, and improvement of the commune dewties, and reve-
" news thairof, heve resolved, concluded, and ordered, and
" hereby resolves, concludes, and ordores, That the *Ladle* full
" of victwall (as the famyne is now maid) extending to the
" *fourt part* of ane peck (or theirby) shall be furthwith, in all
" tymes comeing, exacted, levyed, and collected of each fake
" of beir, malt, meill, peis, beines, wheat and aitts which,
" heirefter, shall be bowght in the country, and browght within
" this burgh for common sale, by any of the inhabitants and
" burgesses thairof, or by whatsimever persone or persones
" duelland without the said burgh. And the partie buyer and
" inbringer of the forsaid victwalls, at the incomeing thairof, is
" and shall be, hereby, astricted & obleidged to acquaint the
" takfman and keiper of the said *ladle* that he may come and
" ladle the said Victwall, befor any sale or use be maid thairof;
" With power to the takfman or keiper of the *ladle* to conveine
" the buyers and inbringers of victwalls out of the country as
" said is (in caice of their deficience in paying of the *ladle* for-
" said) befor the Magestrats and to prove the quantities, by
" witness, oath of pairtie, or any other legall way of probatione
" they pleafe. And orders the said *Ladle* to be roiped and sett
" out to these wha shall offer to pay most for the saime.

THE effects of this act were but of short continuance, for the custom ceased to be levied soon after
the weekly market was not frequented.

IN

In Glasgow, however, the Ladles are still exacted at the commuted price of half a peck per load; and, besides defraying the charges of collecting, produce to the revenue of the city, between six and seven hundred pounds sterling per annum.

The *Trone* was a duty paid for the use of trone weights, appointed by the Magistrates, for weighing certain goods that were sold at the markets and fairs. The balances were suspended from a large beam, of the shape of a cross, that was erected in the market place. The weights were generally made of whin-stone, and hence called the trone-stones; they were " ringed with iron rings," and stamped by authority to shew that they were just. This duty, for the time of Luke's fair, 1622, produced, to the revenues of the town, the sum of " fowrtie " pund ten schilling Scots," besides defraying the charges of collecting. But so much was the state of the fair changed, in the year 1690, that it fell so low as seven merks. It is now altogether annihilated.

The fairs of Rutherglen have undergone very material changes. Horses seem to have been the chief article of sale, at a time prior to the date of the old ballad already mentioned. Afterwards they were frequented mostly for wool and woollen cloth, from the west country, about Ayr and Galloway,

and which was purchased for Glasgow, the Lothians, &c. This species of traffic, being now bought up in Ayr, Maybole, &c. is almost at an end, and has given place to cows; but chiefly to horses, for which the fairs of Rutherglen have become famous. The horses are mostly for the draught, and are deservedly esteemed the best, for that purpose, in Europe. They are generally of the Lanark and Carnwath breed, which was introduced into the county more than a century ago. It is said, that one of the predecessors of the present Duke of Hamilton, brought with him to Scotland six coach horses, originally from Flanders, and sent them to Strathaven, the castle of which was, at that time, habitable. The horses were all stallions, of a black colour, and remarkably handsome. The farmers in the neighbourhood, readily embracing the favourable opportunity, crossed this foreign breed with the common Scotch kind, and thereby procured a breed superior to either. From this, a strong and hardy race of horses was soon spread through the country, but in many places, owing to neglect, was left to degenerate. By want of proper attention, we often let slip the most favourable opportunities of improvement, and suffer unmanly indolence to deprive us of many blessings we might otherwise enjoy. A high degree of merit, however, is due to the farmers in the upper part of the county, for their unremitting endeavours to improve this excellent

cellent breed. They pay strict attention to every circumstance respecting the colour; the softness and hardness of the hair; length of the body, neck and legs; but chiefly to the shape of the back, breast and shoulders of their breeders. No inducement whatever, can lead them to encourage the breed of a horse, that is not possessed of the best qualities. Providence commonly favours the attentive and the diligent. Their laudable attempts have proved to be successful, and Britain is now reaping the merited fruits of their well directed care. Every farm, almost, through the extent of several parishes, supports 6, or at least 4 mares, the half of which are allowed, annually, to foal. The colts* are mostly sold at the fairs of Lanark and Carnwath, and bring to the owners from 5, to 20 l. each. They are generally purchased by farmers from the counties of Renfrew and Ayr, where they are trained for the draught, till they are about five years old: they are then sold at the fairs of Rutherglen and Glasgow, from 25, to 35 l. each; from thence they are taken to the Lothians, England, &c. where they excel in the plough, the cart and the waggon.

---

* The colts, when a year old, are called Tomontals, a provincial contraction for twelve-month-old.

The following is a list of the Fairs of Rutherglen, with the times of the year in which they are, at present, held.

MARCH, first Frid. *old style.* Not frequented.
APRIL, last Frid. *o. s.*
JUNE, first Tuesd. after Trinity Sunday.
JULY, third Frid. *o. s.*
AUGUST, third Frid. *o. s.*
OCT. third Mond. *o. s. whole week.*
NOV. third Frid. *o. s.*

BUT, independent of every other circumstance, Rutherglen acquired a considerable degree of influence, from the share which it had in the management of political matters. It has, for some centuries past, been the " Head Burgh of the Netherward of " Clydesdale, or shire of Lanark; and all the edicts " in the parishes of Bothwell, Barton-Shotts, Cam- " busnetham, Glasfoord, Strathaven, Blantyre, Cam- " buslang, Carmunnock and Rutherglen are served " at its cross."*

THE influence of this borough must formerly have added considerable weight to the political affairs of the nation; for in the year 1617 it sent two

* McUre's Hist. of Glas. p. 88.

two Commiſſioners to the parliament of Scotland. At preſent it is united with Glaſgow, Renfrew and Dumbarton, in conjunction with which, it ſends one Commiſſioner only, to the Britiſh parliament.

From the following copy of a Letter, ſent to the Magiſtrates, by *Gen. Monk*, we may learn, what ideas the General had formed of the importance of Rutherglen.

---

*For My verie loveing freinds The Proveſt
and Baillies of the burgh
of Rutherglen.*

Gentlemen,

HAVEING a call from God and his people to marche into England to aſſert and maintayne the libertye and being of parliaments, our ancient conſtitutione and thairin the friedome and rights of the people of theſe thrie Nationes from arbitrary and tyrannicall uſurpationes upon their conſciences, perſones and eſtates, and for a godly Miniſtry. I doe thairfor expect from yow the Magiſtrates of the burgh of Rutherglen, that yow doe preſerve the peace of the Common wealth in your burgh. And I heirby athorize yow to ſuppreſs all tumults, ſtirrings, & unlawful aſſemblies, and that yow hold noe correſpondency with any of Charles Stewarts pairtye or his adherents, bot apprehend any ſuch as ſhall make any diſturbance and ſend them unto the nixt gariſone. And doe further deſyre yow to countenance and to encowrrage the godly Miniſtry, and all that

trowlie

trowlie feare God in the land. And that yow continow faithful to owne and assert the interest of the parliamentary government in yowr severall places and stationes. I hope my absence will be very short, bot I doe assure yow that I shall procure from the parliament whatever may be for the good government & reliefe of this Natione, and dowbt not bot to obteane abatements in yowr asessements and other public burthenes according to the proportione of England. And what further service I may be able I shall not be wanting in what I may promote the happines & peace of this afflicted people. I shall not trwble yow further, bot beg yowr prayers and desyre yow to assure yowrselffes that I am

Yowr faithfull friend and humble servand

(Signed)   J George Monk.

Ed. the 15th Nover. 1659.

*Postscript. I desyre yow to send me word to Berwick under yowr hands how farre yow will comply with my desyres by the 12th of Decer. nixt. I desyre yow that what is behind of the last fowr moneths of the twelff moneths asesfment may be in a reddines against it be called for.**

THERE are few things, respecting this ancient borough, that merits greater attention than the free and unembarrassed election of its Magistrates and council. The evils arising from a self-elected magistracy, and their uninterrupted continuance in office,

* *Council Records*, ann. 1659.

office, were, at an early period, severely felt by the community. They found by experience, that the guardians of the rights and liberties of the town, too often neglected the charge committed to their trust, and basely undermined the constitution they were sworn to support. Negligence on the one hand, and undue exertions of power on the other, did, at length, excite the complaining burgesses to trace out the true cause of these evils, and to seek for a proper remedy.

THERE are times when the multitude, deprived of their natural rights, will neither be intimidated by the threats, nor subjugated by the artifices of political influence, and overgrown power. They will think for themselves: they will lay schemes to regain their liberty; and, they will dare to put them in execution. Such a spirit of freedom is inspired by the Author of nature, for the good of mankind in general, and of smaller communities in particular.

A REFORM with respect to the magistracy, and set of the borough, was begun by the inhabitants, soon after the beginning of the last century. In the execution of their design they were greatly assisted by Mr. David Spens, town-clerk, whose office gave him many opportunities of defending the interest of the community.

HAPPY

HAPPY would it be for the complaining burgesses in Scotland, were it now in their power to follow the laudable example of the citizens of Rutherglen; and like them, effectually to check the public abuses of which they so much complain. But the period in which this could be done, is, probably, long since past.

AFTER repeated struggles, and a long train of well adapted political exertions, the majority of the Magistrates and council enacted, in the year 1660 " That no Provest nor Baillie shall continue longer " in office than twa ziers togidder." This act which at first met with violent opposition, was renewed, ann. 1670. In the mean while it was ordered, " That no more than twa persones be upon " the Provest Lyte in place of thrie or fowre or " more that was formerly." Before this it was also enacted, that the Provost and Baillies should reside in the town or royalty all the time they were in office.

THESE favourable beginnings opened the way for a thorough reform; the chief clauses of which were laid before the Corporation for their perusal; and, next year, meeting with the approbation of the inhabitants, were appointed to be the *Set* of the town in all time coming.

RUTHERGLEN. 57

A copy of the new Set or Constitution of the town of Rutherglen, as it is recorded in the council books, and extracted from them into the records of the general Convention of the Royal Boroughs of Scotland.

"AT Rutherglen the Twelt day of October, One
" thousand sex hundred thriescore ellevin zeirs.
" Andrew Harvie Provest, W^m· Riddell baillie, Robert Spens,
" George Fairie, George Wyllie, W^m· Riddell fischer, Thomas
" Willkie, Johne Fairie, Johne Riddell elder, Johne Shaw,
" James Wyllie, Robert Bowman, Johne Riddell tailzeor,
" Johne Mwre, Johne Smith, and Robert Awldcorne Coun-
" sellors of the burgh of Rutherglen. With the speciall advyse
" and consent of the haill inhabitants therof now conveened.
" Considdering the debates, differences and divisiones of this
" incorporatione In order to the electione of the Magistrats and
" toun Counsell therof, And that it hath beine the constant and
" continwall practise of, the Provest and Baillies of the said
" burgh thir many zeires bygone efter there electione zeirlie,
" to Nominat and elect a Counsell, by, and to themselffes,
" whairby some leiding and factious men have brought in on
" the Counsell all there freinds, allayes, relationes and adherents;
" And so have practized and endevored to inhawnce and perpe-
" tuat the Magistracie to themselffes for a long tyme; and to
" make use of and dispose upon the commone goodes, revenewes
" and casualities of the burgh as they thought fitt, without
" controlement, to the great prejudice and ruine of the publict
" interest of this poore incorporatione. For preventing whairof
" and for removeing and setleing of all the differences and divi-
" siones of this burgh, in relatione to the electione of there
" Magistrats and toun Counsell. And for establishing a con-
" stant and solid order to be inviolablie observed thereanent in
" all tymecoming IT is now inacted statut and Ordained by

H " the

" the faids Proveft, Baillie and Counfell With the confent of
" the deacones of trades and haill Inhabitants of the faid burgh
" foirfaid; That the toun Counfell of this burgh, confifting of
" ffyftein perfones for this fucceiding zeir and in all tymecome-
" ing fhall be elected and choifen in maner following To wit,
" that ilke ane of the thrie deaconries; Viz, of the fmiths,
" weivers, and mafones and wrights, fhall give in a Lift of fex
" perfones, and the fowrt deaconrie, Viz, the tailzeors fhall
" give in a Lift of fowr perfones; And the remanent burgeffes
" inhabitants within the faid burgh and territorie therof (beiring
" fcott and lott within the famyn) fhall give in a Lift of eight
" perfones to the Proveft and twa Baillies of the faid burgh,
" Wha fhall choyfe thrie out of the feverall thrie fexes, and twa
" out of the fowr, and fowr out of the eight, which makes upe
" the number of ffyftein perfones wha are to be the commone
" Counfell of the faid burgh. And the foirfaid forme of elec-
" tione of the faid commone Counfell is to be unalterable in all
" tymecomeing. And the faids fowr trades and remanent bur-
" geffes fhall be holden and obleift to meit and give in there
" refpective Lifts of perfones foirfaid to the faids Proveft and
" Baillies upon the thretein day of October inftant for this in-
" ftant zeir, And upon the firft thurfday nixt efter the electione
" of the Magiftrats zeirlie, in all tyme therefter. Whairin if
" the faids trades, or any of them, fhall failzie, That the faids
" Magiftrats fhall have power to choyfe the Counfellors for the
" trade, or trades, and remanent burgeffes, ane, or other, of
" them that fhall happin to failzie to give in there Lift to the
" faids Proveft and Baillies upon the faid firft thurfday nixt
" efter the faid electione.———Item, It is inacted, ftatut
" and ordained, that the Magiftrats of the faid burgh fhall be
" choyfen within the tolbwith of the faid burgh upon the twelf'
" day Immediatlie efter Michailmes, In this maner. Viz, at
" the electione, in the zeir 1672, And in all zeirs therefter,
" The Proveft and Baillies fhall be elected and choyfen be a frie
                                                    " voyce

" voyce of the than Magiſtrats and Counſell of the ſaid burgh,
" and of threttie perſones of additionall Counſell to be choyſen
" be the ſaid commone Counſell. And that the ſaid Proveſt
" and Baillies ſhall only continow in there Office for the ſpace
" of ane zeir. And ſhall not be capable to be continowed bot
" ſhall be changed zeirlie.———And the toun Theſawrer to
" be thairefter choyſen be the Proveſt, Baillies and Counſell ſo
" eſtabliſhed.———And for auditeing, comptrolling and ſtate-
" ing of the Theſawrer accompts zeirlie, Thair ſhall be choyſen
" thrie be the Proveſt, Baillies and Counſell; and thrie be the
" deacones and maſters of the foirſds fowr crafts, and eight
" perſones of the remanent burgeſſes foirſaid; And the ſaids
" ſex perſones to be ſtentmaſters for proportionating and laying
" on of all publict burdings to be impoſed upon the ſaid
" burgh.———And whatevir perſone or perſones refuſſes to
" accept of any of the foirſds offices of Proveſt, Baillies and
" Theſſr: foirſaid (being lawfully elected yrto) ſhall pay to the
" Theſſr: for the commone uſe and behwiſe of the ſaid burgh
" The ſowme of Ane hundreth Pundes Scotts money,———And
" it ſhall be Liſſime and lawfull to the preſent Magiſtrats and
" Counſell, for the tyme being, to elect and choyſe fitt and
" able men to ſupplie the places of ſuch of the ſaids Proveſt,
" Baillies, and Theſſr: and Counſell whoe refuſſes to accept
" the ſaids offices, and of theſe deceiſand in the intervall of
" electiones.———And this order to be inviolablie obſerved
" and keiped in all tymecomeing.———And whatevir perſone
" or perſones Proveſt, Baillies, Counſellors and burgeſſes, within
" this burgh, ſhall anywayes heirefter indevore to repaill or
" anywayes infringe this ordor, He or they ſhall not only be
" reput and holden as infringers of the liberties and priviledges
" of this burgh, And thereby, *ipso facto*, ſhall forfawlt there
" burgeſſhipt and be reput and holden as infamows and perjured
" perſones, Bot ſhall alſo be lyable in ane ſyne of ane Hundreth
" Pundes to be payed to the Theſſr: for the publict uſe of this
incorporatione.

"incorporatione.———And farder, all such facts and deids to
" be done in prejudice of the foirsaid sitt and established forme
" of electione of the saids Magistrats and Counsell choyseing of
" the Thessr: Auditors and stentmasters, It shall be voyd and
" null, and of nane availl, force, strenth, nor effect as if the
" samyn had never bein thowght upon or made. And Ordaines
" the above wryttin act and sett to be recorded in the said
" commune Counsell bookes of the said burgh of Rutherglen,
" and in the bookes of the fowr respective deaconries above
" mentionat."

" *Act of the town Councill of Rutherglen relative to the Sett of the
" said burgh.*

" Rutherglen: 27: Apryle: 1710: yeirs.

" JOHN MWRE and Patrick Withersponc Baillies;
" Andrew fleming, James parke, Johne Witherspone, James
" ffriebairne, William Harvie, Andrew Harvje elder, John
" Scott, James pedie, and Robert Bowman Counsellors, now
" Conveened; taikeing to thair serious Considderatione, that
" this burgh, and the publick good and utilitie thairof, Hath
" suffered by persones being advanced Into the Magistracie
" thairof, without knowledge, and experience of the touns
" effaires and circumstances of the samyn.———And which
" evil practisses may be yett againe Renewed, and be of dan-
" gerous Consequence to the toune and publick good thairof,
" and, Consequentlie, to everie privat burges of the samyn,
" unles remeid be provydit, Which the saids Baillies and Coun-
" sell ar willing to doe, To the Utmost of thair power, In
" Mainer underwryttin. THairfor, the saids Baillies and
" Counsell, have statuit, and ordained, and heirby, with advyse,
" and

" and Consent, of the ffowr deacones and thair Mafters of croft,
" Reprefenting the saids trades, and the Reft of the hereitors
" and burgefs wha ar not incorporat within the ffowr deaconries;
" Statutes and ordaines, that in all tym cumeing, no perfone
" shall be Capable of beireing office, as Proveft of this burgh,
" untill firft he have borne office as baillie thairin, for ane yeir
" at Leift.———And that no perfone shall be Capable to beir
" office, as baillie of this burgh, unlefs ffirft he hes served as
" toune thefs^r· thairof.———And Becawes, It will alfoe be of
" evill and dangerous Confequence to this burgh and the publick
" weill and utilitie thairof, if any perfone fhall be advanced to
" be aither Proveft, Baillie, or thefs^r· of this burgh, except ane
" ordinarie burges thairof, Haveing alwayes his duelling and
" refidence Within this burgh, and threttine pund land thairof,
" dureing the haill tyme of his beiring office in any of the for-
" saids stationes. For preventing whairof, THe saids Baillies
" and Counfell, with Confent forsaid, Have statuit, inacted,
" and ordained, And heirby statuits, inacts, and ordaines, that,
" in all tyme cumeing, no perfone fhall be capable to beir office,
" Within this burgh, aither as proveft, baillie, or thefs^r·, except
" ane ordinarie burges of this burgh; Haveing always his duel-
" ling place and residence within the same, and threttine pund
" land, belonging thairto, dureing the haill tyme of his beirand-
" office In any of the forsaids stationes. And that none but
" fuch fhall be Capable to be yotted upon to beir office In any
" of the forsaids stationes.———And the saids Baillies and
" toune Counfell, With advyfe forsaid, Have Inacted, Statuit,
" and ordained, And heirby inacts, statuts, and ordaines, that
" it fhall not be lawfull for any Magiftrat, Counfellor, or vther
" burges q^tfumevir, In all tymcumeing, to vote, plott, or Con-
" tribute, anent the Incrocheing vpon, or Contraveening this
" pnt act, vnder the paine of being declaired Incapable to beir
" office, In any publick ftatione, within this burgh, for ever
" thairefter, and of Lofseing his friedome: and vnder the paine

" of

" of Ane Hundred punds Scotts of fyne. ffarder, for the
" publick ufe, weill, and behove, of this burgh, And, to the
" effect this act may be more readly maid effectuall, It is heirby
" declaired, that it shall be in the power of any of the privat
" burgefs of this burgh, quther Counfellor or not, as weill as
" the Magiftrats, or Counfellors thairof, to cawes the fame be
" put to executtione at thair inftance, and that vpon the expenfs
" of the Contraveeners heirof,———And that thefe prefents
" fhall be Recorded In the Counfell bookes; and extracts heirof
" given, gratis, by the toune Clerk thairof, to the ffowr trades,
" that the famyn may be Recorded in each trades bookes: And
" ane vther extract given by the Clerk, gratis, to the heretors;
" and this prefent act, with the wrytt, Comonlie called the act
" of eftablifchment of this burgh, daittit the twelf day of oct^{r},
" Jaj vi & Sevintie ane zeirs, shall be opinlie red, yeirlie, In
" all tymcumeing, In prefence of the Magiftrats, Counfell, and
" burgefs, that fhall be prefent vpon the Election day of the
" Magt^{s}, efter the additionall Counfell hes given thair oathes,
" and before the Magiftrats be elected.———And that the
" prefent Magiftrats of this burgh, with the prefent Counfellors,
" fhall subfcrive this act: And that all fucceiding Magiftrats,
" and Counfellors, of this burgh, shall, in all tymcumeing, im-
" mediatlie efter giveing thair oathes *de fideli*, and befoir they
" exerce, Subfcrive this act.———And ordaines the Clerk to
" extract ane dowble heirof, vpon parifchment, which is to be
" signed by the prefent Magiftrats, and toune Counfell, and the
" ffowr deacones, and y^r m^{rs} of croft, and the reft of the here-
" tors, and burgefs, who ar not Incorporat within the ffowr
" deaconries. And which, with the forsaid act, called the act
" of eftablifchment, Is ordained to be put into the touns charter
" cheift,

    (Signed)   John Muir.
           Pat: witherfpone.

              " This

"This Act, ratified and approven be the provost Baillies, and Councill, upon the twenty fourth of October, One thousand Seven hundred and ten years. And ordains ye same to stand in all tymcumeing. And Alsoe, of new againe, Enacts, Statutes, and ordains, that no persone, or persones, whatsomever, except he be an Burgefs, and Constant Induellar within this Burgh and territorie thereof, shall not be capabell to be elected to represent this Burgh, either as Elector for the Burgh, or any other manner of way q'fumever, Intymcumeing, And that under the pains and penalties therein contained."

The above Set is inserted in the records of the general Convention of the Royal Boroughs of Scotland. A judicial extract of it is taken from thefe records, and laid up in the charter-cheft, to be annually read on the day when the Magiftrates are elected.

The following qualifications are requifite, in all who are allowed to vote for the Magiftrates and Council, according to an act, in the year 1775, and recorded in the council books.

"ENACTED, that no perfon be allowed to vote for the Magiftrates, unlefs he lives within the royalty; and none to be admitted a burgefs unlefs he has refided within the royalty four months, previous to the time of his admiffion: but if he has a family he muft refide year and day. Alfo, that the abfence of any perfon from the burgh, year and day together, fhall have the effect to preclude him from being entitled to be entered a burgefs, untill he refide the forefaid periods, in the
"events

" events above mentioned. But in the event of his having been
" a burgess formerly, four months residence, or with his family,
" six months."

The Fines, upon entering Burgess, are as follows.

	l.	s.	d.
A Stranger pays	1	2	2¼
A Burgess' eldest son, if his father is in life	0	8	4
but if his father is dead	0	0	6½
A Burgess' 2ᵈ· 3ᵈ· &c. son, and son in law	0	11	1⅓

As every person has not an opportunity of seeing the laws, by which the property, service, and morals of the inhabitants of royal boroughs, were sometimes regulated, I have thought proper to give the following examples, extracted from the records of the Council of Rutherglen.

1660. *Act anent the pryce of labor.*

" THE Provest, Baillies, and Counsell, in pursuance of the
" trust reposed in yᵐ·, being no less desyrous that servands,
" workmen, and others, should have, from there maysters, that
" which is just and equall; as that a remedye may be gevin to
" these abuses, and grivances, concerneing the excessive pryces
" of fies, and waidges, introduced of late, in tymes of plentie,
" by the covetousnes, idlenes, and other corrupt practices of
" some evill affected servands, and workmen. Doe thairfor
" order, and appoint, that, dureing the scarsnes of money and
                                                    " cheapues

"cheapnes of victwall, no persone within this burgh, give
"nor take, more fie, or waidges nor is heir efter prest.
"To witt.

A commone able man Servand, for all forte of husbandrie, is to have, termly, for fie and bounteth, ten punds Scotts; with a paire of dowble solled shooes, and a paire of hoife, and no more.

A man Servand, of younger zeires, commonlie a halflang, is to have, for fie and bounteth, ten merkes, termly, with a paire of shooes and hoife, and no more.

A able woman servand, for all necefferie worke, ten merkes, termly, with a paire of shooes, ane ell of lining in winter, and ane ell of playding in Sommer.

A lafs, or young made, fowr punds Stotts, with a paire of shooes, termly, and no more.

The herveft fie of an able man sheirer, is not to exceid eight punds, and a peck of meill; with meit and drink: and if he be hyred by dayes, halfe a merke, and twa mailles, for ilk dayes worke. And the able woman sheirer is not to exceid fex punds, and a peck of meill; with meit and drink; or fyve schilling, and twa mailles, for ilk day.

A woman, or lafs, for a dayes worke, in weiding of Lint, cloveing, fpining, cardeing, yarnewinning, or any fuch worke, is to have twelff pennys Scotts, and thrie mailles, and no more.

A thrasher is to have fowr schilling Scotts, and twa mailles ilk day, and no more.

Massones and wrights are not to exceid a merke Scotts without; and halfe a merke with, meit and drink, for the dayes worke.

A Barrow man is not to exceid halfe a merke without, and ffowrtie pennyes with, meit and drink, for the dayes service.

A theiker of howfses is to have ten schilling without, and fyve schilling with, meit and drink, for a dayes service.

Tailzivours are not to exceid ffowrtie pennyes and ther dyet, for a dayes worke.

I A

A commone workeman, or laborer, who workes for daylie waidges, is to have halfe a merke without, and 40 pennies with, meit and drink, for a dayes fervice.

Iff any workeman, woman, or laborer within this burgh, fhall refufe to worke, and ferve, upon the pryces refpective, abovewryttin, they fhall be imprifoned, and further punifhed, as the Magiftrats fhall thinke fitt. And if any workeman, or fervand, man or woman, fhall requyre, and exact, greater fies, and waidges then thefe befor expreft, they are to be fynned according to the difcretione of the Magiftrats.

Ordered, alfo, that no man fervand, or woman fervand, un-married, upon any pretence, fhall take upe howfs, and worke at there own hand, without a warrand from the Magiftrats.

Ordered, lykwayes, that Noe inhabitant, or fervand, man or woman, within this incorporatione, Prefume to fie themfelffes, in herveft tyme, to any perfone, or perfones, dwelling without this burgh, Without a fpeciall Licence from the Magiftrats had thereunto; Under the paine of ffyve pundes money."

The price of labour, at the above period, if we confider the value of money at that time, will appear, in fome inftances, to have been very good. A mafon, or wright, for example, received fix fhillings and eightpence fter. for his week's work, a much higher wage than double the fum at prefent.

The following quotations will give us fome idea of the value of money, at the dates affixed to them.

1619. Price of a harrow; " Ten fchilling Scotts."

1621. Price of tilling an acre of land; Ten fchilling Scotts.

ABOUT a century ago the value of oatmeal was exceedingly variable, as appears from the price of the tiend boll, in the following periods, as it is mentioned in the council records, and according to which the stipend was paid.

Ann.	*l.*	*s.*	*d.*	*Scotts.*	*Ann.*	*l.*	*s.*	*d.*	*Scotts.*
1660.	6 :	6 :	8	per Boll.	1682.	7 :	3 :	4	per Boll.
1663.	8 :	6 :	8	do.	1684.	4 :	6 :	8	do.
1671.	6 :	6 :	8	do.	1689.	6 :	5 :	0	do.
1672.	4 :	13 :	4	do.	1699.	10 :	0 :	0	do.
1674.	9 :	12 :	0	do.	1705.	5 :	0 :	0	do.
1677.	4 :	2 :	0	do.	1709.	8 :	17 :	0	do.

IN the year 1719, it was 5L. 17s. 4d. at which price it continued for several years.

1656. This zier the grave digger is to dig a meikle grave for fowre schilling, and a lytle ane for twa schilling Scotts.

1660. Grafs maill for a kow pastureing in the griene, thrie pund Scotts; by and attour nyne schilling for the heirds sieall.

1665. Resolved upon, be the Provest, Baillies, and Counsall, that a Mortcloathe be bowght: and nominates and appoynts Thomas Wilkie, tailzeor, to goe est to Ed^{r.} and bwy alfs much of the best forte of black velvett as will be a lardge Mortcloathe, with frinddges, and all other necessaries thereabout. And ordains Cloud Riddell, Thressaurer, to provyde moneyes for the said mortcloathe, againft the said Thomas his returne, Conforme to his accompt;* and to advance money to him for his charges.

---

* By the account it appears to have cost £ 260 : 18 : 10 Scots.

The pryce, for the use of the mortcloathe, is to be, for each inhabitant within the burgh, thrie shill. sterl. and for any other without the burgh, the pryce is remitted to the Magistrats, or any ane of them to considder thereof; and to give orders thereanent, as they shall thynke fitt.——In the year 1689, the price was reduced to two shill. ster. In the year 1702, it was enacted, "That the pryce of the Mortcloath, for the inhabitants of the town, is to be thrietie shilling Scotts: and to any other ffyftie shilling." The price, ann. 1716, was ordered by the Magistrates to be as follows. "For ye large on, halfe a croune: for ye midmost on, ffyftine shilling Scotts: and for ye littall on, eight shilling Scotts; in all tym comeing, and no more."

1673. "Contracted with David Spens, to furnish a sufficient Troope horse; and to provyde him with a rider, with sword, saddle, pistolls and all furniture requisite; for which he is to have fourscore punds money of Scotland." Ann. 1683, "The sume of ffyftien pund Sterl: given to bwy a troope horse, for Lanark shire Militia; and to furnish sword, saddle, pistolls and all other necessarie furnitre."

1682. "A man and horse, for lieding sand for the calsway, 18 schilling Scotts, every day."

1713. "Anent the charges and expenss payed be John Witherspone to John Bowman Merchant in Glasgow, and vthers, for cloath, Lyneing, buttones, thried, silke, bucroom, binding, stenting and hair for the two Officers, thair Coattes; and to the tailzor for makeing of them. Extending in the haill to the sowme of ffowrtie ane pund ten shilling Scotts."

1710 "A new Drum for the use of the toun was made be Geo: Murdoch, in the Gorbals for 7 : 5 : 8 £ Scotts."

The Magistrates of Rutherglen not only regulated the prices of provision and labour, but they also enacted certain prohibitory laws, of which the following are examples.

1660. " Every person within the burgh is forbid to bwy malt from any vther maltmen than the towns maltmen."

1677. " Ordered that nane of the inhabitants give or sell, to outtentouns, any Muckmiddins, or foulzie. The Council, 1703, " ratifies ane old act, ordering the inhabitants, that nane of them sell, on any pretence, Muckmiddins, or foulzie, to any persone, not a burgess or inhabitant of the touns territorie."

" *Act of the Counsell obliging parents to put there children to schoole.*

Rutherglen, the first of March, 1675.

" THE Provest, Baillies, and toun Counsell, now conveened; Considdering the great carelesnes and neglect of dewtye of diverss parents in this place, towards there Children, throw not keiping, and educating them at schooles, and learneing, q^{r}by they might become more fitt and usefull instruments, bothe for kirk and kingdome.' For remeid q^{r}of Intymcomeing The saids Provest, Baillies, and toun Counsell Statutes, and Ordaines, all the inhabitants of this burgh, from this furth, to send all there children, betuixt sex and twelff zeirs of aige, to the comune schoole of this burgh, to be educat y^{r}at. With this certificatione, that whaevir neglects there dewtye heirin, shall be compelled to pay the quarter waidges, used and accustomed to the schoolemaster, alsweill, and as if, there children were at the schoole. And these that sends there children to uther schooles,

out

out of the toun (except to the Gramer fchoole) fhall pay dowble quarter waidges for them. And that, furth and from, the terme of Candlemes laft bypaft. And for that effect, Orders and authorizes the officers of this burgh, upon a lift fubfcrybed and delyvered to them be the fchoole Mafter, without any farder orders, to requyre and charge all fuch perfones, as fhall be gevin upe in lift to them, as faid is, To make payment to the fchoolemafter of all bygane quarter waidges than dew, from Candlemes laft, alfweill as if there children, had bein learneing at this fchoole.———And incaice of there refufeall to make prefent payment, Than Imediatlie to poynd, and diftreinzie, the deficients reddieft goodes and geir, for the famyn. Or utherwayes (Incaice the officers can not gett goodes ftreinzie, able) to apprehend the perfones of the deficients and comittt them prifoners within the tolbooth of the faid burgh, thairin to remayne ay and quhill payment be made.———And ordaines this order and act to ftand in full force for the prefent fchoolemafter, and all uthers fucceiding him Intymcomeing. And orders Intimatione to be made heirof by towk of drum throw the toun. Accordinglie upon the feventein day of Marche, 1675 zeirs inftant, Intimatione was made heirof."

The good effects of the above regulation were very difcernible in Rutherglen and the neighbourhood. Children of every defcription were educated in reading; and many of them in writing and arithmetic. So much has the regular education of youth been attended to, that no fmall degree of infamy is fixed on the character of every perfon, come to age, who cannot read and write. Happy will it be for pofterity, if, in the prefent advanced progrefs of manufactures in this country, children are not

neglected

neglected in their education. If they are, the lofs that will be fuftained, not only by individuals, but by fociety at large, cannot be made up by any confideration whatever.

Besides the education of youth, the morals of the people were ftrictly infpected by the Magiftrates.

1668. "The Proveft, Baillies and Counfell, confiddering the frequent drinking and drunkennes of J—— P——, Cowper; and the feverall abufes committed be him frequentlie; and that no admonitione, nor punifhment, can gett him reftrained theirfra. Whairfor the faides Proveft, Baillies and Counfell doe heirby Inhibit, and difcharge, all the brewers and fellers of drinke within this burgh, That they, nor ane of them, prefume to give or fell any drinke to the faid J—— P——, except what they fell to his wyfe and bairnes, for the ufe of the howfe and familie: Under the paine of ffyve punds money, *toties quoties*, as they contravene heirin. And ordaines intimatione to be made heirof be towke of drum."

These prohibitions, and others that might be mentioned, will, perhaps, to fome men appear to have been rather fevere. But let us fufpend our cenfure till we take a view of many ftatutes, at prefent, in force, though made on a larger fcale, in almoft all the nations of the world. The prohibitory laws concerning corn, fpirits, falt, game, coal, &c. are equally abfurd, if there is any abfurdity in the cafe.

Our criticism on the conduct of royal boroughs will be greatly moderated, when we consider, that to them, we are much indebted for the privileges we at present enjoy. They were, at first, erected, by the wisest of our Monarchs, with a view to rescue mankind from under the oppressive power of the barons. For this purpose, certain portions of the King's lands were bestowed upon them. These lands, being commonly adjoining to royal garrisons, is the reason why the greatest number of ancient boroughs are situated in the immediate neighbourhood of places of strength. They were put in possession of certain rights and privileges, the management of which was committed to the inhabitants. They are consequently to be viewed as so many free, and almost independent, communities, existing in the midst of oppression and slavery. Justice was to be found in their courts; the lives and properties of the inhabitants were secured from the rapacity of the haughty barons; arts, commerce and industry, prospered within their territories; and from them, the cheering rays of liberty were widely diffused. It is a pity that any of these free societies, established for such noble purposes, should now, in the present enlightened period of the world, and in a land of freedom, give just reason to complain of oppression and tyranny.

But in whatever point of light we are disposed to view the above mentioned arbitrary regulations; the

the following acts respecting the gleaning of fields, in time of harvest, will, it is hoped, meet with general approbation.

"*Rutherglen.* the 18. June 1668.

"The Provest, Baillies and Counsell, Considering the pykries, and other abvses comitted be the gatherers of beir, peis, and other cornes in hervest; and be hirds and other persones, who begs and seikes shaiffes of corne; and who, vnder cullor and pretext of gathering and seiking of cornes, they pyke, steill and rub the stowckes, to the great skaith of the maisters and owners of victwall. THairfor it is heirby ordered that no persone, nor persones, presume heirefter to gather: nor no Landlord, maister, or owner of victwall, suffer or permitt any to gather beir, peis, or other cornes in hervest tyme, upon there ground, or feild, quhill the corne and stowckes be removed; Under the paine of ffyve punds, *toties quoties*, as the premisses shall be contraveined, either be the m^{r.} or owner of the cornes, or be the persone gatherer.——And that no Landlord, M^{r.} or owner of victwall presume heirefter to give any shaiffes of corne to hirds, or to any other persone, or persones q^rsumevir; Under the said paine of ffyve punds money. And, with this certificatione also, to the saids hirds, and seikers of shaiffes; That if they seike, and receive any shaiffes from any persone q^rsumevir, the samyn shall be helden as stollin, and they condignlie punished y^rfore, as accords."

"*Rutherglen*, 12. Octor. 1674. It is Ordered, that nane of the inhabitants w^tin this burgh, suffer or permitt any strangers to bring in w^tin there howss^{s.} or stables, any shaiffes of peis, or corne, for there horss^{s.} the tyme of the faire. Under the paine of ten punds money, *toties quoties.*"

"*Rutherglen,* 10. *Aug.* 1675.

"The Proveſt, Baillies and toun Counſell, now conveened. Ratifies, and approves, all the former acts, ſtatuts, and ordinances of this burgh, made anent the pulling upe, and deſtroying of peis, beines, and wther cornes; makeing of peis kills, burning of peis; againſt gatherers of beir, peis, and wther cornes; giveing of ſhaiffes to birds.——And ſpeciallie that act made thereanent upon the 18. June, 1660.——Attor, for the better ſuppreſſing of all pyckrie, and ſteiling, and deſtroying of peis and wther cornes, It is ordered be the Proveſt, Baillies and Counſell; That no maner of perſone, or perſones within this incorporatione, friedome and territorie thereof, preſume to ſheir, ſtowke, takaway, or leid cornes, aff the ground whair the ſamyn groweth, or byie furth workeing amongſt the victwall late, or airlie, within the night, in any ſorte, upon any pretext q'ſumevir. Bot allanerlie betwixt ffyve in the morning, and eight at night; the bell is heirby appointed to be rung; and whaevir beis found out ſheiring, leiding, or doeing any worke amongſt the victwall, befor the bell ringing in the morneing, and efter the ringing thairof at night, Shall not onlie be lyable in the afoirſaid value of ten punds money, *toties quoties,* Bot alſo be repute and holden as a pycker, and one that wrongeth there neighbors."

The cuſtom of gleaning the fields, during harveſt, ſeems to have anciently prevailed in many nations of the world. However harmleſs and inoffenſive, on certain occaſions, ſuch a practice may have been, it has generally been found to open, among the lower claſſes of mankind, a wide door for idleneſs, revenge,

revenge, and injuftice. Every attempt, therefore, to remove the caufe of thefe evils, merits our approbation. Much praife is due to the community of Rutherglen, for what they have done in this refpect. Their vigorous exertions procured, indeed, the loud imprecations of the idle and profligate, but at length met with defired fuccefs. The practice of gleaning, has, through the weft of Scotland, been, for a long time, difcontinued, and, it is to be hoped, will never be permitted to revive.

There is nothing on record, by which we can precifely afcertain, what was, anciently, the extent of Rutherglen; or the number of houfes it contained. When digging, occafionally, at the eaft end of the town, the foundations of buildings are fometimes met with, in places which were never known, in the memory of any now living, to have been occupied by houfes. One principal ftreet, and a lane, called the Back-row, both lying parallel, in a direction nearly eaft and weft, conftitute the greateft part of the town. The main ftreet, which is very ftraight and well paved, is nearly half a mile in length; and is, in general, 112 feet broad. From both fides of it go off a few lanes, as, the Caftle-wynd, School-wynd, &c.

About 150 yards to the fouth of the main ftreet, is a kind of lane, known by the name of Dins-dykes.

A circumstance which befel the unfortunate Queen Mary, immediately after her forces were routed at the battle of Langside, has, ever since, continued to characterize this place, with an indelible mark of opprobrium. Her majesty, during the battle, stood on a rising ground about a mile from Rutherglen. She no sooner saw her army defeated than she took her precipitate flight to the south. Dins-dykes unfortunately lay in her way. Two rustics, who were, at that instant, cutting grass hard by, seeing her majesty fleeing in haste, rudely attempted to intercept her; and threatened to cut her in pieces with their scythes if she presumed to proceed a step further. Neither beauty, nor even royalty itself, can, at all times, secure the unfortunate, when they have to do with the unfeeling, or the revengeful. Relief, however, was at hand; and her majesty proceeded in her flight.

The town of Rutherglen consists, at present, of 255 dwelling-houses, which are inhabited by 400 families, containing 1631 persons; of whom 270 are children under six years of age: males, 801; females, 830. The population, owing to the progress of manufactures, is on the increase.

There are four incorporated trades in the borough, *viz.* Hammermen, Weavers, Masons and Wrights, and Tailors.

The corporation of *Hammermen* is governed by a deacon, a collector, and four masters.

	l.	s.	d.
Freedom-fine for a stranger is	1	0	0
Upon serving an apprenticeship	0	13	4
A Burgess' son, serving an apprenticeship	0	10	6
If he is a freeman's son, or son-in-law	0	3	4
Booking an apprentice	0	3	4
Each journeyman pays to the corporation	0	3	4
Each freeman pays *per annum*	0	1	0

The Corporation of *Weavers* is governed by a deacon, collector, four masters and five directors, of whom the collector makes one.

	l.	s.	d.
Freedom-fine for a stranger	0	16	4
Upon serving an apprenticeship	0	10	0
Burgess' son serving an apprenticeship	0	5	0
Freeman's son and son-in-law	0	3	4
Booking an apprentice if a burgess' son	0	2	6
——————————if not a burgess' son	0	3	4
Each journeyman pays at entry	0	1	0
Each freeman pays per quarter	0	0	8

The Corporation of *Masons* and *Wrights* is governed by a deacon, four masters, and a collector.

	l.	s.	d.
Freedom-fine for a stranger	1	13	4
Upon serving an apprenticeship	0	13	4
Burgess' son serving an apprenticeship, in the burgh	0	6	8
——————————if out of the burgh	0	13	4
Booking an apprentice, if a burgess' son	0	5	0
——————————if not a burgess' son	0	10	0

The Corporation of *Tailors* is governed by a deacon, two masters, a collector, and an assay-master.

	l.	s.	d.
Freedom-fine for a stranger	1	5	0
Entering an apprentice	0	5	6¼
Entering a journeyman	0	8	10¼
A freeman's son entering an apprentice	0	2	6
———————————a journeyman	0	1	8
Burgess' son entering an apprentice	0	5	0
Each journeyman not entering pays quarterly	0	5	0
Each freeman pays yearly	0	1	0

Besides the incorporated trades, there are a few societies: as, two Mason Lodges; namely, the Operatives, and Rutherglen Royal Arch: Lanark-shire Friendly Society: Coalminers; and Invalids. Their funds are not great; but, under proper management, are sufficient for supplying the wants of any of their members, who may be occasionally in need.

To the charters of the corporations are suspended seals, containing impressions of the Town-coat of Arms. It consists of the Virgin and Babe, attended by two Priests, holding up thistles in their hands. On the reverse is a ship with two mariners on board. In the modern seal the ship is placed on the back ground; it is greatly diminished in its size, and deprived of its mariners. The Virgin has undoubtedly a reference to the church. The ship represents the river Clyde, which is navigable up to
the

the town. It is impossible now to ascertain to what extent the trade of Clyde was anciently carried; and what proportion of it belonged to Rutherglen, at the time when it was erected into a Royal Borough. It is highly probable, that Rutherglen, at that time, was the only town of mercantile importance in the strath of Clyde; and that to it any trade that might be in the river chiefly belonged. That the channel of Clyde was then naturally much deeper than at present, we have no reason to doubt, when we reflect that many million cart loads of mud and sand have been since thrown into it from the land. Trading vessels therefore, which at that period were of a small construction, might be carried with ease up to the town. We are sure, however, that, till of late, gaberts of considerable burden sailed almost every day from the quay of Rutherglen to Greenock, &c. The freight was chiefly coals. The ship, therefore, with propriety constituted a principal part of the coat of arms. On the old seal, which is long ago lost, the human figures were ill executed, but the form of the ship was somewhat uncommon. It resembled the *navis antiqua* of the ancients, and is known by the name of the Herald's ship, because it was introduced by heralds into the blazoning of coats of arms. It is hoped that the draught of the impression, pl. I. fig. 1. will not be unacceptable to the curious.

THE

The *Crofs* and *Trone*, the two chief ornaments of the main ftreet, were in 1777, removed as incumbrances. The Crofs was of ftone, about 13 or 14 feet in height: it ftood on a pedeftal about 14 feet diameter at the bafe; 4 at the top, and 6 in height. The afcent to the Crofs was by 12 fteps all round the pedeftal. The *Trone* was a folid piece of extremely knotty oak, about 18 feet in height; and the two oppofite branches or arms, on which the balances were fufpended, were each about 6 feet long. This uncommon piece of timber grew in Hamilton wood, and was, about 1660, given a prefent to the town by Mr. Robert Spens.

None of the buildings, excepting the *Town-houfe*, and *Church*, is any way remarkable. The former, which confifts of the council-chamber, prifon-rooms, &c. was built in the year 1766; and is pretty elegant. The latter is a fmall, but very ancient, ftructure; and, by the arms of the borough, feems to have been dedicated to the Virgin Mary. It is 62 feet in length, and 25 in breadth, exclufive of the additions on the back and front. The walls are 4 feet in thicknefs; and about 20 feet high, including the pillars on which they are fupported. Of thefe there are 5 on each fide: they are fmooth and round, except the middle ones, which are octagonal. What reafon there might be for fuch a peculiarity is not, perhaps, eafily known. The fhafts are 6 feet

p. 79

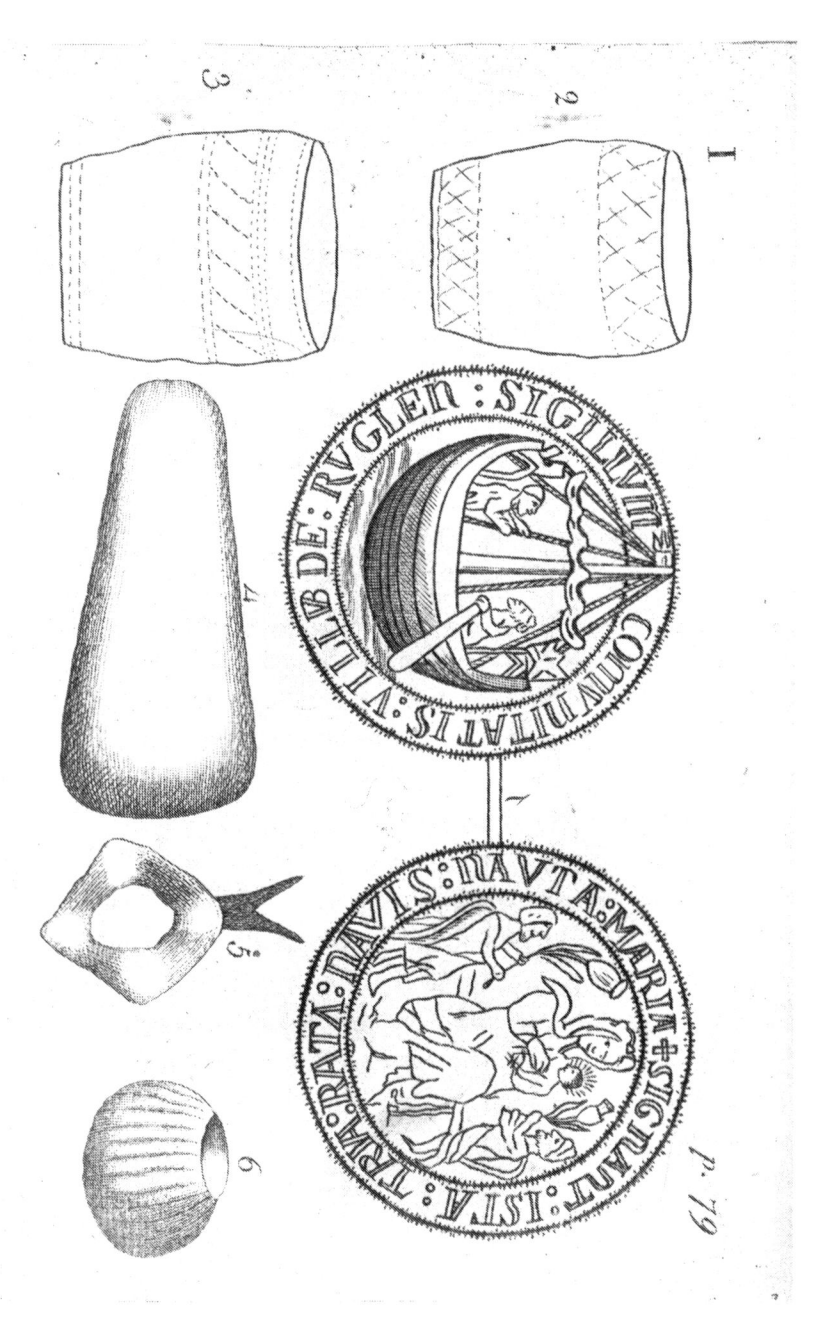

II

in height, and 2 in diameter. The capitals are moſtly a foot and a half in height, and are ornamented with various figures; draughts of which are given in pl. II. fig. 1. The baſe, fig. 2. is about 6, or 8 inches in depth. The arches, fig. 3. are pointed, but the point is hardly difcernible: this, with the conſtruction of the pillars, is a ſtrong proof of the great antiquity of the building, and feems to place its date at a greater diſtance, than the time when the churches, ornamented with high and cluſtered pillars, pointed arches, large windows, &c. were built. Only part, however, of the original ſtructure is at preſent exiſting. The choir, which extended to the ſteeple, at the diſtance of 33 feet, and with which it terminated, was, long fince, entirely demoliſhed. But the ſteeple hath ſurvived the downfall of the choir. It is nearly ſquare: the walls are but a little higher than the roof of the church, and are ſupported by buttreſſes. The clock and bell are of a modern date. The bell is 7 feet in circumference, at the brim, and is ornamented with the following inſcriptions.

Soli · Deo · Gloria · Michael · Burgerhuys · Me · Fecit · mdcxxxv.
Campanam · hanc · Cives · Reutherglenenses · Ecclesiae · suae · parochiali · donant.

The oldeſt account, probably, on record, concerning the church of Rutherglen, is in the hiſtory of the Life of Joceline, bishop of Glasgow; who made a donation of it, with the churches of *Mernis, Katkert,* &c. to the Abbey of Paisley.* That prelate died in the year 1199.

This kirk is rendered famous on account of two transactions, in which the fate of Sir William Wallace, and of his country, was deeply concerned. It was in this place of worship that a peace between Scotland and England was concluded, 8th February, 1297.

> In Ruglen kyrk ye traift yan haiff yai fet,
> A promes maid to meit Wallace but let.
> Ye day off yis approchyt wondyr faft,
> Ye gret Chanflar and Amar yidder paft;
> Syne Wallace come, and hys men weill befeyne,
> With hym fyfty arayit all in greyne;
> Ilk ane off yaim a bow and arrowis bar,
> And lang fuerds, ye quhilk full fcharply fchar, &c.†

It was in this place also that Sir John Monteath contracted with the English to betray Wallace.

> A meffynger Schyr Amar has gart pafs
> On to Schyr Jhon, and fone a tryft has fet,
> At Ruglan Kyrk yir twa togydder met.
> Yan Wallang faid, Schyr Jhon yow knaw yis thing, &c.‡

THE

---

* Keith's Hift. of Scots Bifhops. † Henry's Life of Wallace, B. VI. v. 862.
‡ Life of Wallace, B. XI. v. 796.

The area of the church seems to have been formerly occupied as a burying place. Great numbers of *human bones*, are, occasionally, dug up. A few years ago, when some workmen were laying a floor in the session-house, in the west end of the church, several bones of more than ordinary size were discovered. What struck the attention of all present, among whom was Mr. Lawrie, surgeon in Rutherglen, was a lower *maxillary* bone of uncommonly large dimensions. When, out of curiosity, it was applied to the face of a Provost Paterson, a man of no dwarfish construction, it easily admitted twice the thickness of the Provost's thumb, between its inner surface and his jaw-bone. This relick of the dead, having undergone the above experiment, was, along with several large sculls, and other bones, recommitted to the dust, under the pavement of the session-house.

When digging a grave in the church, ann. 1786, a stone coffin, containing a whole skeleton, was discovered. No inscription could be seen on the stones; nor any amulets in the grave.

The church-yard is not distinguished on account of any uncommon sepulchral monument. The most remarkable are two grave-stones that were, last year, found sunk in a part of the ground, which was never known to have been occupied as a burying place.

Each of them is ornamented with the figure of a sword, having the handle adorned with *Fleurs de Lis, &c.* The execution, for neatness and accuracy, would be no disgrace to the most refined age of sculpture. As there is no date, nor any vestige of letters upon the stones, we have some reason to think that the period in which they were cut, must be at least 500 years back. Each of them is 5 feet 10 inches in length: 1 foot 5 inches in breadth at the head, and 1 foot 1 inch at the foot: they are 10 inches thick. The length of the handle of the swords, (which are of the kind commonly called double handed) is 1 foot 5 inches; and the blade is about 3 feet in length.

The surface of the church-yard is about five feet higher than that of the ground adjoining. A very large *tumulus*, which is said to have anciently stood here, and which was long since levelled, might have considerably augmented the height.

The church with the burying ground, nearly in the middle of which the church is situated, exhibits a beautiful example of a Druid temple, and the grove with which it was usually surrounded. The custom of encircling church-yards with rows of trees is very ancient in Scotland; and is supposed to have been borrowed from the Druids, who made choice of woods and groves, as the most proper places for performing

East

South

The Three Auld Wives Lift, in Baldernock.

performing their sacred rites. This custom, which is not confined to a few places only, may be mentioned as an argument to support the opinion that Druidism, was, prior to the introduction of Christianity, the religion of the inhabitants of this country. This opinion is corroborated by what are thought to be Druid altars, yet remaining, after all the dilapidations that ignorance, avarice, and superstition have occasioned. Some of these altars, which are composed of large stones, may be seen in the neighbourhood of Glasgow.

The *three auld wives Lift*, near Craig-Madden castle, in the parish of Baldernock, is the most remarkable. It consists of three large stones. Two of them are laid along upon the earth, close by each other; and upon the top of these the third is placed, in the same direction, with their ends pointing south and north. The two undermost are of a prismatical shape: but the uppermost seems to have been a regular parallelopepid, and still approaches that figure, as nearly as may be supposed, making allowances for the depredations of time. It is about 18 feet in length; by 11 in breadth; and 7 in depth. It is placed nearly parallel with the horizon, but inclining a little to the north; the upper surface is pretty level. Neither of the two supporters appears to be so large as the stone they sustain: but their just dimensions cannot be easily ascertained, as their

bases

bases are sunk a confiderable number of feet in the earth. Owing to their prifmatical fhape, there is a triangular opening between them and the upper ftone; it is about 3 feet in depth, but fomewhat wider. Through this opening, fo Superftition fays, every ftranger who vifits this place for the firft time, muft creep, otherwife he fhall die childlefs. The ftones are of a grayifh coloured grit, and were taken from the rocks in the neighbourhood. They ftand in a circular plain, of about 250 yards in diameter, and furrounded with rifing ground, forming a kind of amphitheatre. The facred grove hath long ago yielded to the all-fubduing hand of time; yet not without leaving behind traces fufficient to convince us of its exiftence. The plain is of a deep moffy foil. Roots and ftumps of oak trees yet remain in their natural pofition: and fome of them exhibit evident marks that they had been expofed to fire.

The traditional account of the prefent name of this monument is, that three old women, having laid a wager which of them would carry the greateft burden, brought, in their aprons, the three ftones of which it is conftructed, and laid them in the pofition in which they are now found. This tradition probably originated from the Druideffes, who might, at this place, fuperintend the facred rites; and whofe age, fingularity, and more than ordinary fagacity, made them to be looked upon, by the

ignorant

ignorant and grosly superstitious vulgar of these times, as being possessed of supernatural power. Altars, nearly of a similar construction, have been met with in several places of Britain. This monument, which strikes with surprise every beholder, owes its preservation more to the nature of the place where it is situated than to any other circumstance. It is, however, to be hoped that its proprietor will take care to preserve from ruin, this venerable relick of the most remote antiquity.

Not far from the auld wives Lift, but not within sight of it, are two large Cairns, of an elliptical shape. The largest, which is 60 yards in length, and 10 in breadth, is now almost entirely carried away. Through the whole length of it were two rows of broad stones, set on edge on the ground, at the distance of about 4 feet from each other. Between these rows the dead were buried, having flag stones laid over them. The heap raised above them was mostly of pretty large stones, quarried from the adjoining rock. The other Cairn was laid open last year, and, though not so large as the other, was of the same construction, which seems to be Danish. Some of the stones placed in the rows at the bottom are considerably large. Among the contents, upon opening, were found fragments of human bones and urns; specimens of which are preserved by the Rev. James Couper, minister of Baldernock. One of the fragments of an urn is ornamented, near the mouth, with two fhallow grooves. The diameter of the circle of which it is a fegment feems to have been at leaft 20 inches. This *tumulus*, owing to frequent dilapidations, will foon be annihilated. Tradition fays that there was a battle in the neighbourhood, between the Scots and Danes: and that among the latter a perfon of a diftinguifhed character was flain.

A detached piece of whin-ftone in the parifh of Kilbarchan, and about three quarters of a mile north from Caftlefemple, is believed to have been a Druid altar. The fhape is roundifh, but irregular. It is 12 feet in height, at the higheft part; and about 67 in circumference. It is known by the name of *Clochodrig ftone*, a corruption of the Gaelic Cloch a' druigh, the Druids ftone. This, like the auld wives Lift, is reported to have been brought by more than human power. There does not appear to be any remains of a grove with which it might be furrounded.

The *Thugirt-ftone*, in the parifh of Dunlop, may be mentioned with the foregoing. It is called Thugirt, by way of contraction, for *Thou great ftone*. It is reported that even fo late as the time of Popery, the devotees of that religion, in doing penance, ufed to crawl on their knees round the ftone, and to cry, O thou grit ſtaine; from a belief that the deity was, in a peculiar manner, preſent at that hallowed relick. It is not unlikely that this, with ſome other confecrated ſtones, were confidered as idols, and worſhipped as ſuch. Among the Arabians, it is not unfrequent, to meet with great ſtones ſet up for idols.

Having made the above digreſſion, it may not be unneceſſary to obſerve, that of late, owing to various cauſes, the ancient cuſtom of encircling church-yards with rows of trees, is, in many places, diſcontinued. It is otherwiſe in Rutherglen. The church-yard, though ſituated in the middle of the town, is ſurrounded with a beautiful row of trees, about 50 in number; which, beſides being an ornament to the town, adds not a little to the ſolemnity of the church. It appears by the council records, that the Magiſtrates and Council 1660, ordered the trees, then grown old with age, to be cut down, and others to be planted in their room. Theſe, having ſerved their time, were cut down 1715, when the trees at preſent occupying their place, were planted. It is to be hoped that the community of Rutherglen will imitate the praiſe worthy example of their predeceſſors, and take a pleaſure, in ſeeing their borough exhibiting to poſterity, a ſtriking imitation of a religious cuſtom, the moſt ancient, perhaps, next to that of ſacrificing, at preſent exiſting in the world.

The Ministers of Rutherglen, since the Reformation, as their names are found in the records of the presbytery of Glasgow, are the following.

Mr. *John Muirhead*, of the family of Lauchap, admitted on the 16th Decem. 1586. He left Rutherglen and went to Glasford, or "parsonage of Castle Sympell, the 8th Dec. 1587."

Mr. *Alexander Rowatt*, from Dalziel, admitted 25th April, 1592. He went, ann. 1595, to the Barony of Glasgow, in which he was the first minister. He left the Barony and went to Cadder, 1611.

Mr. *Archibald Glen*, admitted 30th March, 1596. He was a man of great abilities and learning. He left Rutherglen and went to Carmunnock, 1603.

Mr. *William Hamilton*, son of John Hamilton of Newtoun, admitted 18th April, 1604.

Mr. *Robert Young*, admitted 21st Aug. 1611.—His son, Mr. *William Young*, was ordained assistant and successor to his father, 28th May, 1647.——Mr. William was succeeded by another assistant, of whom Principal Baillie, in his Letters, says, " He " was a manikin of small parts."

Mr. *John Dickson* was third assistant to Mr. Robert Young, and succeeded him in his charge. He was turned out at the Restoration, and his church given to Mr. *Hugh Blair*, jun. who was ordained, 1661: and continued until the Revolution, when he was turned out, and Mr. Dickson replaced; where he continued till his death, Jan. 1700.

Mr.

Mr. *Alexander Muir*, ordained 17th Dec. 1701.

Mr. *Alexander Maxwell*, ordained 22d Sept. 1719.

Mr. *William Maxwell*, his brother, admitted 19th Aug. 1742.

Mr. *James Furlong*, the prefent incumbent, from the Chapel of Eafe in Glafgow, admitted, 1780.

THE *ftipend*, including the allowance for communion elements, is 147 bolls, 14¼ pecks of victual: of which, 55 bolls are of oats; 34 of barley; and the reft of oatmeal. It is, however, moftly paid in money, according to the market price of the victual. It appears from the records of the prefbytery of Glafgow, that the ftipend, ann. 1586, was no more than 60 marks. But the mark, at that period, contained double at leaft the quantity of filver that it does at prefent; and was, it is probable, eight or ten times more valuable.

THE glebe contains 4¼ acres; part of which is occupied by the manfe and offices. The manfe was rebuilt, ann. 1781: and, befides the materials of the old manfe, coft the parifh the fum of L. 187.

THE right of patronage was anciently lodged in the abbot of Paifley. After the Reformation it belonged to the Hamiltons of Eliestoun, and, having paffed through feveral families along with the eftate, was, 1724, fold by Daniel Campbell of Shawfield, Efq; for the perpetual retention of eight bolls

of tiend meal, payable from his lands within the royalty." "The Magiftrates and Council; the heri-
" tors refiding within the borough and thirteen pund
" land thereof; the members of the kirk-feffion;
" and the tenants of Shawfield, have jointly the
" right of prefentation."

The public School is generally well frequented. The falary is L. 10 fter. yearly. The ftated wages are two fhillings, per quarter, for Englifh: and half a crown for Writing, Arithmetic and Latin.

Rutherglen gives the title of Earl, to Douglas, Duke of Queenfberry. The firft who was honoured with that title was Lord John Hamilton, third fon of William and Anne, Duke and Duchefs of Hamilton. He was, by king William, created Earl on the 15th April, 1697. He left only one child, Anne, Countefs of Rutherglen, who married William, Earl of March, grandfon of the firft Duke of Queenfberry, to which title his defcendants fucceeded, upon failure of the elder branch.

The following account of a few ancient cuftoms, ftill obferved in Rutherglen, will, it is hoped, be acceptable to the public.

One of no fmall antiquity is, riding the marches on Laudemer day. The Magiftrates, with a confiderable number of the council and inhabitants,

affemble

assemble at the cross; from which they proceed, in martial order, with drums beating, &c. and in that manner, go round the boundaries of the royalty, to see if any encroachments have been made on them. These boundaries are distinguished by march-stones, set up at small distances from each other. In some places there are two rows, about seven feet distant. The stones are shaped at the top, somewhat resembling a man's head; but the lower part is square. This peculiar form was originally intended to represent god Terminus, of whom they are so many rude images. Every new burgess comes under an obligation to provide a march-stone, at his own expence, and to cut upon it the initials of his name, and the year in which it was set up.

It has been a custom, time out of memory, for the riders of the marches to deck their hats, drums, &c. with brooms, and to combat with one another at the newly erected stone; out of respect, perhaps, to the deity whose image they had set up, or that they might the better remember the precise direction of the boundary at that place. This part of the exercise is now postponed till the survey is over, and the company have returned to the cross, where, having previously provided themselves with broom bushes, they exhibit a mock engagement, and fight, seemingly with great fury, till their weapons fail them, when they part in good friendship, and frequently,

quently, not until they have teftified their affection over a flowing bumper. They ride the marches at leaft once in two years.

Another ancient cuftom, for the obfervance of which Rutherglen has long been famous, is the baking of *four cakes*. Some peculiar circumftances, attending the operation, render an account of the manner in which it is done, not altogether unneceffary. About eight or ten days before St. Luke's fair, (for they are baked at no other time of the year) a certain quantity of oatmeal is made into dough, with warm water, and laid up in a veffel to ferment. Being brought to a proper degree of fermentation and confiftency, it is rolled up into balls, proportionable to the intended largenefs of the cakes. With the dough is commonly mixed a fmall quantity of fugar, and a little anife feed, or cinnamon. The baking is executed by women only; and they feldom begin their work till after fun-fet, and a night or two before the fair. A large fpace of the houfe, chofen for the purpofe, is marked out by a line drawn upon it. The area within is confidered as confecrated ground: and is not, by any of the by-ftanders, to be touched with impunity. A tranfgreffion incurs a fmall fine, which is always laid out on drink for the ufe of the company. This hallowed fpot is occupied by fix or eight women, all of whom, except the toafter, feat themfelves on the ground,

in

in a circular figure, having their feet turned towards the fire. Each of them is provided with a bake-board, about two feet square, which they hold on their knees. The woman who toasts the cakes, which is done on a girdle suspended over the fire, is called the Queen, or Bride; and the rest are called her maidens. These are distinguished from one another, by names given them for the occasion. She who sits next the fire, towards the east, is called the *Todler:* her companion on the left hand is called the *Hodler;** and the rest have arbitrary names given them by the bride, as Mrs. Baker, best and worst maids, &c. The operation is begun by the todler, who takes a ball of the dough, forms it into a small cake, and then casts it on the bake-board of the hodler, who beats it out a little thinner. This being done, she, in her turn, throws it on the board of her neighbour; and thus it goes round from east to west, in the direction of the course of the sun, until it comes to the toaster, by which time it is as thin and smooth as a sheet of paper. The first cake that is cast on the girdle is usually named as a gift to some well known cuckold, from a superstitious opinion, that thereby the rest will be preserved from mischance.

* These names are descriptive of the manner in which the women, so called, perform their part of the work. To todle, is to walk or move slowly like a child. To hodle, is to walk or move more quickly.

mifchance. Sometimes the cake is fo thin as to be carried, by the current of air, up into the chimney. As the baking is wholly performed by the hand, a great deal of noife is the confequence. The beats, however, are not irregular, nor deftitute of an agreeable harmony; efpecially when they are accompanied with vocal mufic, which is frequently the cafe. Great dexterity is neceffary, not only to beat out the cakes, with no other inftrument than the hand, fo that no part of them fhall be thicker than another; but efpecially to caft them from one board on another, without ruffling or breaking them. The toafting requires confiderable fkill: for which reafon the moft experienced perfon in the company is chofen for that part of the work. One cake is fent round in quick fucceffion to another, fo that none of the company is fuffered to be idle. The whole is a fcene of activity, mirth and diverfion; and might afford an excellent fubject for a picture.

As there is no account, even by tradition itfelf, concerning the origin of this cuftom, it muft be very ancient. The bread thus baked was, doubtlefs, never intended for common ufe. It is not eafy to conceive why mankind, efpecially in a rude age, would ftrictly obferve fo many ceremonies, and be at fo great pains in making a cake, which, when folded together, makes but a fcanty mouthful. Befides, it is always given away in prefents to ftrangers

who

who frequent the fair. The cuſtom ſeems to have been originally derived from Paganiſm, and to contain not a few of the ſacred rites peculiar to that impure religion: as the leavened dough, and the mixing it with ſugar and ſpices; the conſecrated ground, &c. &c. But the particular deity, for whoſe honour theſe cakes were at firſt made, is not, perhaps, eaſy to determine. Probably it was no other than the one known in ſcripture, Jer. vii. 18. by the name of the " *queen of heaven,*" and to whom cakes were likewiſe kneaded by women.

Besides baking ſour cakes, it has, for a long time paſt, been a cuſtom in Rutherglen to prepare *ſalt roaſts* for St. Luke's fair. Till of late almoſt every houſe in town was furniſhed with ſome dozens of them. They were the chief article of proviſion aſked for by ſtrangers who frequented the market; and were, not without reaſon, conſidered as a powerful preventive againſt intoxication. But the high price of butcher meat has now, in a great meaſure, brought them into diſuſe.

The town, however, continues to be famous for making *ſour cream* of an excellent quality. It is made in the following manner. A certain quantity of ſweet milk is put into a wooden veſſel, or vat, which is placed in a proper degree of heat, and covered with a linen cloth. In due time the ſerous, or watery part of the milk begins to separate from the rest, and is called *whig*. When the separation is complete, which, according to circumstances, requires more or less time, the whig is drawn off by means of a cock and pale, or spigot in fauset, as it is called in England, and which is placed near the bottom of the vessel. The substance that remains is then beat with a large spoon, or ladle, till the oleaginous and caseous particles of which it is composed are properly mixed. A small quantity of sweet milk is sometimes added, to correct the acidity, if it is overmuch. The cream, thus prepared, is agreeable to the taste, and nourishing to the constitution. It finds a ready sale in Glasgow, where it is sold at four-pence the Scotch pint; the same price which it brought 40 years ago.

From the above account, it appears that Rutherglen cream is greatly superior to that which is procured from butter-milk; either by means of placing the vessel containing it among hot water, or by milking among it warm milk from the cow. Cream made in the latter of these ways is, in this country, called a *hatted coag*. Both kinds are destitute of the fat part of the milk, which part chiefly constitutes the richness of good cream.

Before I finish the account of the borough, it will be necessary to make a few remarks on the character

character of the inhabitants. It may, in general, be observed, that they were always attached to the interest of government. Perhaps the only circumstance that seemingly contradicts this assertion, was an affair which happened on the 29th of May, 1679. On that day, both the birth and restoration of the King, was, at Rutherglen, celebrated with bonfires,* and other marks of rejoicing. A body of men,

about

---

* In the council records of Rutherglen, bonfires were, till of late, generally called bailfires, a contraction for Baalfires, meaning fires kindled up to the honour of Baal. The making of bonfires, as tokens of rejoicing, seems to have originated from a festival dedicated, by the Druids, to the sun. "On the first day "of May, which day was dedicated to Belinus or the Sun, they "held an annual festival; and kindled prodigious fires in all their "sacred places, and performed sacrifices, with many other so- "lemnities. It is thought, that at midsummer, and again early "in November, other annual festivals were held; on the first, the "people assembled to implore the friendly influence of Heaven "on their fields and pastures: on the latter, they came to return "thanks for the favourable seasons and the increase with which "the gods had blessed their labours." Strutt's Chron. of Eng. vol. I. p. 196.

It would appear that so late as two centuries ago, great fires were superstitiously kindled, in this part of the country. The presbytery of Glasgow, to put a stop to this idolatrous rite, ordered all the ministers within their bounds "to try who made "Beannefires last midsummer-even." Records of the presb. of Glas. ann. 1586.

This custom, which must have prevailed in Scotland, long before the introduction of Christianity into the nation, gave rise to

the

about 80 in number, who were incensed at government on account of the persecutions to which it gave its sanction, assembled at the cross of Rutherglen, with a fixed resolution to execute a plan they had previously concerted: but whether any of them were inhabitants of the town is uncertain. Having chosen a leader, they sung psalms and prayed. The acts of parliament against Conventicles were committed to the flames of the bonfire, which was immediately extinguished. This was the first public appearance of the *Bothwell-bridge* association, or rebellion, as it is sometimes called.

The following is the account which Guthrie, in his history of Scotland, gives of the above-mentioned transaction. " In the year 1679, immediately after " Sharp, Bishop of St. Andrew's death, that the " cruelty of Lord Lauderdale and his party arose " to such a height against the Presbyterians, that " many

the expression *Belten*, the name given to the first day of May, and a well known term of the year. The word is derived from the Gaelic *Baal tien*, which means the fires of Baal. To this day the custom of making great fires, *Taanles*, or *Bleazes*, about the beginning of summer, or Belten time, as it is commonly expressed, is continued all along the strath of Clyde. On some nights a dozen or more of these fires may be seen at one view. They are mostly kindled on rising ground, that they may be seen at a greater distance. They are not, however, attended now with any superstitious rite; but only in compliance with an old custom, the original meaning of which is not generally known by the commonalty.

RUTHERGLEN.

"many of them resolved to assert their liberty by
"taking up arms. About 80 of them assembled in
"Rutherglen: a young preacher, one Hamilton,
"was declared their head; and on the 29th of May
"they drew up a declaration against all the acts of
"parliament relating to religion, and publickly com-
"mitted them to the flames of the bonfires that had
"been lighted up in commemoration of the day.
"After a succefsful engagement with Capt. Graham
"of Claverhoufe, they took poffeffion of the town
"of Hamilton. After a flight fkirmifh they made
"themfelves mafters of Glafgow, but were foon
"afterwards totally defeated at Bothwell-bridge by
"the Duke of Monmouth. This was on the 22d
"of June, fo that the whole lafted no longer than
"14 days."

The inhabitants of Rutherglen are confiderable adepts in borough politics. This, however, does not, in general, obftruct an induftrious application to their feveral employments. But their tranquillity meets, at times, with fhort interruptions. A competition for their influence, in a vote for a member of parliament, fometimes convulfes the community; enervates the finews of induftry; and brings ruin on fome few individuals. On thefe occafions one would be ready to think, that liberty was turned into licentioufnefs, and that the privileges of royal boroughs were curfes, inftead of bleffings, to the perfons poffeffed of them. But where is the conftitution

that

that is free from defects? or where the people that may not in some instances go wrong?

It may, however, be observed, that the inhabitants are so far from being bad members of society, that none of them have, in the memory of man, committed any crime, for which they were brought to public punishment.

The community of Rutherglen is strongly attached to the established church of Scotland. There is not, in the whole town, above seven or eight families belonging to the different parties of the Secession.

To this part of the history properly belongs an account of the different trades and occupations of the inhabitants. That account, however, shall be reserved for the next chapter, in which is given a table containing the number of individuals employed in each, through the whole parish.

The following is a list of the Commissioners from Rutherglen, to the Parliament of Scotland, as their names are inserted in the records of Parliament. It may be observed that sometimes, in these records, the boroughs, whose representatives were present, are only mentioned, but the names of the Commissioners themselves are omitted. As for example, the names of the Commissioners from Rutherglen, who

RUTHERGLEN.

who were present at the Parliaments held, 1st June, 1478:———19th March, 1480-1:———18th March, 1481-2:———2d Dec. 1482:———6th Oct. 1488:——— 10th Nov. 1579, are not mentioned in the records. But the following are marked.*

23d Oct.	1579,	Rob. Lindsay.
13th July,	1587,	David Spens.†
20th Sept.	1612,	And. Pinkertoun.
28th June,	1617,	Rob. Lindsay, & James Riddell.
25th July,	1621,	John Pinkertoun.
20th June,	1633,	John Scott.
1st Jan.	1661,	David Spens.
19th Oct.	1669,	James Riddell.
22d July,	1670,	James Riddell.
12th June,	1672,	James Riddell.
12th Nov.	1673,	David Spens.
14th March,	1689,	John Scott, in the Convention.
5th June,	1689,	do.
15th April,	1690,	do.
18th April,	1693,	do.
9th May,	1695,	do.
8th April,	1696,	do.
19th July,	1698,	do.
21st May,	1700,	do.
29th Oct.	1700,	do.
6th May,	1703,	George Spens.
6th July,	1704,	do.
28th June,	1705,	do.
3d Oct.	1706,	do.

* The Commissioners had their charges paid, out of the town's revenues, at the rate of 3 l. Scots, *per diem*, during their attendance at parliament.

† This Gentleman was an ancestor of Major John Spens the present Provost.

THE following are the names of the *Provosts* of Rutherglen, as these names are recorded in the Council books. Most of the records of the Borough, prior to about the year 1570, are irrecoverably lost.

1616, John Riddell.	1642, John Scott.
1617, Andrew Pinkertoun.	1643, do.
1618	1644, do.
1619, John Riddell.	1645, do.
1620, Andrew Pinkertoun.	1646, do.
1621, John Pinkertoun.	1647, do.
1622, do.	1648, do.
1623, do.	1649, do.
1624, do.	1650, Andrew Pinkertoun.
1625, Thomas Wilkie.	1651, John Scott.
1626, do.	1652, do.
1627, John Pinkertoun.	1653, do.
1628, do.	1654, do.
1629, do.	1655, do.
1630, do.	1656, do.
1631, do.	1657, Walter Riddell.
1632, do.	1658, Robert Spens.
1633, do.	1659, Andrew Pinkertoun.
1634, do.	1660, do.
1635, Thomas Wilkie.	1661, John Scott.
1636, do.	1662, do.
1637, John Pinkertoun.	1663, do.
1638, Thomas Wilkie.	1664, do.
1639, John Pinkertoun.	1665, Robert Spens.
1640, Thomas Wilkie.	1666, do.
1641, John Scott.	1667, do.
	1668,

RUTHERGLEN.

1668, Andrew Harvie.
1669,   do.
1670, James Riddell.
1671, Andrew Harvie.
1672, Robert Spens.
1973, William Riddell.
1674, John Robisone.
1675, Andrew Leitch.
1676, William Riddell.
1677, Robert Spens.
1678, William Riddell.
1679, Robert Spens.
1680, William Riddell.
1681, Andrew Leitch.
1682, Robert Spens.
1683, Andrew Harvie.
1684, Andrew Leitch.
1685, Andrew Harvie.
1686,   do.
1687,   do.   }*
1688,   do.
1689, Robert Bowman.
1690, John Witherspone.
1691, Robert Bowman.
1692, John Scott.
1693, David Scott.
1694, John Witherspone.
1695, John Harvie.
1696, John Witherspone.
1697, George Spens.
1698, Andrew Leitch.
1699, George Spens.

1700, Andrew Leitch.
1701, George Spens.
1702, Andrew Leitch.
1703, George Spens.
1704, Andrew Leitch.
1705, George Spens.
1706, Andrew Leitch.
1707, George Spens.
1708, Andrew Leitch.
1709, George Spens.
1710, John Moore.
1711, Robert Bowman.
1712, Andrew Leitch.
1713, Patrick Witherspone.
1714, Andrew Leitch.
1715, George Spens.
1716, John Moore.
1717, George Spens.
1718, David Scott.
1719, George Spens.
1720, David Scott.
1721, George Spens.
1722, David Scott.
1723, George Spens.
1724, David Scott.
1725, George Spens.
1726, David Scott.
1727, George Spens.
1728, Andrew Leitch.
1729, David Scott.
1730, Andrew Leitch.
1731, David Scott.

* By the order of the King no Provost was elected, during 3 years, and Andrew Harvie was continued in office.

THE HISTORY OF

1732, George Spens.
1733, David Scott.
1734, George Spens.
1735, David Scott.
1736, George Spens.
1737, David Scott.
1738, Andrew Leitch.
1739, James Farie.
1740, Andrew Leitch.
1741, James Farie.
1742
1743, David Pinkertoun.
1744
1745, William Moor.
1746, Andrew Leitch.
1747, William Moor.
1748, John Paterson.
1749, David Scott.
1750, Robert Spens.
1751
1752, John Paterson.
1753, David Scott.
1754, Robert Spens.
1755, David Scott.
1756, Robert Spens.
1757, Allan Scott.
1758, Robert Spens.
1759, Allan Scott.
1760, Robert Spens.
1761, Allan Scott.

1762, Robert Spens.
1763, Allan Scott.
1764, Robert Spens.
1765, George White.
1766, Robert Spens.
1767, Gabriel Grey.
1768, Robert Spens.
1769, Gabriel Grey.
1770, Allan Scott.
1771, Gabriel Grey.
1772, Robert Spens.
1773, James Fleming.
1774, Gabriel Grey.
1775, James Fleming.
1776, Gabriel Grey.
1777, Neil M‘Vicar.
1778, George White.
1779, James Farie.
1780, George White.
1781, Gabriel Grey.
1782, William Parkhill.
1783, Gabriel Grey.
1784, George White.
1785, Gabriel Grey.
1786, George White.
1787, Gabriel Grey.
1788, George White.
1789, Archibald Reid.
1790, George White.
1791, Major John Spens.

CHAP. II.

OF THE PARISH OF RUTHERGLEN, ITS EXTENT, AGRICULTURE, ANTIQUITIES, TRADE, &c.

THE parish of Rutherglen, of which the Borough is the capital, extends, on the south bank of the river Clyde, about 3 miles in length, and 1¼ in breadth. Clyde is the boundary on the north: the parish of Govan on the west: Cathcart on the south-west: Carmunnock on the south: and Cambuslang on the east. The whole is arable, and is mostly inclosed, chiefly with thorn hedges. It lies in a pleasant situation, forming the lower part of the declivity of Cathkin hills; and is beautifully diversified with a regular succession of small hills, and narrow dales; excepting next the river, where it forms itself into some very delightful and fertile plains. It belongs to about 140 heritors: but the greatest part of these have their property within the borough. The valued rent is 2100 l. Scots: the real rent, at the average price of 2 l. ster. per acre, allowing 200 acres for roads, rivulets, &c. comes to 4720 l. ster. exclusive of the rent of houses in the town, which, at 3 l. ster. per family, amounts to 1200 l.

The plains next the river comprehend the estates of *Shawfield, Farme, Hamilton Farm,* and *Rose-bank*.

Shawfield extends about a mile in length, from the town of Rutherglen to Polmadie; having Clyde for its boundary on the north. Sir Claud Hamilton was, 1615, Laird of Shawfield. It was, about 1657, adjudged to John Ellies, and other creditors of the family: and afterwards, in 1695, conveyed, by said John Ellies, to Sir Alexander Anstruther of Newark; who sold it, in 1707, to Daniel Campbell, Collector of his Majesty's customs at Port-Glasgow; whose descendant, Walter Campbell of Shawfield, Esq; sold it, 1788, to Robert Houston of Aitkenhead, Esq; now Robert Houstoun Rae, Esq; of Little Govan. None of the above proprietors took the title of Shawfield but the Hamiltons and Campbells; with the latter of whom it still remains.

The greatest part of the estate consists of a rich plain, which formerly was exposed to frequent inundations from the river. The present proprietor, no sooner got the estate into his possession, than, excited by a laudable ambition of improving his purchase, he caused a bank to be raised along the side of the river, by which his land is not now in any danger of being laid under water. This bank is about 1600 yards in length: the height is 20 feet
above

above the level of Clyde, at low water; being 3 feet 6 inches higher than the height of the great flood in the year 1712: and 18 inches above the height of the flood, 12th March, 1782, the greatest ever known in Clyde. This bank contains 62535 solid yards of earth, the raising of which cost 600 guineas.

Next to the town, on the east, and along the side of the river, is the estate of Farme. It is said to have been once the private property of some of the Stuarts, Kings of Scotland. It afterwards belonged to the family of Crawford, who, naming it from themselves, called it Crawford's Farme. It came afterwards into the possession of Sir Walter Stuart of Minto, who dwelt in the castle, about the year 1645. He is reported to have been a gentleman of extraordinary prudence and humanity; and, during the commotions of the times, to have obtained for Rutherglen many favours. The Flemings had it for some time in their possession. It is now called Farme, and has, for some time past, been the property of James Farie, Esq; of Farme, who made a purchase of it from the Duke of Hamilton. On the estate, and nearly in the middle of the beautiful plain of which it makes a part, is an ancient castle, the family-seat of Mr. Farie. The period in which it was built is unknown; but the thick walls, the few, narrow, and irregularly placed windows, the strong battlements, &c, &c. are evidences of its an-

tiquity,

tiquity, and that it was erected as a place of strength. Being kept in excellent repair, it is wholly habitable, and may continue for ages to come, a beautiful pattern of the manner, after which, the habitations of the powerful barons of Scotland, were anciently constructed. Mr. Farie, to prevent his lands from being injured by inundations, has lately raised a bank about 600 yards in length.

FARTHER up the Clyde is *Hamilton Farm*, the property of Will. Somervile of Hamilton Farm, Esq; It is also secured from the river by a bank about 1500 yards in length. This, with the two already mentioned, includes more artificial imbankment, for the sake of improving land, than is, perhaps, to be found any where else, on both sides of Clyde.

ADJOINING to Hamilton Farm is *Rosebank*, the property of John Dunlop, Esq; of Rosebank. This place occupies one of the most pleasant situations in the country, and richly merits the additional improvements which are begun to be made on it.

IN the higher part of the parish are some considerable estates, as *Galloflat*, which belongs to Mr. Patrick Robertson of Galloflat, writer in Glasgow. *Scotstoun*, the property of John Gray, Esq; of Scotstoun. *Stonelaw*, the property of Major John Spens of Stonelaw. *Bankhead*, which belongs to to George White, Esq; of Bankhead. On the most of these estates are elegant and commodious dwelling houses.

The only part of the town's lands, now belonging to the community, is the *Green*, a plain of about 36 acres, lying between the town and Clyde. In the old records it is sometimes called the Inch;* because at first it was only a small island. The soil is rich and deep; owing to the accumulation of mud and decayed vegetables carried down by the river. The Magistrates and Council, anno 1652, to defray the expences incurred by Cromwell's troops, rouped the green to be ploughed, for the sum of 20 l. Scots, per acre. The inhabitants believing that the ploughing of the green was contrary to their interest, as individuals, made such a formidable opposition that the Magistrates were forced to retract what they had done. It was not broken up till about 30 years ago, when it was let at nearly 4 l. ster. per acre. The crops which it then produced were very great. Like most other commons, however, it is now suffered to lie a disgraceful waste, producing fertile crops of thistles and other hurtful weeds. But as every burgess has a right to have his cow pastured upon it, for the annual grass-mail of a guinea; and as there is a considerable number of cattle kept by the inhabitants, for the purpose chiefly of making sour cream,

there

* The word Inch signifies an island.

there is no probability that its condition will soon be rendered much better. It brings, at present, to the revenues of the town the sum of 50l. yearly.

The state of agriculture in the parish affords few things that merit particular attention. The old method of dividing farms into croft and out-field land is now laid aside: but some of the borough land is run-rig; a custom highly detrimental to improvement. Inclosing, draining, and liming is now become universal. An easy access to lime and dung, of the best qualities, may be had at all seasons of the year. The excellent roads, with which the parish abounds, encourages the farmer to proceed in his improvements. The easy and ready access to Glasgow market, at present one of the best in Scotland, is greatly in his favour. But his chief encouragement arises both from the soil and climate. The former is generally of a good loam, and in some places a light mould, free from stones: the latter is as warm and dry as any in the west of Scotland. The seed time is usually about the end of March; and the harvest in the end of September. Oats, barley, pease, beans, wheat, potatoes, and grasses yield frequently very great returns. Oats, however, is of all the other grains the most commonly sown, because the crop is the most certain and prolific. Potatoes are cultivated by almost every family in the parish: the round white kind is commonly preferred.

The

The *Curl*, a disease extremely hurtful to this useful root, is hardly known here. A rotation of crops is generally observed; and the laying the land under grasses, proper for pasture, is in universal practice. The method which is now followed at Rosebank, may be mentioned as an example. Two years, oats: the third barley and grasses, after dung: then two years grass, cut for hay: and two, pastured. Then oats, &c. as before. The want of a leguminous crop is, perhaps, a defect in this plan. The turnip is not yet brought into cultivation.

No person in the parish is, at present, carrying on improvements in agriculture, with greater spirit and success, than Major John Spens of Stonelaw. Finding, on his leaving the service, that his estate was not in the very best condition, his first care was to lay it out in proper inclosures; the largest of which does not exceed 16 acres. He incloses chiefly with ditch and hedge. In planting the thorns he is at great pains; especially in those places that are unfavourable for their growth. He opens a small cast or drill, which he takes care to have well drained; and then fills it up with a compost of lime, dung and earth. In this the quicks are planted in a perpendicular direction, the one that nature, the surest guide in these matters, hath pointed out as the best. Care is taken that they shall not be cut, at least on the top, for some years after they

P   are

are planted; a treatment, although contrary to the common practice, is, however, highly beneficial to quickset fences. The attention of the Major was next directed to remedy the faults of the surface of the ground. This he does by draining, levelling, trenching, and straightening the ridges. These operations, with the covering some pieces of bad soil with good earth, are executed at a considerable expence. Besides liming and dunging in the ordinary way, he finds it his profit to purchase all the oyster shells he can procure in Glasgow. These he spreads in the gin-tracts, at his coal-works; where, being broken to pieces by the feet of the horses, and mixed with their dung, they are reduced to an excellent manure. He summer-fallows his land by five ploughings; and usually works the plough with three horses. He ploughs as deep as he can, to raise as much new earth as possible. Not having as yet completed his improvements, he has not followed any fixed mode of rotation. He has at present 25 acres sown with wheat, and 20 with wheat and grass-seeds: all of them are after summer-fallow, except about 5 acres after potatoes. Immediately before the wheat, (which is all of the white kind) is sown, it is steeped for the space of 12 hours in water saturated with common salt. This is designed to prevent the *Smut*, a disease, however, that is little known in this part of the country. Some fields which he had laid down with grasses have yielded

profitable

profitable returns. The Calf-ward, for example, a small field containing five acres Scottish, was, after summer-fallow 1788, sown with wheat and grasses. The wheat crop was very good; and next year, each acre produced no less than 400 stone of hay, of the best quality.

The Major, both for the ornament and shelter of his lands, has planted several thousand trees of different kinds. The ground, before being planted, is usually cropped a year, at least, with potatoes: and frequently, after the trees are planted, a crop or two are taken from between the rows. This method, when care is taken not to disturb the plants, is thought to be of great service; and is getting into practice in several parts of the country.

About 20 acres may contain all the growing wood in the parish. The trees are mostly disposed in form of clumps and belts. There is also a considerable number in hedge rows. At Hamilton-Farm and Rosebank are some pretty old and thick trees, the most uncommon, though not the largest of which, are a few white willows, at Rosebank: they are about 50 or 60 feet tall; and 3 in diameter.

The ploughs, at present in use in the parish, are the Scottish, chain, and Rutherglen ploughs. The last

last mentioned is peculiar to this part of the country. It was first made in Rutherglen, about 50 years ago; and consequently, according to Lord Kames, must have been among the first improved ploughs in Scotland. The plan after which it is constructed was proposed by Lady Stewart of Coltness, who at that time lived in the Farme, and was uncommonly active in promoting improvements in agriculture. From this place it found its way into the neighbouring parishes, where it still continues to be known by the name of the Rutherglen plough. It is usually about 11 feet in length, and 19 inches in depth, from the beam to the sole. The sheath is not mortised in the head; and is placed at a more oblique angle than in the Scottish plough. The sock is of an oval form, and is fixed both on the sheath and head. A screw bolt of iron goes through the beam and sheath down through the head. The mouldboard is covered with iron: and the whole is not much heavier than the chain-plough. It answers well in a light soil free from stones. The Scottish plough, however, is, of all the rest, the highest in repute for a stiff soil.

Country servants, owing to the rapid progress of manufactures, are very scarce, and their wages uncommonly high. A man-servant receives, besides bed, board and washing, 5 l. per half year: and a woman-servant from 40 to 50 shillings. A labourer,

when

when hired by the year, receives 15 l. 12 s. A single day's wage, if he is not hired by the year, is, at an average, one shilling, and three-pence. Artificers, as masons and wrights, generally get two shillings a-day. But the practice of undertaking by the piece, almost universally prevails.

The progress of agriculture in this place, and the rise of the value of land, may be estimated from the East-field, the property of John Grey, Esq; of Scotstoun. About the year 1780, it was let for about 10 l. per annum, and was purchased for 500 l. It now pays above 100 l. sterling yearly.

The only *Mill* in the parish is the Town-mill, to which are astricted, or sucken, all the borough lands, at the thirlage, or multure, of the 40th part of the *grana crescentia*, seed and horse corn excepted. The miller is entitled to half a peck, for bannock-meal, out of every 6 firlots, grinded at the mill; and the multurer, or miller's servant, has additional, what is equal to the half of the bannock-meal, for his fee.

Rutherglen *Bridge*, which, in 1775, was thrown over Clyde, between Shawfield and Barrowfield lands, is the only bridge in the parish that is deserving of notice. It consists of 5 arches; and is not burdened with any pontage, being built by a
free

free subscription, to which the town of Rutherglen contributed about 1000 l.

Of the extensive manufactures at present carrying on in the west of Scotland, Rutherglen has only a small share. Most of the inhabitants who engage in business, on a large scale, find it their interest to settle in Glasgow. The state of trade, however, will appear by the following list of mechanics and labourers, who reside in the parish. The number of individuals, employed in each occupation is subjoined.

Trades.	N°.	Trades.	N°.
Bakers,	2	Hosiers,	8
Barbers,	1	Labourers,	55
Brewers,	2	Millers,	2
Carters,	18	Shoemakers,	15
Coal-hewers,	60	Smiths,	37
Coopers,	3	Surgeons,	1
Farmers,	26	Taylors,	11
Flax-dressers,	1	Watchmakers,	1
Fleshers,	3	Weavers,	154
Gardeners,	4	Wrights and Masons,	34
Hatmakers,	10		

Of the weavers 10 only continue at customary work: the rest are employed in the muslin branch. Most of the masons profess also the wright business. About three fourths of the smiths are nailers, and work

work to employers in Glasgow. Mr. *Robert Bryce* hath distinguished himself for making edge-tools, especially augers and screws, both black and polished. He sells the black from 3s. 6d. to 1l. 5s. per doz. wholesale: and the polished from 13s. to 2l. 9s. 6d. per dozen. His carpenters and coopers axes and adzes are sold from 5d. to 8d. per lb. All his tools, on account of their excellent workmanship, and extremely good temper, are, in Glasgow and Greenock, preferred to any from England. His demands are always greater than he can execute. For grinding his tools he prefers the stones from Hamilton-hill, in the neighbourhood of Glasgow, to Newcastle grind-stones. The former are composed of a smaller grit than the latter, but take down remarkably fast: they wear equally round, because no part of them is harder than another; and they are not intermixed with nodules and streaks of martial-pyrites, which are extremely hurtful to edge-tools, and frequently render grind-stones totally useless. Mr. Bryce hath also acquired a peculiar skill in the dexterous management of *Bees*. He can, without killing the queen-bee, unite different swarms, or parts of swarms, and make them keep together in harmony. His apiary is sometimes stocked with 24 hives.

Rutherglen and Shawfield printfields, lately begun in the parish, give employment to about 200 persons.

persons. The former is carried on by Mr. Cummin and Co. and the latter by Mr. Dalglish.

All the women in the parish find abundance of suitable employment. Every 3 looms afford work to at least one woman, who winds the yarn for them. There are no fewer than 22 tambouring machines in the town. Four young girls commonly work at each; and gain, by their united labour, about two shillings per day.

The coal-works carried on at Stonelaw, by Major John Spens, are of long standing. There is no account when coals were at first wrought in this place. But from the number of old wastes the period must be very remote. At present about 126 persons are employed in the works. The water is raised by a steam engine, which, about 1776, was erected by Gabriel Grey, Esq; of Scotstoun. The coals turned out are of different qualities, but all of them are very good. They are sold on the hill at 10d. per hutch, weighing 400 lb. but it commonly exceeds that weight: carriage to Glasgow is 4d. so that a cart-load of 3 hutches, weighing about 13 Cwt. is laid down in the street for 3s. 6d. But two wheeled waggons, containing 6 hutches, are commonly used. Some of them, that lately were occasionally weighed, contained no less than 26 Cwt. of soft coal; which, however, is specifically heavier than

than hard coal. The empty waggon generally weighs about 8¼ Cwt. It is commonly 2 feet in depth; 3¼ in breadth; and 5¼ in length; the wheels are 4⅔ feet in height. The whole amounting to about 34¼ Cwt. is drawn by a single horse, which goes to Glasgow three times a day. Glasgow is distant from Stonelaw three miles and a half. Such heavy draughts, drawn by one horse, even for a greater length of road, is not unfrequent in this country. The horses employed are of the Lanarkshire breed. Their superior excellency, after the above-mentioned exertion of their strength, to which they are daily accustomed, need not be called in question.

A considerable quantity of iron-stone is turned out along with the coal, at Stonelaw. It sells at 5s. 6d. per ton on the hill, and is delivered at Clyde Iron-work for 6s. 6d.

THE persons employed in the above-mentioned works reside mostly in the town; for which reason the country part of the parish is but thinly inhabited. There are in it, however, 31 dwelling-houses, containing 44 families; inhabited by 229 persons, of whom 106 are males, 123 females, and 27 are children under 6 years of age. The population of the whole parish, therefore, amounts to 1860 persons, of whom 907 are males; 953 females;

males; and 297 children. The increase since the year 1755, if the return made to Doctor Webster was accurate, is no less than 891.

Although the parochial register of births is, with respect to population, not much to be depended upon, yet I shall give the following list of baptisms, taken from the Sessional Records.

Years.	Births.	Years.	Males.	Females.	Total.	Burials.
1699,	11.	1781,	29,	38,	67,	45.
1700,	10.	1782,	30,	37,	67.	
1701,	11.	1783,	20,	24,	44.	
1702,	18.	1784,	33,	24,	57.	26.
1703,	21.	1785,	36,	34,	70.	32.
1704,	16.	1786,	27,	34,	61.	54.
1705,	18.	1787,	42,	35,	77.	63.
1706,	27.	1788,	35,	37,	72.	41.
1707,	25.	1789,	33,	37,	70.	40.
1708,	26.	1790,	52,	32,	84.	35.
1709,	27.	1791,	40,	31,	71.	

The number of *poor* in the parish, considering its population, is not great. There are only 26 on the poor funds. They are mostly aged and infirm women. Each receives from 2s. to 5s. per month. There are besides a few indigent families, who are occasionally assisted, as the kirk Session, to whose care the oversight of the poor is intrusted, sees proper. The funds for answering the above purposes

are

are raised from the weekly collections at the church-door on Sabbaths; from proclamations of marriage; and the annual interest of a small sum, accumulated chiefly by pious donations of charitably disposed persons. These different sources, for there is no poor tax in the parish, procured to the Session, from February 1790, to February 1791, the sum of l. 52-13-3¼. The disbursements, during the same period, were l. 46-16-0. Balance added to the stock l. 5-17-3¼. One or two of the poor are allowed to beg within the bounds of the parish, but no where else.

RUTHERGLEN is by no means destitute of *grocery shops*, and *public houses*. Of the latter there are no fewer than 26 within the town. These, although more than sufficient for ordinary demands, are not able to accommodate strangers that frequent the fairs. To supply the deficiency, every inhabitant claims a right, now established by immemorial practice, of selling ale and spirits, licence free, during the time of the fairs. This custom which is hurtful neither to the revenues of government, nor the interest of the community, is profitable to some industrious families who inhabit large houses.

THERE are few remains of *antiquity*, at present existing in the country part of the parish. A *tumulus* of earth, supposed to have been originally a burying place, was lately demolished in the estate of Shawfield, a few yards from Polmadie; and the place where it stood converted into a mill-dam. None of its contents attracted the particular attention of workmen employed in removing it.

A *tumulus*, likewise of earth, still remains at Galloflat, about half a mile east from the town. This name, the Gaelic orthography of which is *Gallouflath*, or more properly *Callouflath*, is compounded of *Callou*, a safe retreat; and *flath* a hero. This mound was anciently surrounded with a ditch, the traces of which were visible so late as the year 1773. At that period the proprietor, Mr. Patrick Robertson, writer in Glasgow, ordered the ditch to be enlarged and converted into a fish-pond. During the operation, a passage 6 feet broad, and laid with unhewn stones, was discovered, leading up to the top of the mound. Near to this passage was dug up two brass or copper vessels, shaped like a porringer. Each held about a choppin, and was full of earth; they were white on the inside; but from what cause I could not learn. They had broad handles, about 9 inches in length, having cut upon them the name *Congallus*, or *Convallus*. These antique vessels, owing to negligence, are now irrecoverably lost. The mound, close to which they were found, is about 12 feet in height; 260 round the base; and 108 round the area on the top.

In the middle of this area, and a foot and a half under the furface, was difcovered a flat whinftone, about 18 inches in diameter, having a large hole cut through in the middle, and a fmaller one near the edge. Befide the ftone were found three *beads* of an antique fhape. One of them is preferved by Mr. Patrick Robertfon writer to the Signet, Edinburgh. The colour is a fine green of a verdigreafe hue; and the enamel is, in general, pretty entire. The perforation in the middle is remarkably wide; and the external furface is, fet off to advantage by a ribbed ornament, as in pl. I. fig. 6. in which the true dimenfions of the bead are preferved. This ancient amulet exhibits a beautiful example of the firft, but rude method, of cutting and graving upon ftones, that is known in the world. Cutting upon ftones and making ftraight lines, preceded engraving, or making any other kinds of figures upon them. " With a fharp-pointed ftone the early inhabitants of the world might fcratch ftraight lines upon the polifhed furfaces of other ftones, of a fofter texture; nay, with fuch a diamond, properly fet in a handle, they might make fuch lines and dotes even upon the hardeft." The bead being made of the old Egyptian pafte, anciently fo much admired in Europe, there is every reafon to believe that it was originally brought from the Eaft; and afterwards worn as an amulet by perfons of the firft diftinction in the nation. " The famous old

" glafs

"glafs manufactures of Egypt, Tyre, and Sidon,
"which furnifhed the Phoenicians with great and
"various objects of exportation to all Europe, and
"to the remoteft nations, would of courfe very
"foon furnifh their fagacious neighbours, the
"Greeks, with the very beft materials for fpecula-
"tion and imitation. In Egypt they made, in
"remoteft antiquity, rich coloured glafs and ena-
"mels, of which various proofs are found amongft
"the Egyptian antiquities; and the traders dif-
"perfed them over all the world in various forms,
"even in that of glafs-beads; and, we have very
"good reafons to apprehend, for purpofes fimilar
"to thofe for which our chriftian traders in flaves,
"manufacture and export them to the coaft of
"Guinea and Madagafcar. Such glafs-beads, fome-
"times curious and apparently Phoenician work-
"manfhip, and here in England erroneoufly enough
"called Druids' beads, are frequently found in the
"urns and fepulchral monuments of the barbarous
"nations, which the Phoenicians formerly vifited,
"for the laudable purpofe of bartering baubles for
"amber, gold, tin, flaves, girls, and other valua-
"ble commodities." †

THESE beads are, both in England and Scotland, commonly called *fnake*, or *adder* ftones. "Of
"thefe

---

† Introduction to *Taffie's* Gems, by *R. S. Rafpe.*

" these the vulgar opinion in Cornwall and most
" part of Wales is, that they are produced, through
" all Cornwall, by snakes joining their heads toge-
" ther and hissing, which forms a kind of bubble
" like a ring about the head of one of them, which
" the rest by continual hissing blow on till it comes
" off at the tail, when it immediately hardens and
" resembles a glass ring. Whoever found it was
" to prosper in all his undertakings. These rings
" are called *glain nadroedh*, or *gemma anguinæ*.
" *Glune* in Irish signifies *glass*. In Monmouthshire
" they are called *main magl*, and corruptly *glaim*
" for *glain*. They are small glass amulets, com-
" monly about half as wide as our finger rings, but
" much thicker, usually of a green colour, though
" some are blue, and others curiously waved with
" blue, red, and white. Mr. Lhuyd has seen two
" or three earthen rings of this kind but glazed
" with blue and adorned with transverse strokes or
" furrows on the outside. The smallest of them
" might be supposed to have been glass beads worn
" for ornaments by the Romans, because some
" quantities of them, with several amber beads,
" had been lately discovered in a stone-pit near
" Gardford in Berkshire, where they also dig up
" Roman coins, skeletons, and pieces of arms and
" armour. But it may be objected that a battle
" being fought between the Romans and Britons,
" as appears by the bones and arms, these glass
" beads

"beads might as properly belong to the latter.
"And indeed it seems very likely that these snake-
"stones, as we call them, were used as charms or
"amulets among the Druids of Britain on the same
"occasion as the snake-eggs among the Gaulish
"Druids. For Pliny, who lived when these priests
"were in request, and saw one of these snake-eggs,
"gives the same account of the origin of them as
"our common people do of their glain nair. There
"is, says that naturalist, *a kind of egg in great re-
"pute in Gaul disregarded (omissum) by the Greeks.
"A number of snakes in summer rolling together,
"form themselves into a kind of mass with the saliva
"of their mouths and froth of their bodies, and pro-
"duce what is called the anguinum, or snake's egg.
"The Druids say this, by their hissing, is borne up into
"the air, and must be caught in a mantle before it
"reaches the earth. The person who catches it must
"escape on horseback, for the snakes will pursue him
"till they are stopped by a river. The proof of it is,
"if it floats against the stream even when set in gold.
"As the Magicians know how to conceal their secret
"arts, they pretend it must be caught in a certain
"period of the moon, as if it was in the power of man
"to influence the operation of the snakes. I have
"seen one of these eggs, about the size of a small round
"apple, covered with a cartilageneous crust, like the
"claws of the arms of the polypus, and used as a drui-
"dical symbol. It is said to be wonderfully efficacious

"in

" *in promoting of law suits and procuring favourable*
" *audience of princes, insomuch that I am well assured*
" *a Roman Knight among the Vocontii was put to death*
" *by the late Emperor Claudius, merely for having*
" *one of them in his bosom as a trial.* Thus, conti-
" nues Mr. Lhuyd; we find it very evident that the
" opinion of the vulgar concerning the generation
" of these adder-beads, or snake-stones, is no other
" than a relic of superstition, or, perhaps, imposture
" of the Druids; but whether what we call snake-
" stones be the very same amulets that the Bri-
" tish Druids made use of, or whether this fabulous
" origin was ascribed formerly to the same thing
" and in aftertimes applied to these glass-beads I
" shall not undertake to determine. Dr. Borlase,
" who had penetrated more deeply into the druidi-
" cal monuments of this kingdom than any other
" writer before or since, observes, that instead of the
" natural *anguinum*, which must have been very
" rare, artificial rings of stone, glass, and some-
" times baked clay * was substituted as of equal
" validity. †

THE account which, in Scotland, is usually given
of the formation of the *adder-stone* is not much

more

* In the year 1790, one of Cornelian was found at Easter
Glentore, in the parish of New Monkland. It is in the posses-
sion of John Watt of Luggiebank, Esq.
† Cambden's Britannia, Lond. 1787. Vol. II. p. 571.

more rational. The common report is, that, at a certain season of the year, a great number of adders assemble themselves together, and that the largest among them casts his skin, which he does by quick convolutions of his body. Through this *exuviæ* the rest of the serpents force their way with great agility; every one, at passing through, leaving a slime or slough behind it. By degrees the skin becomes considerably thick, and, upon drying, takes the form in which it is afterwards found. To come near the adders whilst thus employed is said to be attended with no small danger. A circumstance which is reported to have happened in Mossflander, a well known peat-moss, lying in the counties of Stirling and Perth, is frequently mentioned as a proof of this. A man travelling through the moss, as the story says, chanced to go hard by the place, where a great number of serpents were employed in making a stone. Being perceived by them, they instantly set up a horrid hissing, and, with one accord, darted after the man, who was forced to flee with all his might, to save his life. At length, finding himself about to be overtaken by his incensed pursuers, he threw away his plaid, that he might run with greater speed. By this circumstance he made a fortunate escape: for, returning next day, in search of the plaid, he found it full of holes made by the adders, who had forced themselves through it, and thereby wrecked their vengeance on their imaginary enemy.

THE

The adder-stone, thus produced, or the beads and rings substituted in its place, is thought by superstitious people to possess many wonderful properties. It is used as a charm to insure prosperity, and to prevent the malicious attacks of evil spirits. In this case it must be closely kept in an iron box to secure it from the *Fairies*, who are supposed to have an utter abhorrence at iron. It is also worn as an amulet about the necks of children to cure sore eyes, the chincough and some other diseases; and to assist them in cutting their teeth. It is sometimes boiled in water as a specific for diseases in cattle: but frequently the cure is supposed to be performed by only rubbing with the stone the part affected. These foolish notions, however, are now happily exploded; being retained by none but a few credulous people, who, although without design on their part, exhibit a striking proof of the gross absurdities of the former ages of superstition, and tell us, in the most persuasive language, how much we should value the superior knowledge that now prevails.

A small mound of earth, at Hamilton Farm, was, about 25 years ago, levelled with the ground. In the bottom of the mound was a stone coffin containing human bones.

DRUMLAW, a small hill which stands in the middle of a plain called *Drumlaw-holm*, near the South-west boundary of the parish, was thought to have been artificial. A trial, to ascertain the truth, was lately made by digging a pit on the top of the hill. It was found to be composed of a coarse gravel, with a considerable mixture of earth, without any appearance of stratification. The search was left off in uncertainty. This little hill, being of an oblong form, resembling a sow's back, is beautifully descriptive of the etymology of its name.

CROSSHILL probably derived its name from a cross that was erected on its top. Near the cross was a stone about 10 feet high, by $3\frac{1}{4}$ broad. It was ornamented with various figures. The most remarkable was that of our Saviour riding upon an ass. There were several ornaments and inscriptions round the figures. This religious monument, during the last persecution in Scotland, fell a sacrifice to the fury of a mob, exasperated at the violent methods that were then used to enforce a mode of religion contrary to the consciences of the people. In one night the whole was broken in pieces, and not a fragment preserved.

THERE was, a good while ago, raised up by the plough, in a field called the *Pants*, an earthen pot, containing a considerable number of coins, chiefly
of

of Alexander III. and Edward I. Along with the coins were a few rings and other trinkets. Two persons, into whose hands this little treasure happened to fall, were prosecuted by the Sheriff of the county, and imprisoned in Hamilton, until they delivered up the whole. Some, however, both of the coins and rings are preserved by Major John Spens, a gentleman possessed of a laudable ambition, to save from destruction the remains of antiquity in his native country.

There was, till of late, a kind of fort, or semicircular intrenchment in the South-west corner of the parish: but no account of its origin was preserved. It is now levelled with the ground.

At a little distance from this place, and in the estate of Castlemilk, is *Maul's Myre*, where *Watling-street*, a Roman military way, in this county, according to Cambden, terminated. The name Watling is given to this road from one *Vitellianus*, supposed to have superintended the direction of it, the Britains calling Vitellianus, in their language, *Guetalin*.* In many places of England it is called *Mitchell Scott's Causeway;* and is believed by the credulous vulgar there, that the devil and his friend Mitchell made it in one night. Maul's Myre signifies a low ditch or marsh, from *Maul* or *Maol*, a

servant,

* Cambden's Britannia, Vol. I. p. 47.

servant, or whatever is low or mean; and *Myre* or *Meer*, a ditch. This etymology is descriptive of Maul's Myre in the western boundary of Rutherglen. Watling-street hath been traced from Errickstone to several other places in the county.† All the attempts to discover it in this parish, through which it must have gone, if the commonly supposed line of its direction is true, have been fruitless. This may be owing to the cultivated state of the parish, where not a stone that can obstruct the plough is left unremoved. That it went not far from Chesters is highly probable, as the word is acknowledged by all to be a corruption of *Castra*.

In May, 1792, one of the principal rooms in the old castle, at the Farme, was ordered to be repaired. The workmen, having torn down an old stucco ceiling, discovered above it another of wood. It was painted with water colours; but the figures were so much effaced, that excepting a few waved lines and stripes, it was impossible to form any distinct idea of what they consisted. Several lines of writing, in the old English characters, were observed on the sides of the great beams that lay across the house. The letters were black upon a white ground. Some of the lines were so greatly obliterated that they could not be read. The following, however, which were legible, are here offered to the public.

† Cambden's Brit. Vol. III. p. 348.

public, as a literary curiosity; and as an example of the way which the inhabitants of Scotland anciently used to inculcate the principles of morality and good breeding.

> Faire speiche In presence, with guid report in absence; And maners In to fellowschep, obtian grait reurence.
>
> ——————— Gyf thou heinsousnes dois or vice also; for scheme remanis quhen pleisour is ago.
>
> He that sitis doun to ye bend for to eite,
> forzetting to gyf god thankis for his meite;
> Syne rysis upe and his grace oure pass,
> Sitis doun lyk ane oxe, and rysis upe lyk ane ass.
>
> Thir armes that is heir, that ar abuine pentid; At the nobill hous that the lard of this bows is descendit. I, C, A, D. written 1325.

Each of the above stanzas is, in the painting, comprehended in a single line. The epitome of the rules of good breeding, that is contained in the first, is so admirably concise, that it probably would have puzzled Chesterfield, and his numerous admirers, to have made a better. The former part of the second stanza is obliterated, but the latter contains a lesson so important, that to have suppressed it would have been a crime. From the last it appears probable that all of them were written when the family of Crawford dwelt in the Farme.

I shall conclude this chapter with two Tables: the one containing the local names in the parish;

and

and the other the firnames of the male heads of families, with the number of families belonging to each name.

A TABLE,

Containing the Names of Places in RUTHERGLEN.

Alleys.	Drum-law-holm.	Moorfide.
Balloch-mill.	Eaft-croft.	Pants, *or St. Mary's*
Bankhead.	Eaft-field.	*croft*.
Bencath-hill.	Farme.	Pyet-fhaw.
Blackfauld.	Galloflat.	Quarrel-law.
Blairbath.	Gallomoor.	Quarrelholm.
Blairtum.	Gillgove.	Quarrel-fide.
Boultree-burn.	Green.	Rofebank.
Bullions-law.	Hamilton Farm.	Rutherglen-mill.
Calf-ward.	Hanging-croft.	Scotstoun.
Chapel-croft, *or*	Hanging-fhaw.	Shawfield.
Trinity-croft.	Horfe-croft.	Sheriff-rigs.
Chefters.	Killdale.	Stonelaw.
Clinkert-hill.	Kings' Crofshill.	Temple-crofs.
Cock-moor.	Kirk-rigs.	Tongues.
Cowans-loan.	Lemonfide.	Warlaw.
Crofs-hill.*	Lochbrae.	Weft-field.
Crofs-flat.	Lunniefide.	Weft-moor.
Drum-law.	Mill-rigs.	

* Of thefe there are more than one in the parifh.

A TABLE,

Containing the Sirnames of the Male Heads of Families in RUTHERGLEN, *with the number of Families belonging to each Name.*

Those marked with the *asterisk* are of long standing in the parish.

Sirnames.	N°.	Sirnames.	N°.	Sirnames.	N°.
Adam,	3	Cairn,	1	Elles,	1
Aiton,	1	Calder,	1	Farie,*	1
Allan,	1	Chalmers,	1	Findlay,	1
Allison,	1	Clerk,	1	Finnie,	1
Anderson,*	2	Cochrane,*	2	Fleming,*	4
Atkin,	3	Corbet,	1	Forrest,	1
Atkinhead,*	1	Craig,*	9	Fram,	1
Auldcorne,*	1	Crane,	1	Friebairn,*	3
Bain,	2	Crawford,*	1	Fullford,	1
Baird,	3	Cross,	2	Furlong,	1
Barkley,	1	Cummin,*	1	Fyfe,	1
Barr,*	1	Currie,	1	Gardner,	1
Bennie,	2	Dalglish,	1	Gemmil,	1
Bisset,	1	Dickieson,	1	Gilchrist,	1
Blair,	1	Dickson,	1	Gilmour,	1
Boddin,	3	Dinsmuir,	1	Glen,	2
Bowie,	1	Donald,	1	Graham,	1
Bowman,*	6	Dugald,	1	Grey,	1
Boyd,	1	Duncan,	3	Hamilton,	10
Brown,*	8	Dunn,	3	Hart,	1
Brownlie,	2	Dyer,	1	Harvey,	4
Bryce,	2	Dykes,*	1	Hodgeson,	1
Bryson,	3	Edmifton,	1	Hosie,	2

Sirnames.	Nº.	Sirnames.	Nº.	Sirnames.	Nº.
Hunter,	4	Melvin,	1	Sawers,	1
Hutchifon,	1	Mercer,	1	Scott,*	7
Jack,	1	Millar,	3	Scouller,	2
Jackfon,	2	Montgomery,	2	Shaw,*	6
Johnfton,	1	Morrifon,	1	Shearer,	2
Kelfo,	1	Morton,	1	Shields,	2
Kerr,*	9	Motherwell,*	2	Smith,*	4
Key,	2	Muir,*	8	Sniddon,	1
Kirkwood,	1	Murdoch,	2	Somervile,	2
Knox,	2	Nifbet,	3	Spens,*	2
Lang,	6	Noble,	1	Steven,	2
Lawfon,	2	Park,*	14	Stewart,	1
Letham,	1	Parkhill,*	3	Stirling,	1
Lietch,*	1	Paterfon,*	8	Swan,	1
Lindfay,	6	Pedie,*	1	Tenant,	1
Lochhead,	3	Perfton,	1	Thomfon,	3
Love,	4	Pettigrew,	1	Turnbull,*	5
Lowfon,	1	Pinkertoun,*	3	Urie,	3
Lyon,	1	Pitcairn,	1	Walker,	3
McAllafter,	1	Purdon,	1	Wallace,*	2
McAuley,	2	Rae,	1	Wark,	3
McDonald,	2	Ralfton,	1	Warnock,	2
McEwing,	1	Ramfay,	2	Watfon,	2
McFarlane,	2	Rankin,	3	Weir,	1
McKenzie,	2	Reid,	2	White,*	4
McKey,	1	Riddell,*	11	Williamfon,	5
McMath,	1	Ritchie,	1	Wilfon,*	14
Mair,	1	Robertfon,	4	Wingate,	2
Maitland,	1	Roger,	2	Wifeman,	1
Mark,	1	Rofs,	1	Young,	2
Meiklejohn,	1	Ruffel,	1	Yuil,	3
Melvil,	1				

HISTORY

OF

EAST-KILBRIDE.

THE HISTORY OF EAST-KILBRIDE.

CHAP. III.

OF THE EXTENT OF KILBRIDE, ITS POPULATION, PLACES OF NOTE, &c.

THE county of Lanark is commonly divided into the upper, middle, and lower wards. In the second of these divisions is situated the parish of Kilbride. It is bounded on the north by the parish of Carmunnock: on the west by Eaglesham: on the south by Loudon, Avendale, and Glasford: and on the east by Blantyre, and Cambuslang. It is about 10 miles in length, from south to north; and from 2, to 5, in breadth, from east to west.

It consists of the united parishes of Torrance and Kilbride;* and is subdivided into 446 horse-gangs, according to which the statute work is paid, each horse-gang being rated at 3s. 6d. sterl. The valuation, as it stands in the Cess-book of the county, is 7679l. 13s. 3d. Scots. The real rent, however, may, on an average, be estimated at 4s. 6d. per acre: which, on a general calculation, may amount to 5040l. sterl. The number of heritors is about 135, nearly 30 of whom are non-residents. The parish is inhabited by 587 families, which contain 2359 persons, of whom 1065 are males; 1294 females; and 488 children under 6 years of age. The return made to Dr. Webster, in 1755, was only 2029. The upper part of the parish, however, was, some time ago, greatly depopulated by the accumulation of small farms into large ones. The parochial Register of baptisms commences in the year 1688, but no accurate calculation can be instituted upon that, as the childrens names have not been uniformly enrolled. I have, however, extracted from the session-books a list of baptisms in the following periods.

* The parish of Torrance was, in 1589, annexed to the parish of Kilbride, "as being a pendicle thereof, and as next adjacent to the said kirk." Records of the presb. of Glasgow, anno 1589.

Years.	Males.	Females.	Total.
1688,	27,	20,	47.
1689,	25,	22,	47.
1700,	21,	16,	37.
1710,	23,	30,	53.
1720,	17,	31,	48.
1740,	26,	30,	56.
1770,	30,	25,	55.
1780,	39,	35,	74.
1785,	29,	42,	71.
1788,	32,	31,	63.
1789,	31,	34,	65.
1790,	30,	32,	62.

No regifter of burials has been kept in the parifh, the difference, therefore, between the births and burials is not known. In the form of regiftration the mother's name is omitted, a circumftance which, in many cafes, renders ufelefs the chief defign of regiftrating births. As feffional regiftrations bear legal evidence in courts of law, the community fhould pay attention to the form in which they are made.

This parifh is called Eaft-Kilbride to diftinguifh it from Weft-Kilbride, in the county of Ayr. The name is compounded of *Kill*, a Gælic word for a church or burying place, and *Bride*, or *Bridget*, the name of a faint greatly famed in the Romifh legends. Scottifh and Irifh writers contend about the

place

place of her nativity. Hect. Boethius* maintains that she was born in Scotland: that she received her education in the Isle of Man: and at her death was interred at Abernethy. This opinion is supported by B. Leslie,† who takes great pains to distinguish her from the Swedish Briget. It is asserted on the other hand, "That she was born in a village belonging to the diocese of Armagh, and became one of the greatest ornaments of the kingdom of Ireland. Her father, who was one of the principal chiefs of the country, intrusted her to the care of a christian woman, who educated her (says the historian) in the fear of God, and love of virginity. Her father, after she was come of age, brought her home to his house; which rather served to confirm the resolution she had taken to consecrate her virginity to God. Being asked in marriage by a young man, she prayed to the Lord, to render her so deformed, that he would think no more of her. The prayer was heard, and a disease in her eyes delivered her from his solicitations, and induced her father to permit her to take the vail. Three other ladies of the country joined her in this design, who, after their vow of perpetual virginity, received the vail and a peculiar dress from St. Niel, a disciple of St. Patrick. She was, during her lifetime, the founder of many monasteries, in different provinces of Ireland. She instituted a religious order, called the

* Lib. 9. fol. 158.   † Lib. 4. p. 142.

the *Holy Saviour*, and gave the order rules, contained in 31 chapters, dictated, as it is reported, by Jesus Christ himself, and approved by the holy See. This order prevailed very much in Britain, Ireland, and the low countries. She persuaded Pope Gregory XI. to transfer the holy See from Avignon to Rome, where she died."* An Irishman who writes her life, under the title of *Bridgida Thaumaturga*, (8vo Paris, 1620) tells us, that one of her chief miracles was restoring, by a touch of her hand, a withered and dry tree, to a flourishing state. † Arch^{b.} Usher seems to think that there might be two saints of the same name, one belonging to Ireland, and the other to Scotland; and so each kingdom might value itself on account of its own saint. But, to whatever kingdom she belonged, one thing is certain, that many places in Scotland have been dedicated to her honour: and that the firnames *Bride*, and *M'Bride*, are by no means unfrequent in this country.

CROSSBASKET, the least elevated ground in the parish, is about 200 feet above the level of the sea: the top of *Eldrig*, at the distance of about 7 miles south of Crossbasket, is computed to be at least 1600. From Crossbasket to Eldrig there is a gradual ascent,

but

---

* Histoire du Clergé feculier et regulier. Tome troisieme. p. 316.

† *Nicolson's Histor. Librar.*

but confifting of a regular fucceffion of fmall hills, with very little level ground between them. The moorland part of the parifh commences about 2 miles to the north of Eldrig, and continues a confiderable way down the fouth fide of the ridge, where Kilbride borders with Loudon. Eldrig is the higheft part of that ridge formed by the hills in Eaglefham, Mearns, Nielfton, &c.

THE moft remarkable waters,* and rivulets in the parifh are, *White-Cart, Calder, Pomillan, Kittoch,* and the water of *Irvine.* The Cart, Calder, and water of Irvine, derive their origin from the Eldrig, and its vicinity. Calder takes its courfe by Torrance, Calderwood, Crofsbafket, and joins Clyde in the parifh of Blantyre. Cart runs by Eaglefham, Cathcart, Paifley, &c. and enters Clyde below Inchinan Bridge. Pomillan runs through Strathaven, and joins Aven about half a mile from the town. Kittoch, which rifes from the neighbourhood of the Shields, out of a marfh commonly called Kittoch's Eye, runs by the village of Kilbride, Kittochfide, Piel, &c. and joins Cart near Bufbie; to which place the weft boundary of the parifh anciently extended: but the lands of Bufbie are now allocated, *quo ad facra,* to the parifh of Carmunnock. Over thefe rivulets are feveral good stone

† The term *water,* as a proper name, is generally ufed in Scotland to denote a fmall river.

stone bridges, but none of them are so remarkable as to require a particular description.

The village of Kilbride is 7¼ miles south of Glasgow, 5 of Rutherglen, and 6 west of Hamilton. It consists of 71 dwelling-houses, which form the chief street and two lanes. It is inhabited by 167 families; which contain 524 inhabitants. This village, of which the proprietor of Kirktounholm is superior, was constituted a burgh of barony, about the end of Queen Anne's reign. By the grant the inhabitants are empowered to hold a weekly market on Tuesday, besides four fairs in the year. The market-day is not observed, but the fairs are tolerably well frequented.

About a quarter of a mile west from Kilbride is the mansion-house of *Kirktounholm*. The old building was, about 30 years ago, destroyed by lightening: a very elegant modern structure now occupies its place. Lord Lyle, formerly Sir Walter Cunningham, Bart. of Corsehill, is the proprietor.

Adjoining to Kirktounholm is *Limekilns*, the family-seat of William Graham of Limekilns, Esq; About a mile and a half west from Limekilns is *Kittochside*, the most pleasant village in the parish.

In the neighbourhood of this place are the remains

mains of two ancient Fortifications, on two hills, now known by the name of Caſtlehill and Rough-hill. The former is ſituated on the north, and the latter on the ſouth-ſide of Kittoch: the diſtance between them is about 200 yards. The intervening plain, through which the rivulet runs, is called Caſtleflat. The area on the top of the Caſtlehill is 122 feet in length, and 63 in breadth. There are no remains of buildings on it. The natural ſituation of the hill renders it not eaſily acceſſible but on one ſide: at each end there is a ditch, about 57 feet wide, and 11 deep, cut quite acroſs the hill, or rather narrow ridge of which the Caſtlehill originally made a part. The area on the top of the Rough-hill is 129 feet in length, and 71 in breadth. On this are the remains of a building that meaſures 73 feet, by 63. The ruins of this ancient ſtructure have, for a long while paſt, ſupplied materials for the dykes, and roads in the neighbourhood. It was built of free-ſtone, but the ſtones do not appear to have been hewn. Some labourers, about 50 years ago, as they were collecting ſtones for the above-mentioned purpoſes, diſcovered, among the ruins, a pretty large vault. On making this diſcovery they were greatly elated with the hopes of finding a treaſure. After the moſt diligent ſearch, however, they found nothing but rubbiſh. In a few days the ſubterraneous apartment, which had been concealed for time immemorial, was no more. It

is

is probable that other vaults may lie buried in the ruins, as they have never been thoroughly searched. Two sides of the hill are almost inaccessible, the rest have been secured by *fossæ*, of which there are yet some distinct traces. It is not known whether any stones having inscriptions on them were ever discovered among the rubbish: it is probable that no attention was paid by the workmen, to so minute, and, in their apprehension, so trifling a circumstance. Not far from the ruins I lately found a *Celt*, or stone-hatchet, of a coarse kind of iron-stone: it is 6¼ inches in length, and 3 in breadth, at the face, but only 1 at the other end, pl. I. fig. 4. It is worthy of notice that celts, from every part of the world where they have been found, are nearly of the same shape. This rude instrument, being used by the inhabitants of this country before they knew the use of iron, carries back our ideas to the most remote antiquity.

When, or by whom, these hills were occupied, as places of strength, cannot easily be discovered. Tradition says, that they were built by the Romans; but their elliptical form seems to put a negative upon that report. Nor is it certain but that both of them belonged to the same fortification. This is the more probable as there are no remains of building on the Castlehill, which might be used as an exploratory mount, or a *prætorium*.

Although

Although the above-mentioned ruins are, probably, the most ancient in the parish, yet there are others of considerable antiquity. One of these is the *Mains of Kilbride*. This extensive habitation of a rich and powerful family is situated about a mile north of the kirk, and is wholly in ruins, except the tower which is pretty entire. This, like the abodes of the great in former times, appears to have been built for defence. It is 56 feet high, 37 long, and 27 broad: at the west end is a dark and dismal vault, which seems to have been used as a prison: the wall near the ground is about 6 feet in thickness: the windows are extremely narrow and irregularly placed. This tower was habitable till about 70 years ago, when the roof was taken off to procure slates for some office-houses at Torrance. It was surrounded by a deep *fossa* which is yet visible: the chief entry was by a narrow draw-bridge on the east, and strongly guarded by a beautiful arched gate, over which was placed a stone having the Arms of Scotland cut upon it. The workmanship is good, considering the period when it must have been executed: the tails of the unicorns, however, are made to bend downwards between the hind legs, similar to the direction given them in the title page of Bassandyne's folio Bible, printed at Edinburgh 1576. This stone was, about 50 years ago, taken down by order of *Col. Stuart*, and removed to Torrance, where it is placed in the front of the house, above the chief entry.

The old, and, probably, the first edifice of the Mains, stood about 70 yards north of the tower, and is now lying in ruins. The *fossa* within which it was inclosed is more perfect, and much larger than the one round the castle.

An aged *Yew*, which stands a few yards to the south-east of the Mains, is the only tree worthy of notice about the place. The trunk is 5 feet in circumference, and 10 feet high; the branches into which it divides itself rise to a considerable height, and extend over a large space of ground. What contributed greatly to the beauty, and, at the same time, to the grandeur of the Mains was an artificial lake, a little to the south of the tower. It covered a space of about 20 acres. A small island, composed of earth and stones, was raised in the middle of the lake; which, besides beautifying the scene, afforded a safe retreat for the water-fowl with which the place abounded. This little eminence is now covered with planting; and, instead of being the pride of the lake, is become a useful ornament to a rich and extensive meadow, in which, since the water was drained off, it now stands.

The castle, the age of which is unknown, was probably built by the Cummins before the reign of King R. Bruce. At that period nearly two thirds of the lands of Kilbride belonged to that powerful family.

family: But the whole was forfeited by the treachery of John Cummin, whom Bruce killed at Dumfries. They were afterwards, in the year 1382, given to John Lindfay of Dunrode, fucceffor to James Lindfay, who affifted the King in killing the traitor, at the altar. This family preferring the Mains to Dunrode, their ancient family-feat, near Gourock, took up their refidence in Kilbride. They flourifhed in great wealth and fplendour till a little more than a century ago, when the eftate was fold to pay the debt which the extravagance of its owner forced him to contract. The Mains, with a few adjoining farms, belongs at prefent to Alexander Stuart, Efq; of Torrance.

This ancient building hath now undergone a very great change: for, inftead of being the well-fortified habitation of a powerful and fplendid family, it is converted into a pigeon-houfe. It is reported, that the laft proprietor, in the Dunrode family, greatly exceeded all his predeceffors in haughtinefs, oppreffion, and every kind of vice. He feldom went from home unlefs attended by twelve vaffals, well mounted on white fteeds. Among the inftances of his cruelty, it is told, that, when playing on the ice, he ordered a hole to be made in it, and one of his vaffals, who had inadvertently difobliged him in fome trifling circumftance, immediately to be drowned. The place hath ever fince

been

been called Crawford's hole, from the name of the man who perished in it. Tradition mentions this cruel action as a cause, in the just judgment of God, that gave rise to his downfall. In a short while after, it is reported, his pride was brought very low. This haughty chieftain was, at length, forced by penury to apply for charity to the tenants, and domestics he had formerly oppressed. We have reason to believe that they would not give a very kind reception to so cruel and overbearing a tyrant. It is told, that, having worn out the remains of a wretched life, he died in one of their barns. Such was the miserable end of one of the greatest, and most opulent families in this country.

To the Lindsays belonged also the lands of *Basket*, and the castle of *Crossbasket*, in the vicinity of Blantyre. This ancient building, the age of which is not known, was the jointure-house of the family of the Mains, but is now the property of Capt. Thomas Peter of Crossbasket. It is about 54 feet high, 38 long, and 22 broad. The whole is kept in good repair. A commodious dwelling-house, of a modern construction, is built close to the east end of the tower. The situation is pleasant and healthful. Considerable attention had once been paid to the gardens and inclosures; but they have, for some time past, been greatly neglected. Soon, however, will they put on a quite different appearance, when the Captain shall have finished the improvements he has begun to make on the estate.

The word Crofsbafket is derived from a Crofs that stood at a small distance from the tower, and in the lands of Bafket. Near the foot of this religious monument was a sacred Font. Both were of stone. On the font was a long inscription, but so much obliterated that the characters have not been legible, more than a century past. These hallowed remains of superstition, like many of the greatest monuments of antiquity, fell, about 50 years ago, a sacrifice to avarice and ignorance: and report says, that the person who destroyed them, never after did well.

About a mile south from Crofsbafket, and on the banks of Calder, stands the house of *Calderwood*, the seat of Sir William Maxwell of Calderwood, Bart. The estate came into the family of Maxwell by a marriage of *Eumerus*, or *Homerus de Carlaveroc*, a cadet of the family of Nithsdale, with *Mary*, daughter and heirefs of *Roland de Mernis*, in the reign of Alexander III. Sir Robert Maxwell, second son of Eumerus, was, in his father's lifetime, designed by the title of Calderwood; and from him the present Sir William Maxwell is lineally descended.

Close to the mansion-house stood the castle of Calderwood,

Calderwood, the date of which is not known. It was 87¼ feet in height; 69 in length; and 40 in breadth. The rock upon which it stood was 60 feet perpendicular. A great part of the tower fell, of its own accord, on the 23d of January, 1773. The downfall of that ancient edifice, did not induce the family to abandon a spot, which nature had been pleased to decorate with a great variety of her undisguised beauties. The ruins were, without loss of time, converted into a modern building.

Although the situation of Calderwood is low, in comparison of the ground adjacent, and although the prospect from the house is greatly confined, yet the place is not unhealthy or unpleasant. It is surrounded with banks through which the Calder, in a variety of beautiful meanders, takes its course. A delightful *cascade*, formed by nature, fronts the house, at the distance of about 200 yards. The fall, which is interrupted by small breaks, renders the landscape exceedingly agreeable. The scene in general, being a mixture of the GRAND, the ROMANTIC, and BEAUTIFUL, would, in ancient poetry, have been celebrated as the inchanted abodes of the rural Deities. That a spot like this, surrounded with so many natural beauties, should have been fixed upon, at a very early period, for the seat of a rich and honourable family, is a proof of the good taste of the first builder of Calderwood Castle.

Two miles south from Calderwood stood the ancient house of *Torrance*. It was reduced to ruins near two centuries ago, and nothing of it now remains but some scattered rubbish. Adjoining to the ruins is a Holly-tree, which hath survived the downfall of the house. This aged, but living monument, is one of the most remarkable trees in the parish. It is very tall, and covers an area of about 30 feet in diameter. Near a foot from the ground it divides itself into four branches; the least of which is, in circumference, 25 inches; another is 31; the next largest is 37; and the largest of all is 41: the circumference of the trunk, below the branches, measures 6 feet 10 inches.

The name Torrance, which is derived from Tor, a little hill, is taken from an artificial mound of earth, still known by the name of the *Tor*, and which is situated about a quarter of a mile from the house. It is about 160 yards round the base, and 20 of ascent. The area on the top is oval.

The present edifice was built in 1605, when the estate of Torrance belonged to the Hamiltons, cadets of the family of Hamilton. It was sold, about the middle of the last century, to the Stuarts of the family of Castelmilk. The present proprietor, Alexander Stuart of Torrance, Esq; is the great-grandson of James Stuart of Torrance, the original purchaser.

purchafer, who was brother to Sir Archibald Stuart of Caftelmilk, the anceftor of the prefent Sir John Stuart of Caftelmilk, Baronet. They were the two only fons of a Sir Archibald Stuart of Caftelmilk, Caffiltoun, and Fynnart-Stewart, who married Ann, eldeft daughter of Robert, Lord Sempil; which Sir Archibald Stuart was the heir male, lineally defcended from Matthew Stuart of Caftelmilk, Caffiltoun, and Fynnart-Stewart, who died in the year 1474; and of whom mention is made in various original deeds ftill extant.

This Matthew Stuart was the fon of Sir William Stuart of Caftelmilk, who is mentioned in Rymer's *Fœdera Angliæ* as one of the fureties given, on the part of Scotland, in the year 1398, for the prefervation of the peace of the Weftern Marches between England and Scotland; which Sir William Stuart was the brother of Sir John Stuart of Darnley. Thefe two brothers, during the reign of James I. of Scotland, went over to France, to the affiftance of Charles VII. where they performed many gallant actions, and rendered fuch fignal fervices to that Monarch, and the kingdom of France, that they are mentioned with high encomiums by many hiftorians of thofe times: and Sir John Stuart of Darnley, the elder brother, received from Charles VII. the Lordfhip and eftate of *Aubigny* in the province of Berry in France; with many other marks of diftinction.

Both

Both these brothers, Sir John Stuart of Darnley, and Sir William Stuart of Castelmilk, were killed on the   day of February, 1429, at the battle fought that day, near to Orleans, during the famous siege of that place.

Castelmilk, of which a view from the south east is here given, is situated on the northern declivity of Cathkin hills, in the parish of Carmunnock, about a mile and a quarter from the town of Rutherglen. It is the family-seat of Sir John Stuart of Castelmilk, Baronet. This ancient place was, for centuries past, called Castletown, or Casseltown, but now more frequently Castlemilk, or Castelmilk, from the Castle of Milk, a river in Anandale, in the county of Dumfries; which castle was anciently possessed by Sir John's ancestors. The old building, the age of which is not known, is pretty large, and of a very ancient construction. The walls are extremely thick, and terminate above in a strong battlement. Originally the windows were few, and narrow, and the stairs very strait. The whole building is kept in excellent repair, and contains not a few commodious apartments. The most remarkable is one that goes under the name of Queen Mary's room, because, (as report says) her Majesty lodged in it the night before the battle of Langside. The ceiling of this memorable room is ornamented with the Arms of the Kings of Scotland, in the Stuart

line,

S.E. VIEW of CASTLEMILK IN THE COUNTY of LANARK
The Seat of Sir John Stuart Bar.t

III

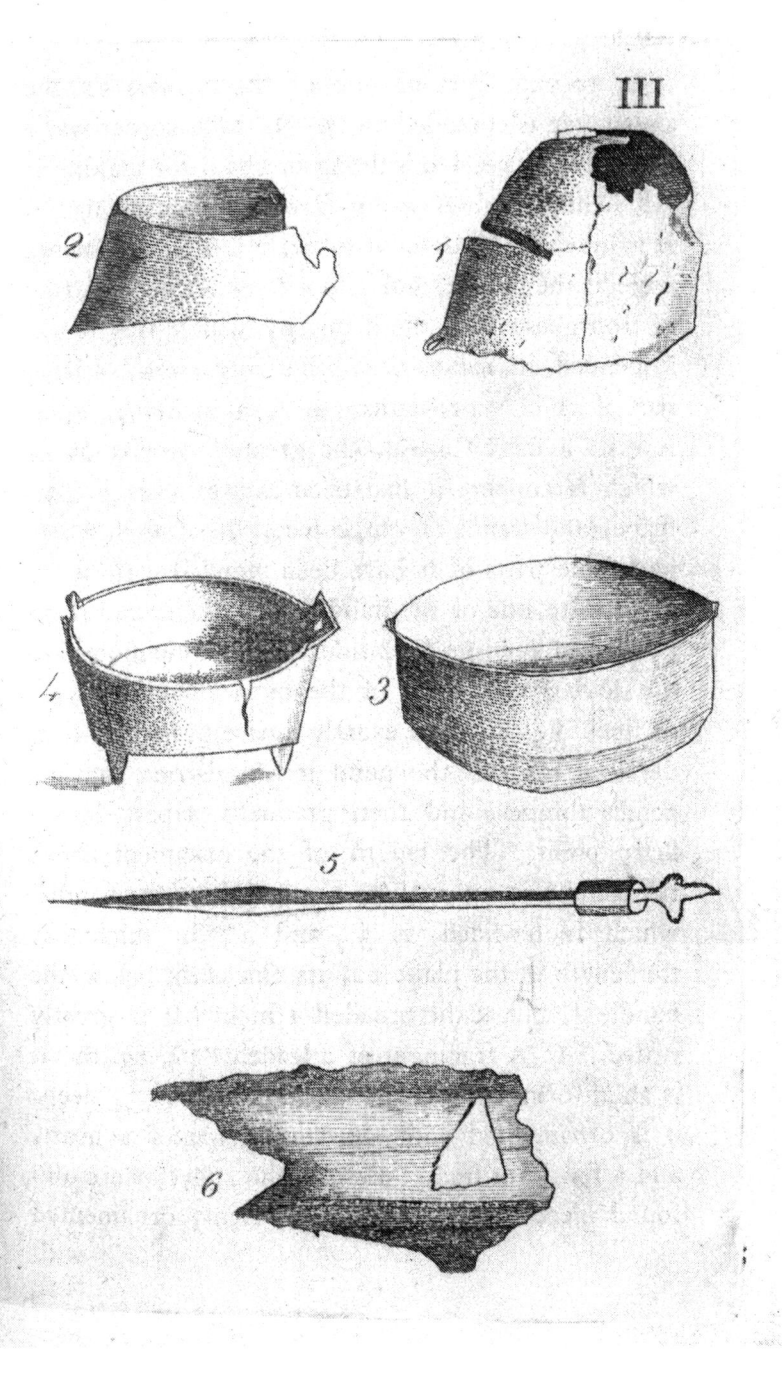

line, and with the Arms of all the crowned heads of Europe with whom the Stuarts were connected. Several additions have been made to the house by which it is rendered very commodious. The pleasure grounds have lately been laid out to the best advantage. Few places in Scotland enjoy a more agreeable situation. It commands a prospect, which, for a mixed variety of extensive, majestic, rich and beautiful objects, is probably not equalled any where in Scotland; as it takes in the city of Glasgow, with the strath of Clyde, filled with prospering manufactures; whilst the vast and far distant mountains of Lennox, Argyle, Perthshire, &c. mingling with the sky, terminate the view.

In the beginning of Summer, 1792, the following pieces of antiquity were found buried in a field adjoining to Castelmilk. 1. An antique *Helmet* of iron, pl. III. fig. 1. It measures from top to bottom, 11 inches: from the face to the back, 16: from side to side, $9\frac{1}{4}$: the opening for the light is $5\frac{1}{4}$ long on each side. The metal on the face is much thicker than on the back, which, in the side exposed to view in the figure, is not entire, owing apparently to corrosion. It weighs 13 lb. 2 ounces, avoirdupois. 2. A *Neckpiece*, likewise of iron, fig. 2: it is $5\frac{1}{4}$ inches deep at the back, and 7 at the face: 11 from the face to the back, at the bottom; but only 9 at the top: it is $10\frac{1}{4}$ in width, and weighs 4 lb.

4 lb. 10 oz. Part of one of the corners on the upper side is corroded away. In each corner was a small slit, to receive a thong or chain for making it fast behind. 3. A camp *Oven*, of copper, fig. 3. It is much worn, and corroded: it is 2 feet 5¼ inches wide at the mouth, and 1 foot 6 inches deep: a ring of iron goes round the brim, by which ring it was suspended, by means of another ring or *bool* of iron, part of which yet remains. 4. A camp *Kettle*, fig. 4. It is of a mixed metal, the greatest proportion of which is copper: it had been cast into its present shape, and stands on three feet. It is much worn, and some parts of it have been mended with pieces of copper: one of the handles is broken, and there is a wide rent on one side. The dimensions are not so large as those of the oven. 5. A *Dagger* of steel, fig. 5. It is exactly square below the handle, but towards the point it spreads out, and becomes thinner, and then gradually tapers into a sharp point. The length of the ornament above the handle is 2¼ inches: the length of the handle, which is six-sided, is 3¼ and 1¼ in thickness: the length of the blade 22, its thickness below the handle ¼, but at the broadest 1 inch. It is greatly rusted. 6. A fragment of a leaden *Vase*, fig. 6. It is about 6 inches long at the mouth, and 3¼ deep: it is ornamented with the rude shape of a heart, and a few faint lines. Besides the above, were also found pieces of *Leathern Belts*, richly ornamented with

with ftuds of brafs. The whole was found among very dry fand, which no doubt contributed to their prefervation. It is known that leather, when well tanned, will, if kept dry, retain its texture and toughnefs for many ages. The ruft, on fome parts of the iron, is fwelled up into fmall protuberances, refembling that kind of *ætites* in which the *nucleus* is wanting. The *tunica* is confiderably thick, and feems to be compofed of very fine *lamellæ*. Thefe protuberances muft have taken their prefent fhape and confiftency, during the evaporation of the ruft, when in a liquid ftate: for as the water, containing the iron, would be abforbed into the atmofpheric air, the ferruginous particles, being left behind, would be confolidated into the form of concentric *lamellæ*. Their emptinefs feems to be owing to the homogeneous quality of the iron ruft; for had fand or clay been fufpended in the liquid, we have reafon to think that they would have been left behind by the more minute metallic particles, and would have formed a *nucleus* below the ferruginous *tunicæ*. This might help to explain fome phenomena in the formation of *ætites*, and other metallic cryftallizations; and might help to prove that many of thefe bodies were formed during a tranfition from a ftate of fluidity, by a *menftruum*, to a ftate of drynefs, by evaporation.

The houfe of Torrance, which is about 5 miles fouth from Caftelmilk, was originally a fquare tower

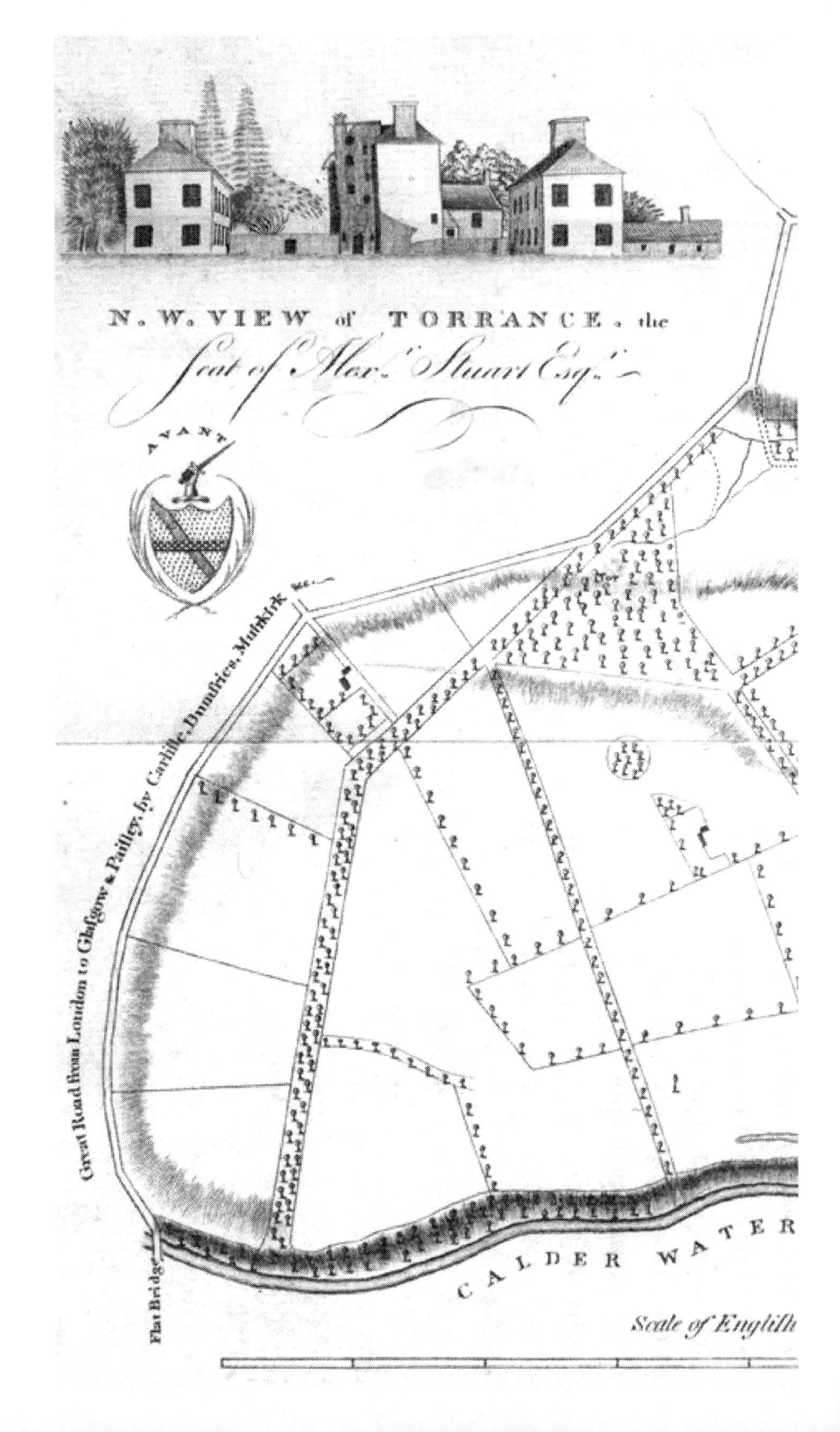

N.W. VIEW of TORRANCE, the Seat of Alexr. Stuart Esqr.

AVANT

Great Road from London to Glasgow & Paisley, by Carlisle, Dumfries, Muirkirk

Flat Bridge

CALDER WATER

Scale of English

Road to Hamilton

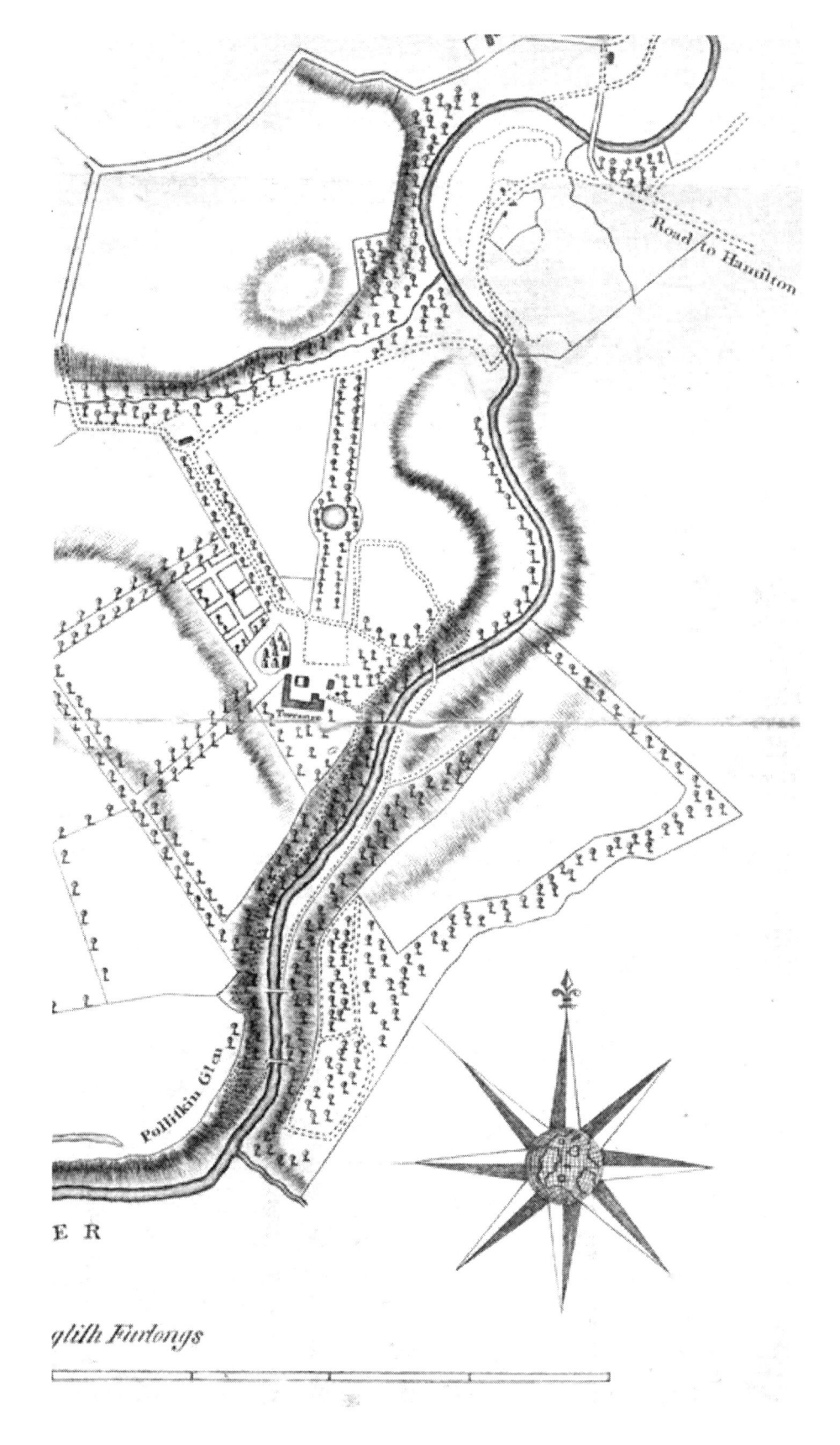

Pollitkin Glen

E R

glish Furlongs

of confiderable height; but has, of late, by feveral improvements and additions, been made both commodious and elegant. The fituation is high, and commands an extenfive and beautifully diverfified profpect to the north-weft. The adjoining banks contain a great variety of natural beauties. Two years ago they were laid out in ferpentine walks, hermitages, &c. which bring into view beautiful cafcades, purling ftreams, rugged rocks, and diftant landfcapes. Such rural and romantic fcenes, fucceeding each other in a manner fo agreeably ftriking, are but rarely met with in this part of the country. What adds confiderably to their beauty is a wooden bridge, of an uncommonly neat conftruction, thrown over the Calder, and by which thefe variegated circumambulations are connected. It is 21 feet in height, and 44 over. A plan of the improvements on thefe banks, with a view of Torrance, is given in pl. IV.

But the late improvements about Torrance are not confined to the banks of Calder only. The prefent proprietor, whofe attention is laudably directed to the ufeful, equally as to the ornamental, has planted many thoufand trees on the eftate, moft of which are thriving well. Thefe, with what were planted, about 60 years ago, by Col. Stuart, are highly conducive both to the beauty and utility of the country.

THE

The old kirk of Torrance, which stood about half a mile from the mansion-house, was left to fall into ruins after the parish was, in 1589, united to Kilbride. It hath long ago been totally demolished. In the adjoining burying-ground human bones are occasionally dug up.

About a mile and a half south from Kilbride are the ruins of the ancient castle of *Lickprivick*. Most of the buildings, already mentioned, must, perhaps, yield to this in point of antiquity. I am sorry it is not in my power to give such a particular description of it as it deserves. The castle and the adjoining lands were, for time immemorial, possessed by the Lickprivicks of that ilk. The family made a considerable figure long before the reign of King Robert Bruce; and continued to flourish a long time after. One of the descendents was printer to James VI. of Scotland.

To this ancient family was granted, for singular services, the heritable title of Sergeantcy and Coronership, in the Lordship of Kilbride; along with considerable emoluments inseparable from the title. The original charter, by which the grant was made to the family, was dated in the year 1397. It was afterwards renewed by James I. of Scotland; James IV. and James VI. The title, with the profits, belongs, at present, to Torrance: the greatest part of the estate is the property of John Boyes, Esq;

At what period the name Lickprivick took its rife, and on what account, is not, perhaps, eafy to determine: it appears to have been very ancient and refpectable in the parifh. But ancient families, like other things, are worn out by length of time: the laft perfon of the name I could hear of in this part of the country, died a few years ago in Strathaven.

The manfion-houfe, or caftle of Lickprivick, had once been no contemptible building. It was conftructed, like the houfes of the great during the feudal fyftem, with towers, battlements, &c. The whole was, about 60 years ago, reduced to ruins, and nothing now remains but fome fcattered rubbifh. Not far from the building is an artificial mound of earth, which continues pretty entire: it is about 14 feet in height; it is fquare at the top; each fide meafures 12 yards.

The *Piel*, which ftands on the fouth bank of Kittoch, at the north-weft boundary of the parifh, is juftly entitled to a place among the ancient buildings in Kilbride. The old caftle, few veftiges of which now remain, ftood about a quarter of a mile to the weft of the prefent building; but when, and by whom it was built, is not known. The moft confiderable part of the prefent edifice was built near two centuries ago. Since that time it has received fome additions which contribute greatly

to

to the beauty of the place. Having experienced a great number of masters, it is now in the possession of Andrew Houston, Esq; of Jordon-hill. The house, though not at present inhabited, is in tolerable repair; and might, at a small expence, be rendered commodious. The Compass, containing the 32 points, is painted on the ceiling of the uppermost apartment: the index, which is fixed to an iron rod that goes through the roof, is directed by the wind in whatever point it blows.

A considerable number of neat and commodious dwelling-houses have lately been built in the parish; as Limekilns, Rogertoun, Dykehead, Kittochside, Braehead, Long-Calderwood, Caplerig, Plat-thorn, Nook, Burnhouse, Crosshill, Browster-land, Browncastle, and Whitemoss.

In mentioning the places of note in the parish, *Mount Cameron*, should by no means be omitted. It is a small eminence about three quarters of a mile south-east from Kilbride; and on which is built a neat and commodious dwelling-house. This place, formerly called *Blacklaw*, takes its present name from Mrs. JEAN CAMERON, a Lady of a distinguished family, character and beauty. Her zealous attachment to the house of *Stuart*, and the active part she took to support its interest, in the year 1745, made her well known through Britain.

Her

Her enemies, indeed, took unjust freedoms with her good name; but what can the unfortunate expect from a fickle and misjudging world? The revengeful and malicious, especially if good fortune is on their side, seldom fail to put the worst construction on the purest and most disinterested motives. Mrs. Cameron, after the public scenes of her life were over, took up her residence in the solitary and bleak retirement of Blacklaw. But this vicissitude, so unfriendly to aspiring minds, did not throw her into despair. Retaining to the last the striking remains of a graceful beauty, she spent a considerable part of her time in the management of domestic affairs. She shewed, by her conversation on a great variety of subjects, that she had a discernment greatly superior to the common. But politics was her favourite topic; and her knowledge of that subject was not confined to those of her own country. The particular cast of her mind, especially during the latter part of her life, was rather melancholy. A vivacity, however, that was natural to her constitution, often enlivened her features and conversation. Her whole deportment was consistent with that good-breeding, unaffected politeness, and friendly generosity, which characterize the people of rank in the Highlands of Scotland. She was not remarkable for a more than ordinary attachment to any system of religious opinions, or mode of worship; which is not always the case with the unfortunate.

unfortunate. She attended divine service in the parish church; in which she joined with becoming devotion. Her brother, and his family, of all her friends, paid her the greatest attention. She died in the year 1773, and was buried at Mount Cameron, among a clump of trees adjoining to the house. Her grave is distinguished by nothing but a turf of grass, which is now almost equal with the ground.

That the names of places in the parish are partly Gælic, and partly English, will appear by a table of proper names subjoined to this chapter.

Several proper names have originated from crosses that were anciently erected in the parish: as Crosshill, Whitecross, Wardlawcross, &c. Near the cross was commonly a heap of stones, which was used as a resting-place for funerals occasionally passing that way. One of these ominous resting-places still remains on the top of Wardlawcross. Some time ago, however, a great part of the stones was carried away, especially the larger ones upon which the biers and coffins were usually laid. Mr. Stuart of Torrance, the proprietor, was no sooner informed of this fraudulent dilapidation, than he ordered the stones to be carried back.

The Market-hill, which is situated about half a mile from Kilbride, on the old road to Glasgow,
received

received its name from a market which, when the plague raged in Glasgow, was held on it, two days in the week. The people in this part of the country, afraid of catching the infection, would not come nearer the city, with their marketable goods, than this hill: to which temporary market the inhabitants of Glasgow resorted; and this circumstance gave rise to the name which hath continued ever since.

That the firnames of *Torrance* and *Calderwood* originated in this parish, is not improbable. Concerning the latter, the following story is handed down, by tradition, among the family of Calderwoods in the shire of Ayr. They say, " that, at a remote period, there lived at Calderwood, in Kilbride, a family of the name of Calderwood, whose forefathers had, for time immemorial, possessed that place. This family, at last, consisted of three sons and a daughter. The sons having unhappily quarrelled with the priest of the parish, and finding it not safe to remain any longer in Calderwood, fled for protection to the Earl of Cassils, who gave them three separate farms; namely, Peacockbank, and Moss-side in the parish of Stewarton; and the Fortyacre lands in Kyle. These brothers had numerous families, which, in a short time, spread the name of Calderwood through the county. The sister, who was left in Kilbride, was married to a
gentleman

gentleman of the name of Maxwell, who got, by the marriage, the whole of her father's eftate." If this ftory (which I had from one of the defcendents of the brother who fettled in Peacockbank) is true, it is probable that Calderwood anciently belonged to a family, bearing the name of the lands they poffeffed.

The name of *Flakefield*, took its rife from a place called Flakefield in the upper part of the parifh. About the middle of the laft century two young men of the name of Wilfon, the one from Flakefield and the other from the neighbourhood, went to Glafgow and commenced merchants. The famenefs of the name had occafioned frequent miftakes in the way of their bufinefs. To prevent this, the one was, for the fake of diftinction, in a fhort time, known from the other by the *cognomen* Flakefield, the place of his birth. His real firname foon became obfolete, and he was afterwards called by the name of Flakefield, which, in place of Wilfon, has defcended to his pofterity.

To this man's fon the city of Glafgow, is, in a great meafure, indebted for her prefent opulence and trade. I hope it will be thought not altogether foreign to our defign, to mention the circumftance by which this was brought about. Wilfon, *alias* Flakefield, put one of his fons to the weaving trade.

The lad, after having learned his bufinefs, enlifted, about the year 1670, in the regiment of the Cameronians, but was afterwards draughted into the Scottifh Guards. He was, during the courfe of the wars, fent to the continent, where he procured a blue and white checked handkerchief, that had been woven in Germany. A thought ftruck Flakefield, that, were it his good fortune to return to Glafgow, he would attempt to manufacture cloth of the fame kind. Accordingly he preferved, with great care, a fragment fufficient for his purpofe. Being difbanded, in the year 1700, he returned to his native city, with a fixed refolution to accomplifh his laudable defign. Happy would it be for mankind, were travellers into foreign countries to pick up what might be ufeful in their own; and, like this praife-worthy foldier, return home poffeffed of fome valuable acquifition. A few *fpindles* of yarn, fit for his purpofe, was all, at that time, William Flakefield could collect: the white was but ill bleached, and the blue not very dark; they were, however, the beft that could be found in Glafgow. About two dozen of handkerchiefs compofed the firft web. When the half was woven he cut out the cloth and took it to the merchants, who, at that time, traded in Salmon, Scottifh plaiding, Hollands and other thick linens. They were pleafed with the novelty of the blue and white ftripes, and efpecially with the delicate texture of the cloth, which

which was *thin set* in comparison of the Hollands. The new adventurer asked no more for his web than the neat price of the materials, and the ordinary wages for his work. All he asked was readily paid him, and he went home rejoicing that his attempts were not unsuccessful. This dozen of handkerchiefs, the first of the kind ever made in Britain, were disposed of in a few hours. Fresh demands were daily made on the exulting artist for more of his cloth; and the remaining half of his little web was bespoken before it was woven. More yarn was procured with all speed, and several looms were immediately filled with handkerchiefs of the same pattern. The demands increased in proportion to the quantity of cloth that was manufactured. Some English merchants, who resorted to Glasgow for thick linens, were highly pleased with the new manufacture, and carried, for a trial, a few of the handkerchiefs to England. The goods met with universal approbation. The number of looms daily increased, so that, in a few years, Glasgow became famous for that branch of the linen trade. A variety of patterns and colours was soon introduced. The weavers in Paisley, and the neighbouring towns, engaged in the business; and the trade was at length carried on to a great extent. Thus, from a small beginning, a very lucrative and useful branch of business took its rise; and which has been the means of introducing others still more extensive.

The Checks were followed by the Blunks, or linen cloth for printing; and to thefe is now added the Muflin-trade; which, at prefent, extends to the amazing fum of nearly two millions fterl. *per ann.* and Glafgow is univerfally acknowledged to be the firft city in Scotland for manufactures. But neither William Flakefield, nor any of his defcendents, ever received any reward, or mark of approbation, for the good fervices done, not only to Glafgow, but to the nation at large. Flakefield, however, having, during his fervice in the army, learned to beat the drum, was, in his *old age*, promoted to the office of town-drummer; in which office he continued till his death.

WHAT is the moft ancient firname in Kilbride cannot now be known. From the following rhyme, which is fometimes repeated by old people, it would appear that fome names are of confiderable antiquity.

> Since fnow was fnow, and grafs was grafs,
> There were *Craigs* in the Park, and *Flemings* in Knowglafs:
> *Watts* in the Claddans, and *Struthers* in the Skioch.

Thefe places, fince they became the property of the Earl of Eglinton, have changed their ancient inhabitants. The *Strangs*, *Wilfons*, and *Reids*, are names

names that have long prevailed in this part of the country. The *Hamiltons* have, for many years, been confiderably numerous. The moſt conſpicuous were the Lairds of Torrance. From them deſcended the Hamiltons of Weſtburn, Ladyland, Aitkenhead, Daichmont, Woodhall, and ſeveral other families of diſtinction.

To know the riſe of ſirnames in Scotland, and where theſe names have, at different times, chiefly prevailed, would be of confiderable advantage. Thereby the connections that have been formed between ancient families might, in ſome meaſure, be traced out: and the migration of names from one part of the country to another laid open to our view. An accurate account of ſirnames, in ſeparate pariſhes, would, in this reſpect, be of confiderable utility. I have, therefore, drawn up the following liſt of the names of heads of families in Kilbride; to which is ſubjoined, the number of families belonging to each name. The names of widows, although they may keep houſe, are not included.

A

THE HISTORY OF

A TABLE,

Containing the Sirnames of the Male Heads of Families in KILBRIDE, *with the number of Families belonging to each Name,* Anno 1790.

Sirnames.	Fam.	Sirnames.	Fam.	Sirnames.	Fam.
Aiton,	1	Caldwell,	2	Graham,	5
Alexander,	6	Campbell,	4	Granger,	7
Allan,	4	Chriftie,	2	Grifbey,	1
Aikfon,	7	Coats,	4	Guthrie,	1
Anderfon,	2	Connell,	1	Hamilton,	28
Arbuckle,	1	Cook,	4	Hart,	1
Arniel,	3	Craig,	7	Hunter,	1
Baird,	4	Crawford,	4	Jackfon,	7
Banantyne,	1	Criechton,	1	Jamiefon,	2
Barclay,	2	Cuthbertfon,	1	Johnfon,	1
Barr,	2	Cutter,	1	Kirkland,	4
Barrie,	1	Davidfon,	1	Knox,	1
Barter,	1	Denham,	1	Kyle,	1
Bowman,	1	Douglafs,	1	Lambie,	1
Brown,	7	Drummond,	1	Lammond,	1
Brouning,	4	Duncan,	1	Law,	1
Brounlie,	2	Dykes,	2	Lawfon,	2
Bryce,	2	Edmefton,	1	Leggat,	4
Bryfon,	1	Fleming,	10	Leitch,	1
Buchanan,	1	Forreft,	1	Lennox,	2
Burns,	4	Fofter,	1	Liddel,	1
Burnfide,	2	Fram,	1	Lindfay,	12
Cairns,	1	Gault,	1	Logan,	1
Calder,	1	Gilmour,	4	Lyon,	3

McAuley,

Sirnames.	Fam.	Sirnames.	Fam.	Sirnames.	Fam.
McAuley,	1	Pollock,	7	Stuart,	1
McKey,	1	Rankin,	3	Sutherland,	1
McLean,	1	Reid,	12	Syme,	2
McMath,	2	Riddell,	9	Symours,	1
Mair,	1	Robertson,	2	Taffie,	1
Marrow,	1	Ruffel,	4	Thomson,	6
Marshall,	2	Sawers,	2	Torrance,	1
Mauchlane,	2	Scott,	5	Turnbull,	1
Maxwell,	1	Scouller,	1	Turner,	1
Millar,	3	Semple,	2	Walker,	1
Mitchell,	1	Shaw,	1	Wallace,	6
Montgomery,	3	Simpson,	1	Warnock,	4
Morrison,	1	Sinclair,	1	Watson,	14
Morton,	1	Smith,	13	Watt,	9
Muirhead,	1	Spiers,	2	Wilkie,	2
Murray,	1	Stark,	1	Wilson,	19
Orr,	5	Steel,	3	Woddrow,	1
Park,	5	Steven,	6	Wood,	1
Paterson,	10	Stevenson,	2	Whyte,	1
Peden,	1	Stirling,	3	Yates,	1
Pedie,	4	Strang,	8	Youll,	2
Pettigrew,	1	Struthers,	15	Young,	18

BUT the parish of Kilbride is honoured, not only with several ancient and extensive families, but with a considerable number of individuals, who have added to the credit of their families, and splendour of their names. The camp and the court are indebted to the MAXWELLS of Calderwood, and STUARTS of Torrance for men of distinguished abilities, who

honourably

honourably supported leading characters in their several departments. An extensive benevolence to mankind, valour and courage untainted by meanness, with a deep penetration into the affairs of state, shine with the brightest lustre on their names. To mention particular instances, in which their abilities and humane dispositions were remarkably displayed, would be to write a history of their lives. Let it suffice to observe, that the enterprizes in which many of them acted a conspicuous part, not only in Europe, but in the East and West Indies, will celebrate their memory, whilst the annals of our nation exist.

Nor will the name of HUNTER ever be forgotten by the Literati of Europe. The late Dr. William Hunter, and John his brother, who are among the first in the list of men of science, in the present age, were born at Long-Calderwood, about a mile and a half from the village of Kilbride. The former is so well known, that it will be needless here to mention particulars. I shall only observe, that, for great abilities and uncommon success, he is distinguished as a physician: and that his name is immortalized, when he is considered as a careful enquirer into the works of nature and art. His collection of antiquities and natural curiosities is not equalled, perhaps, by any private museum in Europe.

HIS

His brother, Dr. John Hunter, who has arrived at the head of his profession in London, is, by his medical investigations, &c. &c. daily adding honour to his name, and place of nativity.

But characters of great worth are not confined to distinguished birth, or liberal education. The parish can boast of several individuals, in the inferior stations of life, whose conduct, on some occasions, would do honour to nobility itself.

The people, in general, are sober, industrious, and frugal. They possess from their forefathers a courageous and independent spirit, which, as it enables them, on the one hand, to bear misfortunes with magnanimity; so it forbids them, on the other, to receive, with impunity, the affronts that may be offered them. Being easy in their circumstances, they know not what it is to cringe or to flatter: they have suffered but few encroachments on their liberty, either civil or religious; of course their spirits are not broken by means hostile to the rights of men, or of christians.

I shall conclude this chapter with a Table of the names of the most remarkable places in the parish.

A TABLE,

Containing the Names of the most remarkable Places in the Parish.

Auchinfin	Burnhall	Crofthead
Ardochrig	Burnhouse	Crofsbafket
Arpoch-hill	Burnfands	Crofshill
Auldhouse	Cadger-rig	Doghillock
Backwardrow	Cairnduff	Duncanrig
Bankfield	Calder	Dykehead
Bafket	Caldergreen	Dykehole
Benthall	Calderwood	Dykenook
Benthead	Cambus-hill	Edwards-hole
Bethern	Cantiflaw	Eldrig
Blackburnmill	Caplerig	Fieldhead
Blackcraig	Carts-hill	Flakefield
Blackland	Caftlehill	Forefaulds
Blazehill	Caftleflat	Freeland
Bogend	Claddans	Gill *
Boghall	Claddengreen	Gillburnfynke
Bogton	Clayheughs	Greenhills
Bofsfield	Clochern	Haighhill
Bottom	Cock-running-mill	Halfmerk
Brachead	Corfe	Hall
Brankamhall	Corfeland	Headhouse
Bridgemill	Cowrochfauld	Herlaw
Browncaftle	Craighall	Herlaw-crook
Brownhill	Craigmulloch	Hermyres
Buchandyke	Craignith	Herflocks

* Of these there are many in the parish.

EAST-KILBRIDE. 179

Highflat	Long-calderwood	Rangerhouse
Hillbank	Mains	Rawhead
Hillhead	Market-hill	Rigfoot
Hills	Mauchlan-hole	Righead
Hillside	Maxwellton	Rogertoun
Huntlawrig	Meadowhouse	Rough-hill
Jacktoun	Midtoun	Shields
Kilbride	Millhouse	Shieldburn
Kirktounholm	Milton	Shorthill
Kittochside	Moss-nook	Skioch
Knocklegoil	Mount-cameron	Startuphall
Knowglass	Muckethill	Stuart-field
Knowhead	Murray	Stuart-Tine
Laighlyoch	Nerston*	Thornton
Laitfad	Nethermains	Todhills
Langlands	Nethertoun	Tor
Langlandhouse	Newfarm	Torrance
Larhills	Newhouse	Tunnelside
Lauriestoun	Nook	Tunnochmoss
Lawknow	Park	Tuphall
Lawmoor	Parkhead	Wardlawcross
Lawside	Pateshall	Whitecross
Lickprivick	Philipshill	Whitehills
Limekilns	Piel	Windichill
Lockarshields	Plat-thorn	Woodside
Logoch	Polliskinglen	

* A contraction for North-East-toun.

Z 2 CHAP.

CHAP. IV.

OF AGRICULTURE, TRADE, DISEASES, POOR, STATE OF RELIGION, SEPULCHRAL MONUMENTS, &c.

INSURMOUNTABLE obstacles, both from the soil and climate, will always obstruct agricultural improvements in this parish. Nearly three-fourths of the arable land is composed of a stiff clayey soil, generally incumbent on till, a substance greatly unfavourable for vegetation: it is likewise, in most places, very much exposed to under-water, and is commonly known by the terms cold and sour.* Many things highly unfavourable to the progress of agriculture naturally arise from such a soil. The season is far advanced before the ground is sufficiently dry to admit the plough: the seed, after being sown, sometimes rots before it has time to vegetate; and not unfrequently the surface of the ground, after seed-time, cakes to such a degree of hardness, especially in a great drought after heavy rain, that the tender blade cannot get through.

It

---

* The term *sour* is, in Scotland, usually applied to a cold and wet soil; and conveys the idea of viscidity, which, in some cases, is a concomitant of fermentation. In this sense it is far from being improper.

In this case the incrustation might be reduced by the harrow; but this method, so far as I know, is not practised. The only preventive against this evil, is to give the land what is called a *rough mould*, that is, breaking it, in time of harrowing, into pieces about the bigness of a hen's egg.

The unfavourable state of the soil is, in some measure, owing to the climate, which, in the exposed situation of Kilbride, is cold and wet. The frost sets in very early in Autumn, and continues late in Spring. The ploughing season usually begins about the middle of March, and the seed is commonly sown about the second week of April.

Besides the soil and climate, there are other circumstances which greatly retard the progress of agriculture. The roads, in general, are in a bad condition: and the farmer complains that he cannot find a sufficient quantity of proper manure. But rooted prejudices in favour of old customs is, perhaps, of all others the greatest obstruction.

The grievance arising from the soil may, in a considerable degree, be removed by drains, properly directed through the wet land. To this the farmer has every inducement from favourable declivities in almost every field in the parish. But unhappily very little attention is paid to this mode of improvement.

provement. Moſt of the lands about Kittochſide muſt, however, be excepted. About 20 years ago, John Reid of Caſtlehill, Eſq; began to drain his lands. His ditches are about 20 inches wide, and 36 deep. In the bottom he makes a drain with two rows of ſtones laid parallel to one another, at the diſtance of about 3 inches, and as much in height: over theſe he places another row, taking care to lay the ſtones in ſuch a way that they cannot eaſily be miſplaced. All the ſtones are gathered from the land. Theſe, being of a roundiſh ſhape, he prefers to flags, ſet on edge either perpendicularly, or in a triangular poſition. Above this concealed drain he throws a layer of ſmall ſtones, and covers the whole with earth ſo deep as to admit the plough. Experience hath taught him that drains made, as above deſcribed, anſwer the purpoſe extremely well; and of theſe he is not ſparing. In one field, not exceeding 5 acres, the drains are ſo numerous that 2000 cart-load of ſtones were not more than ſufficient for making them. The expences, however, (which were eſtimated at fourpence per fall) were nearly repaid by the additional increaſe of the firſt year's crop. The advantages ariſing from this practice are ſo obvious, that moſt of his neighbours are now following his example. It may juſtly be remarked, that the pariſh can never admit of any high degree of improvement, unleſs a great part of it is gone over in a ſimilar manner.

THE

The evils arising from bad roads are now, in some measure, removed, by the generous assistance and extensive influence of the Torrance family. Two turnpike roads were, in 1791, drawn through the parish; the one leading from Glasgow to London, by Muirkirk, Dumfries, Carlisle, &c. and the other from Ayrshire to Edinburgh, by Eaglesham, Blantyre, Hamilton, &c. In consequence of this, the statute work, which is now chiefly converted into money, will be laid out on private roads.

But a long course of time will probably elapse before the other obstacles are removed. The want of proper manure is, no doubt, a great hinderance to the progress of agriculture. Although the parish abounds with lime, which fertilizes the whole country round, yet that useful material is thought to be lost when laid on the lands in Kilbride. It is imagined that lime is of no service, but rather a hurt, to land incumbent on limestone. This, without all question, is ill-founded. It is likewise said, and indeed with some degree of truth, that when lime is thrown upon clay ground of a wet spouty nature, it sinks too far below the surface, and is lost: and that, if the ground is strong enough to suspend it, the fertilizing particles are carried away by heavy rains. Both these objections will be effectually removed by properly draining the land.

PREJUDICES

PREJUDICES in favours of old cuſtoms obſtinately oppoſe improvements in agriculture. The old method of croping land continues in not a few places. According to this, the farm is divided into *Croft*, and *Outfield* land. The method for a clay ſoil is, to divide the croft into three parts, to be cropt every year according to the following ſucceſſion. 1. Oats; 2. peaſe or beans; 3. bear, laid down with all the dung raiſed on the farm; and the ground prepared by two ploughings, the firſt in March, and the ſecond in May. The outfield land, which receives no dung, is laid out in two diviſions; each of which, in rotation, is cropt two years with oats; and paſtured two, with natural graſs.—The method for a light ſoil is, to divide the croft into four parts, and to crop as follows. 1. Oats; 2. peaſe or beans; 3. paſture; 4. bear, laid down with dung. The outfield land is divided into two parts, each cropt with oats two years, and paſtured three.

THIS old method is going out of practice. The moſt approved one ſubſtituted in its place is, to divide the farm, without the diſtinction of croft and outfield, into nine parts, which are laid under the following rotation.

THE firſt and ſecond years, oats: third, barley: fourth and fifth, hay: and the remaining four, paſture.

All the dung produced on the farm is laid down for the barley, along with which the grasses are sown. Beans or peafe are frequently substituted in place of oats, the first year, especially in a stiff soil; and oats in place of barley, the third year, the barley crop being precarious. When lime is used, it is commonly spread hot on the ground, about midsummer, in the third or fourth year of pasture. One defect, in the above method, seems to be a total want of summer-fallow. This is owing to a common notion, that the land, if exposed to new surfaces, during Summer, is much injured. Wheat is objected to, because it is greatly exposed, in Winter and Spring, to frequent frosts, and heavy rains. Not a few allow the ground to lie under natural grass, from a belief, that rye-grass purges the land. This objection will be removed by sowing, along with the rye, a proper quantity of clover, and other plants; whose broad leaves cover the surface of the ground, and thereby hinder the rays of the sun from scorching it. The greatest part of the soil of Kilbride, if left without artificial grasses, is a long time, after ploughing, before it acquires a good sward; and when it does, the natural grasses are not all of the best kind. Carexes, rushes, mosses, &c. bear a considerable proportion to the poas, clovers, plantains, and some other indigenous plants that are good for pasture. It must, however, be observed, that almost all the soils in the parish naturally produce several excellent vetches, as the *Vicia Cracca*, tufted vetch; *V. Sepium*, bush vetch; *Lathyrus Pratensis*, yellow vetchling, &c. This species of the *Lathyrus*, which, in some places, is now in high repute among the cultivated leguminous plants, grows in great perfection, not only in the stiffest soil in the parish, but likewise in the till that is thrown out of the lime-quarries, even almost as soon as it is pulverized. The roots spread themselves very copiously in the earth, and penetrate the stiffest clay; for which reason it may be called the fertilizer of untoward soils. These circumstances, for nature is the parent of agricultural improvements, should induce farmers to pay attention to this wholesome plant.

LINT is cultivated in almost every farm, for the use of the family; but the quantity is small; the crops precarious; and the quality, in general, bad.

No plant is in greater cultivation and use than the *Potatoe*. To fatten cows with this root, is a practice that has of late got into the parish; and in this the farmer believes he finds his profit.

A few trials have been made to raise *Turnips*, but, for want of success, the practice has been discontinued.

FROM

From the present state of the soil, and the grains it is calculated to produce, it is easy to perceive, that the more highly improved instruments of agriculture will be of small utility. The common Scots plough, or the Roman plough, as it is here sometimes called, is in general use; and is always wrought with four horses. A trial was lately made on Bakewell's small wheel plough; but the height of the ridges and the stiff soil were irresistible obstacles to its utility. Other implements of husbandry are nearly in the same state here as in the west of Scotland. There was not, about 70 years ago, a *wheel Cart* in the parish, and very few sledges. The roads were so bad as not easily to admit of either. Lime, coals, &c. were carried on horseback; and a few stone weight constituted a load. The first cart in the parish was, soon after it was made, employed in carrying a few coals from Cambuslang. Crowds of people went out to see the wonderful machine: they looked on with surprise, and returned home with astonishment.

The farmers have, of late, paid particular attention to the management of milk cows, the offspring of an excellent breed introduced into the parish, about 40 years ago, by the late Patrick Graham of Limekilns, Esq; This worthy gentleman procured the first of the breed from a bull that belonged to the late Colin Rae of Little Govan, Esq;

but the cows were of the common indigenous kind. The bull was originally of the breed that has long been reared in the parishes of Dunlop and Stewartoun, and which is now known by the name of the Ayrshire breed. With respect to its origin the common account is, that, about a century ago, the farmers in Dunlop were at great pains to improve the original breed of the country, by paying strict attention to the marks which their experience had led them to make of a good milk cow. Proceeding agreeably to a well known fact that takes place in some tribes of quadrupeds, namely, that the breed improves, or degenerates, according to the good or bad qualities of the male, they singled out, and carefully reared the most promising bull-calves. The consequence was, that the breed improved daily, and is now unequalled by any in Scotland. The marks of a good milk cow are the following: The body is commonly of a brown colour, the face and belly white: the horns small and equally curved inward, and slightly tipped with black: the head little, and the mouth small: the legs short, and the belly big: the veins on the belly large, and greatly branched: the udder rather of a large size, having the *mammæ* inclining a little outwards some few are Mull-eared, that is, having the ears notched at the top: the weight is commonly from 18 to 24 stone, Tron. Cows possessed of these properties, and fed in the rich pastures of Dunlop, Stewartoun,

Stewartoun, and some other places in the county of Ayr, yield, *per diem*, at an average, each 12 pints of milk, Scots measure. The milk is peculiarly rich, and is mostly made into sweet milk cheese, which, for toasting, is surpassed by none in the world. The superior quality of the milk is, no doubt, owing partly to the fine pasture on which the cows are fed. The natural grasses, with which the fields are closely mantled over, consist principally of the *Anthoxanthum Odoratum*, sweet scented vernal grass; *Holcus Lanatus*, meadow soft grass; *Cynosurus Cristatus*, crested dog-tail grass; *Poa Trivialis*, common meadow grass; *Bellis Perennis*, daisy, or gowan; *Trifolium Repens*, white clover; *Lathyrus Pratensis*, yellow vetch; and a small mixture of the *Ranunculus Repens*, creeping crowfoot, or crow-toes; *Achillea Millefolium*, yarrow, or hundered leaved grass; *Plantago Lanceolata*, ribwort; and some other plants not rejected by cows. The fields are, early in Spring, covered with a beautiful verdure. This continues till about the end of May, when the gowan covers them with a snowy whiteness. The flowers of this plant, equally with the leaves, are greedily devoured by cows; and are believed to produce, in abundance, milk of a most exquisitely fine quality. The gowan is followed by the white clover; successive crops of which continue till the end of the season. Even in Winter, the ground being kept dry, the verdure is uncommon.

The

The graffes are feldom allowed to rife high, but they are extremely clofe, and continue fucculent all the year round. The farmer is at pains to promote the luxuriant growth of thefe excellent graffes. The fucceffion of crops is, in general, the following. 1. Oats; 2. oats; 3. oats, laid down with rye and a little foft grafs: next year hay; and then 7 or 8 years pafture, of which the laft crop is reckoned the beft. The crops of oats are commonly very heavy. As the land is dry it is never poached by the cattle. From 16 to 22 milk cows are generally kept on a plough of land; the milk of each cow producing, at an average, 20 ftone wt. of cheefe, or 10 ftone of butter, yearly. The land rents from 15, to 20 fhillings per acre.

The produce in Kilbride is not fo great. The grafs, in general, is too coarfe, and fcanty; and the ground too wet, for the cows to yield more than an ordinary quantity of milk. From 8 to 12 cows are generally kept on a plough of land, and the milk produced is moftly made into fweet milk cheefe, which, in Glafgow and Edinburgh, is fold under the name of Dunlop cheefe. Each farm produces, at an average, about 100 ftone weight yearly. The annual product, therefore, may amount to about 11100 ftone weight, which, at 7s. per ftone, comes nearly to 4000l.

The

The diseases to which black cattle, in this parish, are exposed, are not numerous, and seldom fatal. For most of them *Garlic* is used as a sovereign remedy; and its healing virtue rarely fails. This is verified particularly in the *Tail-slip*, a disease which cold sometimes brings upon cows. This trouble first appears in the end of the tail, by affecting it in such a manner, that it seems soft to the touch. As the disease proceeds upwards every joint has the appearance of being dislocated; and, if a remedy is not got before it reaches the back, death is the unavoidable issue. It is discovered by the straddling manner in which the animal walks; by the softness of the tail, and the feeble manner in which it hangs down. The only remedy used in this part of the country, is, first to make, with a sharp knife, a deep incision, the whole length of the part affected: if the wound bleeds the disease is reckoned not incurable. The incision is then filled with a mixture of bruised garlic, and black soap; and the wound bound up with a piece of woollen cloth. The cure is almost instantaneous. Garlic given by the mouth, for the *Moor-ill*, has met with great success. The *Spalliel*, in young cattle, is sometimes cured by opening a communication between two incisions made, one on each side of the part affected, and filling it up with a mixture of black soap, saltpetre, and bruised garlic. But this disease is effectually prevented, by giving the calves about the

quantity

quantity of half an ordinary head of garlic, once every 3 or 4 weeks, from the time they are 2 or 3 months old, till they are out of the reach of taking the disease. The garlic is bruised, and given them along with their meat, or thrust down their throat. I know not if there is a single instance of a calf, thus treated, taking the disease.

The *Film* is a disease in the eye, and is occasioned by a hurt. It appears like a white scale covering the sight. The remedy commonly applied, is saltpetre pulverized, and mixed with an equal quantity of the yoke of an egg, boiled so hard as to be crumbled down into a powder. This mixture is blown into the eye through a small reed, or a tube of paper. The operation is to be repeated 5 or 6 times; each after an interval of about 20 hours. This remedy seldom fails of success.

Grazing of cattle for slaughter succeeds pretty well in those parts of the parish where it has been practised with judgment. There are few places in Scotland where less attention is paid to the rearing of horses. The farmer supplies himself, with that useful domestic, from the Rutherglen and Glasgow markets. *Hogs* are frequently reared by the whey made from the cheese. They are afterwards fattened by potatoes, or oatmeal mixed with water; fed in this cleanly manner they are highly esteemed and bring a good price.

THE breeding of *Sheep* was, for time immemorial, an object of importance in this parish: but the practice gradually declined as the lands were inclosed for ploughing; and the West Highlands opened for the rearing of sheep. There are only about 110 score, of the black faced kind, fed in the parish, and these are confined to the moorland farms.

THE farmers, in general, pay strict attention to domestic œconomy. Frugality presides over all their family expences. To their honour it may be said, that extremely few of them deserve the name of spendthrifts. The wives and female-servants are very industrious. Besides managing their houses, making cheese, and lending their assistance in many operations in the fields, they bring to the market a considerable quantity of fine linen yarn, of their own spinning. Of this fine yarn, there is, perhaps, more spun in Kilbride than in any neighbouring parish.

SERVANTS wages are double what they were 40 years ago. A man-servant commonly receives 5l. sterling per half year; and a woman from 40 to 50 shillings. The terms for the removal of servants are the 15th of May, and 11th of November, old style. Farmers are under a necessity of keeping cow-herds. These, in general, are an idle set of mortals;

mortals; and, a few inftances excepted, are a drawback on the community at large. Little or no encouragement is given them, to be employed, like herds in fome parts of Scotland, in knitting ftockings. Mafters, from a notion that they would not do juftice to the cattle, forbid them every kind of lucrative amufement: they confequently fpend their time in the moft difgraceful indolence.

LITTLE can be faid in favour of the plan after which the farm-houfes are built. The byre and ftable are commonly in the one end, or rather half of the building; the kitchen in the middle; and the fpence, which ferves for a room, in the other end. The paffages about the houfe, owing to the improper entrance into the byre, are, for the moft part, not very clean. The old, but nafty cuftom, of having the dunghill before the door of the dwelling-houfe, is generally continued. Some good farm-houfes have lately been built on the eftate of Torrance. The furniture of their houfes is, in general, very plain. An univerfal tafte, however, prevails for a *Clock* and a *Cheft of Drawers*. Thefe ufeful articles are to be found in almoft every houfe, even that of a day-labourer not excepted. Delf inftead of wooden veffels, for the table, are commonly preferred.

THE extent of the farms is generally from 40 to 60

60 acres. The duration of leafes feldom exceeds 19 years. A cuftom, which once prevailed in the parifh, of letting farms by two, or three *lifetimes*, is now laid afide. Leafes are moftly fixed by private agreement: lately fome have been let by public roup; a method, equally hurtful to the proprietor, as to the tenant.

The heritors, in general, pay no attention to the cultivation of *trees;* for which reafon the face of the country has the appearance of nakednefs. It was the practice to plough every inch of land that could be broken up; and, were the inclinations of the people to be confulted, the fame cuftom would continue. Lately, however, a few gentlemen have begun to raife wood on their eftates; and their attempts are meeting with deferved fuccefs. Were more of the country laid under wood properly difpofed, there is every reafon to believe, that the crops of grain would be more prolific than at prefent. That planting will not thrive in the cold climate of Kilbride is a miftake; becaufe every houfe almoft, even in the moft expofed fituations, is furrounded with large trees of various fpecies. But confiderable attention was paid to the raifing of them. The foil was prepared by draining off the water. A handful of oats was thrown into the bottom of the hole, dug for the young tree: over thefe about an inch of good earth was laid: upon this

this the roots of the plant were carefully fpread, and covered up with the beft mould that could be got; and the plant fecured from the cattle. The oats, having come to a ftate of vegetation, raifed a proper degree of heat, and thereby made the plant fet forth with vigour. It is not, therefore, a deficiency of nature, but of proper care, that foreft trees will not thrive in Kilbride.

For the fame reafon fences are in a bad condition. It muft indeed be acknowledged, that the foil is, in general, unfavourable for raifing quickfets: when the root ftrikes upon till, or into cold clay, the bufh will never thrive. But no care is taken to prevent that evil. A ditch is dug out: the materials thrown up, are formed into a dyke of earth: in this the young hedge is planted, and very often in that part, where, in the courfe of the operation, the worft of the earth is laid. Seldom either ftake, or rice, is placed on the top of the dyke, by way of fecurity. Thus the tender thorns, imbedded in an improper foil, are left defencelefs. The young hedge undergoes a kind of dreffing for a year or two, but is afterwards left to combat with grafs, thiftles, &c. which greatly injure its growth. The practice of keeping it down by cutting it on the top is continued: the blame of the whole is caft on the foil and climate, and the parifh left, in a great meafure, fencelefs.

SENSIBLE

Sensible of the impropriety of such management, John Reid of Castlehill, Esq; began, about 10 years ago, the following method. A ditch 2 feet deep, and 20 inches wide, is cast and filled with small stones, from the land. Near to this, another ditch, 3 feet deep, and 4¼ wide, is opened, and the best of the materials laid immediately above the stones. In this good soil the thorns are planted, in a sloping direction; and about a foot above the stones. He takes care to weed them twice in the year; and never cuts them on the top, till they are pretty large; when they are sided, topped, and plashed as occasion requires.

Here I cannot but mention an uncommon method of planting thorns, that was practised about 40 years ago, when hedges were beginning to be raised in the parish. The direction being marked out, a small drill was opened. In this was laid a rope of straw, in which, at small distances, were placed ripe seed of the hawthorn: the rope was covered with earth; and the seeds, by the time they began to vegetate, found abundance of good nourishment from the straw, which was then rotten. The seedlings, in proper time, made their appearance, and, in some instances, became very vigorous. The hedge that encloses part of the glebe was planted, or rather sown, in this manner.

Farmers,

FARMERS, in general, are greatly deficient in keeping their land free from hurtful weeds. Forgetting the proverb, *That one year's feeding, is seven years weeding*, they allow thistles, &c. to grow unmolested in the lee-land, road-sides, &c. &c. That the ground spontaneously brings forth weeds; and that, to attempt to eradicate thistles, &c. from the fields, implies a disbelief of the curse, and a fighting against God, are arguments used by some superstitious people as a defence for their negligence. But when these men are seriously asked if they think it to be their duty, and that it is in their power, to keep their fields clear of thorns, (which have a respect to the curse as well as thistles) they are forced to answer in the affirmative, and thereby confute their own hypothesis. Such persons should be taught, that one of the greatest curses entailed on the earth arises from the rooted prejudice, ignorance, and sloth of its inhabitants.

CONSIDERABLE improvements, in all the branches of agriculture, might, by this time, have been made, had the *Farmer Society*, which was instituted in 1772, been properly conducted. To enquire into the best methods of managing land, &c. and to lay in a fund for supporting distressed farmers, were the laudable designs of this erection. But Discord, the infernal pest of every worthy undertaking, put an end to this good institution. The society was, about

about 1786, finally diffolved, and their fmall ftock was *equally divided* among the members, which were 25 in number.

The parifh is well furnifhed with *Mills*, there being no fewer than feven. Some of them are conftructed for lint, as well as for oats and barley; but none of them for wheat. At Kittochfide-mill there is an excellent machine for drying peafe: it is an improvement on the machine that was invented, fome time ago, by *Mr. John Watt* at the Mill of Drips. To thefe mills almoft all the land in the parifh is aftricted, and the dues are, for the moft part, very high. The lands of Torrance, however, were, by the prefent proprietor, relieved from that burden; the tenants paying an equivalent for the freedom.

The value of land, in this part of the country, has been rifing this long time paft; but property is not, in general, often changed. The eftate of Kittochfide confifting of three and a half ploughgangs of land, belonged, about two centuries ago, to Caldwell of Caldwell. The whole was fold for 800 merks to John Reid, a predeceffor of the prefent proprietors. From a circumftance that happened lately after it was fold, it would appear, that the purchafe was favourable on the part of the buyer. The Laird of Caldwell, foon after the bargain

bargain was concluded, propofed to retract what he had done. To this the purchafer, who was formerly his tenant, would not agree. To force compliance, or take revenge, in cafe of a refufal, Caldwell fent a confiderable number of his vaffals to Kittochfide. Reid was fecretly informed of the defign. Fearing that he might be drawn into a compliance, he thought it beft to make his efcape, and leave his houfe to be defended by his *twelve* fons. The young men, though remarkable for courage, feeing a fuperior force coming againft them, wifely refolved to remain quiet. Notwith-ftanding, they foon had the mortification to fee their father's houfe fet on fire. One of them attempting to extinguifh the flames was inftantly killed by the incendiaries. Reid, knowing that he could not withftand fo powerful an adverfary, threw himfelf under the protection of Lindfay of Dunrode; who then lived at the Mains. Happy to have fo numerous a family allied to his intereft, he readily undertook to defend him from Caldwell; and embraced the firft opportunity of reprefenting the whole matter to the King. His Majefty was defirous to fee Reid and his fons. Struck with the decent and manly appearance which they made, he declared, that if any injury was done them, he would caufe Caldwell to be immediately executed. The Reids, ever after, were allowed to poffefs their lands without moleftation.

THE

THE ſtate of TRADE and MANUFACTURES, in this pariſh, will appear from the following liſt of Mechanics, *anno* 1790.

Trades.	Nº.	Trades.	Nº.
Bakers,	2	Maltmen and Brewers,	1
Blackſmiths,	12	Maſons,	21
Clockmakers,	1	Shoemakers,	39
Coopers,	2	Surgeons,	1
Flax-dreſſers,	2	Tailors,	20
Gardeners,	4	Weavers,	63
Hoſiers,	5	Wrights,	14

ABOUT 34 looms are employed in the Muſlin branch, and a few in Counterpane bed-covers. Nearly 2000 pair of ſhoes are annually made for export, by the medium of Glaſgow. The ſhoemakers, a few years ago, conſtituted a charitable ſociety, and have already accumulated a conſiderable ſum for the relief of the diſtreſſed.

ALL the maſons, except two, profeſs the wright trade, at which they ſometimes work during winter. A *Maſon Lodge*, known by the name of *Kilbride Operatives*, was inſtituted in 1738. Although peace and concord ought to have animated this friendly ſociety, yet ill-featured *Contention*, with all her vociferous train, found her way among them. *Confuſion* reared aloft her hideous countenance, which all the powers of their art could not lay. The Lodge was diſſolved diffolved in 1759. Before the beginning of another year, however, a confiderable number of the members, not willing that fo laudable an inftitution fhould be annihilated, and defirous to regain the credit they had formerly loft, were conftituted into a new Lodge. They now conduct their fociety with that *peace* and *concord*, in which no fmall part of the honour of Mafonry confifts. Their annual meeting is at Kilbride, on the 27th of December, old ftyle: on which day they have a parade.

A *Cotton-fpinning manufacture* commenced here in 1783, and employs from 60 to 100 hands. The machinery was, till the beginning of 1792, confined to the vicinity of Kilbride. But the bufinefs increafing, a mill, to go by water, was built a little above the town. This mill, with the other buildings occupied by the company, are the property of *Gen. Stuart*, of the Torrance family, and were built by him, fince his return from fervice, laft war, with the view of encouraging induftry in his native parifh.

The quarrying and burning of *limeftone* has, for time immemorial, given employment to the induftrious labourer in Kilbride. The quarries, of which there is a confiderable number, employ, at prefent, about 50 workmen. The Winter is moftly fpent in *tirring*, a term ufed for removing the earth from off

off the limestone post: and the Summer in raising and burning the stone. The wages are from one penny, to three-pence *per* load of burnt stone, in proportion to the difficulties attending the work. The proprietors are at the expence of the tools, coals, &c. that are necessary; but they furnish only half of the powder used in blowing the stone. The produce of the quarries, in 1790, was no less than 9845 chalders, which, at 6s. 8d. each, amounted to 3281 l. 13s. 4d. sterl. Pot-kilns are, in general, preferred to draw-kilns.

The Iron-stone Mines, lately opened in the banks of Calder, employ about 40 men; the greatest part of whom are under the direction of a few undertakers, who are paid, per ton of the stone, in proportion to the difficulties attending the working it. About 14 coal-hewers are employed in the coal-works, in the lands of Torrance, and Lickprivick.

Kilbride has, for a long time past, been famous for one of the best frequented *sheep markets* in Scotland. It is held annually on the last Friday of May; and two first Fridays of June, old style. The *Common*, on which it is kept, was once very extensive: but, excepting a few acres, is now inclosed. There is, however, abundance of room for all the cattle that are brought to it. Forty, or fifty thousand

thousand sheep were, about the beginning of the present century, annually sold at this market: but the number is now reduced to about 3000. This reduction is owing chiefly to the great number of cattle, now bred in the Highlands. It is thought that Argyleshire is, by nature, better calculated for breeding sheep than the south country, about Muirkirk, Dumfries, &c. the latter, during several weeks in Winter, being frequently close, that is, entirely covered with snow: but the former is generally open, especially in the Glens, and sides of the Lochs, even in the greatest storms.

THREE Fairs are yearly held in the village of Kilbride: one on the fourth Tuesday of June: another on the second Tuesday of August: and the third on the second Tuesday of November. A few cows are the chief article sold at them. The town is furnished with *no fewer* than 13 public houses.

THE inhabitants, in general, are pretty healthy; although none of them have arrived at any uncommon degree of longevity. The disease that chiefly prevails among young people is the consumption. It is asserted that, till about a century ago, this malady was exceedingly rare, and seldom mortal. The distemper that proves most deadly to children is the *small-pox*. In summer, 1787, no fewer than 32 children, in the town and neighbourhood, were

seized

seized with that loathsome disease: 13 with difficulty recovered. Inoculation, the best remedy for that distemper, meets here with a very bad reception. Rooted prejudices, founded upon arguments, some of which are trifling, others absurd, have such a strong influence on the minds of the people, that they sit still, in sullen contentment, and see their children cut off in multitudes. It is to be hoped, that natural affection, and a sense of duty, will, at length, get the better of unreasonable prejudices; and that the period is approaching, when inoculation for the small-pox will be universally practised.

The method of conducting *funerals* stands in great need of amendment. It is tedious, expensive, and laborious. The whole neighbourhood, commonly, is warned to attend at a certain hour; yet little attention is paid to the time. A great company of men and women, meet at the place appointed, and are entertained with ale, spirits, and short-bread: in some wealthy families wine is also used. The corpse is usually carried on spokes; which circumstance, from the badness, &c. of the roads, makes the service exceedingly unpleasant. Although all agree, that a reformation, in this respect, is necessary, yet, on account of being thought singular, few are willing to set an example.

The kirk-session takes the sole management of
the

the funds for supporting the poor. The method in which these funds are managed, is agreeable to the true spirit of the church of Scotland. *Poor-rates*, which, in some places, are a fertile source of dissipation and poverty, were never established here. No encouragement is given to idleness; whilst none are allowed to starve. The average number of individuals, on the session list, is about 16. The monthly allowance to each, is from 1s. to 6s. A few are permitted to beg within the bounds of the parish. Besides the poor on the list, there are commonly about 20 indigent persons, most of whom are heads of families, who get occasional supply, as the session sees necessary. This, although small, added to what they can earn, by any labour they are capable of, enables them to live more comfortably in their own houses, than they could do in the best endowed hospitals. The funds for answering the above charitable purposes are very small: they amounted, from the 6th of May, 1786, to the 6th of the same month, 1787, to 46l. 17s. 4d. Of this 38l. 2s. 11¼d. was collected at the church door: the rest was made up of 2l. 8s. 10d. of proclamation money; with the interest of 1000 merks, that were mortified, by the Calderwood family, to the poor of the parish; and the interest of a small sum accumulated by the session. The annual amount of the contributions is seldom so much as it was in the above-mentioned period.

In

IN the parish are two charitable mortifications. One made by Mr. Aikman, on the lands of Burnhouse, for supporting four old men, in the town of Hamilton. The other by the Earl of Dundonald, of the lands of Milton, &c. for burses to students in the college of Glasgow.

THE public school is endowed with a salary of 200 merks *per annum*. The wages are a merk, *per* quarter, for English: 2s. for Writing and Arithmetic: and 2s. 6d. for Latin. The school-master is commonly appointed session-clerk, for which he has 2s. 6d. for every proclamation of marriage: 6d. for each baptism: and 4d. for writing a certificate. Besides the public school, there are commonly two or three private ones in the parish.

THE state of *religion* in this place, affords few things remarkable. The ministers, since the Reformation, were Mr. *Durroch;* Messrs. *Sharp,* father and son; Mr. *Charters;* Mr. *Burnet;* Mr. *Creighton;* Mr. *Muir;* Mr. *Matthew Connell;* Mr. *David Connell* his son; and Mr. *French* the present incumbent. The Rector of Kilbride was, during Popery, *chantor* to the Cathedral of Glasgow. Mr. Woddrow, in his history of the church of Scotland, observes, that, about the middle of the last century, the people were greatly divided in their religious opinions. This historian, when giving an account
of

of the reverend Mr. Burnet, who was ejected from his charge in Kilbride, says, " Mr. Burnet was a " minister of great solidity and learning; and though " he had no freedom to fall in with the indulgence " himself, yet he was very opposite to division upon " that score, and both heard the indulged ministers, " and pressed his people in Kilbride, among whom " he lived, to do so. He had been singularly use- " ful in that parish, where there were a great many " Quakers and Separatists; and yet by his painful " and excellent preaching, and other labours, he " reclaimed the most part of them." Since that time the people were united in their religious sentiments, and regularly attended public worship, in the parish church, until Mr. D. Connell's death, in 1790. A presentation from the *Crown* was then procured for the reverend Mr. James French of Carmunnock. The disaffected party were very formidable: they left the church, and joined the *Relief.* A meeting-house was immediately built in the village of Kilbride; and the congregation made choice of the reverend Mr. Smith for their minister. Among the dissenters are 45 that adhere to the Reformed Presbytery: 42 Antiburghers; and nearly the same number of Burghers.

For a long time past, the college of Glasgow has been titular of the tithes, which amount, *per annum*, to 32 chalders of meal, paid in money, according

ing to the Fiars of the Commiffariot of Hamilton and Campfie. Of thefe the minifter receives 12 for his ftipend; and 50 merks for communion elements.

From the proprietors of a certain diftrict in this parifh, the minifter of Eaglefham receives, annually, 16 bolls of *Graig-Mulloch* corn; fo called from a hill in that diftrict. The corn which this hill ufually produces is uncommonly bad; hence Craig-Mulloch corn is a proverbial expreffion for corn of the worft quality. The inhabitants of this part of Kilbride have a claim on the minifter of Eaglefham, for a fermon to be preached among them every ten weeks, and a minifterial vifit once a year. This claim, however, is either not made or not complied with: but care is taken that there fhall be no rifk of a profcription, with regard to the payment of the corn.

With refpect to the *Church* of Kilbride, few things merit the attention of the public. It was rebuilt in 1774, but is not yet feated. That part of the old church which fupported the belfry, is allowed to remain, and ferves the purpofe of a fteeple. The bell was caft in the year 1590, by one of the moft celebrated bell-founders in Europe, and bears the following infcription.

PETER · VANDEN · GHEIN · HEFT · MI ·
GHEGOTEN ✢ MCCCCLXXXX ·

This bell was rent by violent ringing, on a day of rejoicing, held by the people of Kilbride, when they heard the news that Lord Dundee, a cruel perfecutor, fell in the battle of Killicrankie, fought on the 17th of July 1689.

Neither the church, nor church-yard, is adorned with large, or expenfive fepulchral monuments. The graves are generally covered with ftones; but very few of them are ornamented with Coats of Arms, or epitaphs for the dead. Nothing is left to diftinguifh the burying-place, at the old church of Torrance, fave a few fragments of human bones, that are occafionally difturbed, when the ground is laboured. A neat burying-place was lately built at Calderwood, in the bank, a little above the houfe; but it is folely appropriated to the family. It is not ornamented with the emblems or *mementos* of death: the folitary fituation indicates its ufe, with the moft convincing language.

The practice of raifing *tumuli* over the deceafed was very ancient in Kilbride. Public marks of refpect, when judicioufly beftowed, have been of great ufe to fociety. By decorating the tombs of worthy characters, the living may receive inftruction from the dead. A confiderable number of thefe *tumuli* were, till about 30 years ago, remaining in the parifh. But they are now almoft totally annihilated.

To find heaps of gold and silver, or to procure materials for building dykes, and making roads, were the chief causes of destroying these hallowed monuments, which had, in remote ages, been raised by industry and pious veneration. The sacrilege, however, was repaid, not with capacious hoards of money, or coffers of jewels, as were fondly expected; but with urns, and stone coffins, containing nothing but earth, and rotten bones. Some, indeed, have been opened with a more laudable view of tracing, by means of the remains of antiquity concealed within them, the progress of the arts and sciences; and of discovering, more fully, the ancient rites and customs observed in burying the dead.

KNOCKLEGOIL, the former name of Limekilns, and probably the modern pronunciation of the Gaelic *Knockillgoill*,* (the hill where foreigners are buried) was perhaps the largest mound in the parish. It was composed of some thousand cart loads of stones, which, on several occasions, answered the purpose of a quarry: but the remains of this large collection were all carried away about 50 years ago. A few urns, nearly half filled with earth and bones, was all the treasure it contained; and were, by the incurious workmen, devoted to destruction.

---

* *Knoc*, a small hill; *kill*, a cell or grave; and *gall*, a foreigner; in the plural *goill*.

Not long ago, another mound, or *law*, as thefe barrows are here called, was demolifhed a little above Kittochfide. It was about 10 feet in height, and compofed chiefly of ftones, but of what dimenfions I could not learn. It contained a large urn, in which were human bones. Clofe by the urn was found what was thought to be an old *Spade*, of a clumfy fhape. The iron, which was pretty thick, and not much corroded by ruft, was too confiderable an object to be neglected by the workmen, who firmly believed that great treafures were concealed in thefe burying-places. Being difappointed in their high expectations, for they fancied that the happy moment was come, when their fortunes would be made, they were refolved to make the moft of every thing they found. But the difficulty was, how to difpofe of the fpade, fo as to fhare the prize equally among them. A confultation was held, with all due deliberation: the fpade, the urn and the bones were lying before them; nor was any regard paid to the *manes* of the dead. The equitable divifion engroffed all their attention. Various methods were propofed. It was, at length, unanimoufly agreed upon that it fhould not be fold: it might, for any thing they knew, be uncommonly ominous; efpecially as it was iron, and taken out of a grave which was generally believed to be haunted. Their invention was for a while ftretched on the rack. At length, after various debates, they came to the
following

following resolution, namely, that the spade should be converted into *tackets* for their shoes. They thought that thereby an equal division would be made, and, were there any thing ominous, it could affect nothing but their old shoes. This wise scheme, (which next day was put in execution) being finally agreed to, the Genius of the tomb had the mortification to see the urn, with its contents, broken in pieces.

NEAR Rawhead are the remains of a very large cairn, called *Herlaw*. Some thousand cart loads of stones have, at different times, been taken from it; and some thousands yet remain. The stones seem to have been gathered from the land. Many urns with fragments of human bones were found in one corner of it, but none of them were preserved. It is about 12 feet in height; and covers a base of 70 feet in diameter: but this must have been far short of its dimensions when entire.

NEAR Nerston, in the year 1788, a small cairn was destroyed, in which was an urn that contained bones which seemed to have been burnt. The consecrated vessel, with its contents, was broken in pieces, and mixed with the materials, which the labourers were collecting for making roads.

THE lands adjoining to the Mains of Kilbride contain

contain a few of these rude, but durable monuments. Owing, however, to the frequent dilapidations that are daily making on them, they will soon be entirely destroyed. One, that some years ago was totally demolished, was about 12 feet in height, and of a gentle ascent. In the bottom was a coffin of large flags, containing a perfect skeleton, which, on being touched, fell to ashes: the teeth were firm, and the enamel in tolerable perfection. The bones were remarkably thick, but of no extraordinary length. The head was lying toward the east. In the bottom of a very small cairn which, in 1789, was annihilated, in the lands of East Rogertoun, the property of his Grace the Duke of Hamilton, were found five urns, not of the ordinary shape. They were about 18 inches high; 6 wide at the one end, and 4 at the other: both ends were open. They were said, by the workmen, to be glazed, and ornamented with flowers; and narrower in the middle than at either end. They stood upon smooth stones, distant from each other about ¼ of a yard, and placed in a circular form. The top of each urn was covered with a thin piece of stone. They were all totally destroyed, by the rustic labourers, so that not a fragment was preserved.

In the boundary between these lands and Cathkin moor, an urn was, in Sept. 1792, discovered a few feet under ground. It was full of earth,
mixed

V

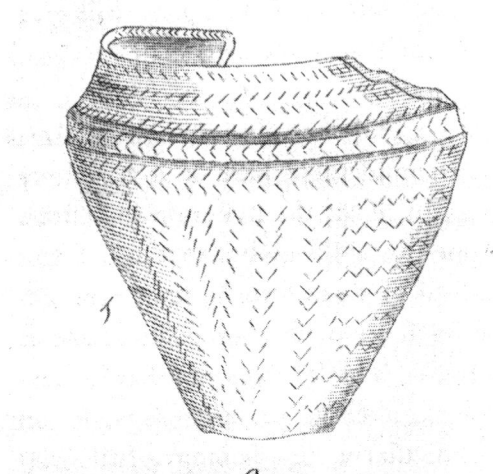

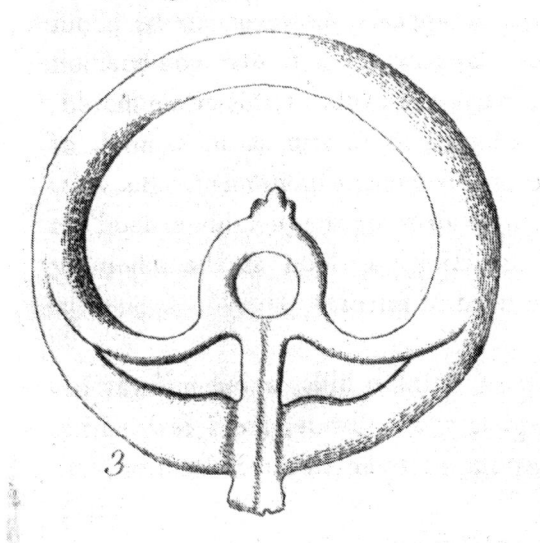

mixed with fragments of human bones. It was about 6 inches in width, and 8 in depth. An outline of this facred repofitory, pl. V. fig. 1. will give an idea of its peculiar fhape, and ornaments.

The largeft at prefent remaining near the Mains, is *Lawknow*. A confiderable part of it has lately been carried away to repair the dykes on the eftate. None of the ftones are fo large but that a man can eafily carry, and all of them feem to have been gathered from the land. No urns or coffins have as yet been difcovered. This cairn is peculiar in having, in the bottom, a circle of large flags, fet on edge, not perpendicularly, but floping a little outward. They are of a hard gritty fchiftus, found plentifully in the neighbourhood. As part only of the circle has been dug through, its diameter is not exactly known: it appears, however, to be about 8 or 10 yards. Barrows of a fimilar conftruction are very rare; what yet exifts of this circle fhould, therefore, be allowed to remain as an example of the peculiarity of this ancient monument. But this, with fome entire cairns in the neighbourhood, is devoted to deftruction, as foon as the adjoining dykes ftand in need of repair.

On the top of Cathkin hills, about midway between Rutherglen and Kilbride, are a few cairns, which, on account of their elevated fituation, are seen at a great diftance. Their fhape is conical. The largeft is called Queen Mary's, from a report that her Majefty fat on the top of it during the battle of Langfide. Several places, in this country, are faid to have been honoured by her Majefty's prefence on that memorable event. That fhe took a view of her army, and the fcene of action, from various ftations, during the courfe of the day, is not improbable. As this confpicuous cairn is in the neighbourhood of Caftelmilk, where fhe is faid to have ftaid the night before; there is nothing marvellous that fhe took a view of her army from this place, which commands a diftinct profpect of Langfide, and the tract of Clyde from near Hamilton to Dumbarton. This cairn was furrounded with a narrow ditch, and a fmall dyke of earth. It was about 18 feet in height, and 120 in diameter. The ftones, of which it was moftly compofed, feem to have been collected from the land; and none of them were very large, except one on the top: it was flat on the upper fide, and weighed feveral ton weight.*

THIS

---

* Different opinions have been formed about the original defign of thefe flat ftones on the tops of cairns. Toland fays, that fires were kindled on them at certain times of the year, particularly on the 1ft of May, and the 1ft of November, for the purpofe of facrificing. At which times all the people, having extinguifhed their domeftic hearths, rekindled them by the

facred

THIS tumulus was interfected nearly in the middle by a ftratum of burnt earth, about a foot in thicknefs. This aged monument afforded materials, thefe many years paft, for building dykes in the neighbourhood. Some workmen, as they were employed, in the beginning of 1792, in taking away what remained of the ftones, difcovered in the weft fide about 25 urns, full of earth and human bones. The earth feemed to have been taken from the adjoining foil. The bones were moftly in fragments, and very white, as if blanched. The urns were of coarfe clay, rudely formed, feemingly with no other inftrument than the hand, and fo foft as eafily to be fcratched with the nail. Externally they were of a faintifh brown colour, as if baked by the heat of the fun: but internally they were black. They were of different fizes, moftly about 12 inches deep, and 6 wide at the mouth. None of them were deftitute of ornaments; thefe, however, were extremely rude, and feem to have been done in a hurry, with a fharp-pointed inftrument. The urns generally fell to pieces when touched: one pretty entire was, however, preferved. Outlines of two of them are given, pl. I. fig. 2. 3. They were all placed with their mouths undermoft upon flat ftones;

---

facred fires of the cairns. In the parifh of Blair-Athol there is a facrificing cairn 60 geometrical paces in circumference, having feveral large flags on the top, which probably conftituted the altar.

stones; and a piece of white quartz was found in the center of the mouth of each. These pebbles were larger and smaller, in proportion to the dimensions of the several urns to which they belonged.*

In one of the urns was found what is supposed to be a *Fibula*. It is of that kind of mixed metal of which the heads of the Roman spears were frequently made, and of which copper makes a considerable proportion. A draught, according to the true dimensions, is given pl. I. fig. 5. In another was found the middle part of a comb; which is likewise of the same mixed metal with the former, and overlaid with a beautiful green enamel, pl. V. fig. 2.

In the bottom of the cairn, and exactly in the center of the area which it occupied, was a *Coffin*, or *Chest*, of large flags. It was about 4 feet every way

* A circumstance somewhat similar to this is mentioned in the Scots Magazine, for February 1790, where we are told, "That in the Cairn of Menzie, in Cairn-Moor in Buchan, was " found, along with earth and bones, in a stone coffin, a Dart-" head of yellow flint, most perfectly shaped, and a little block " also of yellow flint, as if intended to furnish the deceased with " more darts, should he have occasion for them on the passage!" But what was the original intention is, perhaps, out of our power precisely to ascertain. It is more likely that the block of flint, and the pebbles, above-mentioned, were deposited more from a superstitious view than any thing else.

way; and a very large stone, that required the strength of 6 or 8 men to remove, was placed over it for a covering or lid. A small quantity of earth was all the treasure it contained. Close to it, however, was a considerable number of small bones, mostly in fragments. Among them was a tooth quite empty within; but the enamel was entire. The want of the osseous substance affords a proof that it was the tooth of a child. Along with them were found two fragments, both of the same shape, but of what ornament is not known, pl. V. fig. 3. They are of mixed metal, like the *fibula*, and had been overlaid with a green varnish, or enamel, some parts of which retain the original gloss and beauty. They are probably of Roman workmanship. Beside the urns was found a *Ring* of a hard, black schistus, that burns with a clear flame. It is 4 inches in diameter; but the rim is an inch in breadth, and ¼ of an inch in thickness. Rings of a similar shape, and of the same coally substance, have been discovered in several places of Scotland.* It is believed that they were originally worn as ornaments, probably the *armillæ*; and were afterwards used as charms, deriving, no doubt, their virtue from the sanctity of the original possessors. One that was found in a cairn, in the parish of Inchinan,

* Scots Magazine, June 1766.

Inchinan, about 40 years ago, has performed, if we believe report, many astonishing cures. It is to this day preserved in the parish as an inestimable *specific;* and is imagined, by the superstitious, to be more valuable than many ton weight of medicines. Is not superstition so far useful, that it preserves some pieces of antiquity that would otherwise be destroyed?

There are a few cairns yet remaining on Cathkin hills. From off one of them a layer of stones was lately taken; but upon the appearance of a stratum of earth the dilapidation was discontinued.

When the sepulchral tumuli, with which this country abounds, were raised, cannot with certainty be determined. The period was, in all probability, prior to the introduction of christianity. The custom of burning the dead was very ancient in the world. Various opinions are given for its origin. Pliny asserts, that it was practised with a design to prevent the dead bodies of soldiers, slain in the wars abroad, from being raised out of their graves, and inhumanly treated by the enemy. For this reason it would appear that the bodies of Saul, and of his sons, were burned by the inhabitants of Jabesh gilead.*——To prevent the remains of deceased
friends

* 1 Sam. xxxi. 12.

friends from being torn out of the graves, by wild beasts.————To prevent the corruption of the human body,————And to keep the air from being polluted, may be mentioned as reasons for this practice.

Along with the body, the ornaments worn by the deceased, the spoils they took in war, their arms, &c. were frequently thrown upon the funeral pile. The bodies being burnt, the fragments of the bones, and as much of the ashes as possible, were collected, and put into urns, or stone coffins; and generally along with Money, Combs, Buckles, Jewels, Amulets, &c. Owing to this, it may happen that weapons, &c. peculiar to one nation may be found in cairns that were raised by another.

Some urns, especially those that are thought to be Roman, are well shaped; and the clay of which they are made seems to have been extremely well prepared, and thoroughly baked. But the urns of all the northern nations of Europe, are of coarse clay, rudely formed, and ill baked. Of this kind are the urns found in Cathkin. The coffins are either single, or many joined to one another in the same row, as those in Baldernock, formerly mentioned. They are commonly composed of large flags; but some are of a single stone hollowed out, as one described by Mr. Wallace in his history of Orkney.

The construction of the cairns differs considerably. Some are of earth, others of stones. In some the stones are large, in others not; and some are composed of earth and stones. They are of different sizes; whilst not a few urns and coffins have been found buried in the earth, where not the smallest trace of a cairn could be seen. In some places they are oblong, and in others bell-shaped, or conical. Not a few are surrounded with trenches, or rows of stones; and sometimes the top is ornamented with a large stone, thought to have been used as an altar, on which victims for the dead were offered: this probably was the case with the one in Cathkin, already mentioned. Borlase (Antiquities of Cornwall) informs us, that Harold employed his whole army, and a great number of oxen, in drawing one vast stone to crown the monument of his mother. Not unfrequently cairns were erected to the memory of some great personage, who may have died abroad, or perished in the sea. This may be the reason why so many empty coffins are found even in the largest; and why these coffins are accompanied with the bones of victims that were slain to the Shades of the person, whose memory was perpetuated by the mound. Not a few have great stones placed on end at the head of the coffin. This was exemplified in the cairn, in Craig-Madden Moor, already described. One somewhat of a similar construction was, a few

years

years ago, demolished in the parish of Strathblane, in the neighbourhood of Glasgow. This ancient burying-place, the origin of which is unknown, was 60 yards in length; 14 feet in height, and of a confiderable breadth. It was compofed of gravel, and lay eaft and weft. In the bottom were a great many coffins of ftone, placed in a row, and feparated from one another by a fingle flag. Every coffin contained an urn, that was full of earth and burnt bones. Befide each urn was a pillar about 3 feet in height, and 8 inches in thicknefs. They were fragments of bafaltic, five-fided columns, a few rocks of which are found in the parifh. Moft of the pillars are built in a dyke adjoining to the church. The urns on being touched fell in pieces.

But cairns have not always been raifed for the honour of the perfon whofe remains they contain. Murderers, &c. have had, on many occafions, their graves diftinguifhed by heaps of ftones. This practice has been very ancient in the world.*

The accumulation of thefe incredible heaps of ftones was not the work of a day. Paffengers, honouring the memory of the deceafed, and often with a fuperftitious view, added to the heap, by throwing

* Jofh. vii. 16. and viii. 29.

throwing a stone upon it, every time they passed by. Hence the proverbial expression among the Highlanders, alluding to this practice, *Corridh mi cloch air do charne.* I will add a stone to your cairn. As each of the stones, thus collected, could not be large, the heap must necessarily have been composed of small stones, which were, probably, gathered from the land. This circumstance leads us to form a more rational account why so many cairns, every where almost in Scotland, are composed of small stones, than the one mentioned in the false, and ill-natured assertions of a Gothic, or rather a Pickish author, who says, " There is no authority, " and no reason to believe that the Celts ever used " to raise hillocks over their illustrious dead. The " plain Cromlech, or little heaps of stones, was " more consonant to their savage indolence." *
And, " Ancient monuments of the British Scots " there are none, save cairns of stones, used as se- " pulchres, and as memorials. These were adapted " to Celtic indolence: while the Gothic industry " raised vast stones instead of piling small ones: " nor are any cairns found in Gothic countries, " so far as i can learn, except such as are very " large." †

THE

---

* Pinkerton's Antiq. of Scot. vol. I. p. 412.

† Vol. II. p. 140.

The history of the period, when these monuments were raised, is so obscure, that it is not always certain by what people the several kinds of them were erected. Among the many conjectures that have been made on the subject, extremely few are conclusive. It hath been alledged, that the cairns, in which are found urns made of fine clay, and well shaped, were Roman: and those containing urns of coarse materials, and ill shaped, were British. The trinkets found in them have been made another criterion. Cairns of an oblong form, and composed of large stones, are supposed to be Danish, or Saxon: whilst those of a conical shape, and composed of small stones, are imagined to be Celtic. Several marks have likewise been given by authors as characteristic of the station of the person over whom these cairns were raised: as a great one for a Prince; and a small one for a person of an inferior rank. According to Cooke, (*Enquiry into the Patriarchal and Druidical Temples, &c.*) they are distinguished into four kinds. 1. "Circular trenches, with a small tump, or elevation in the center, are supposed to be Druidical barrows. 2. Plain round ones, may be Roman, Saxon, Danish, or British. 3. Such as are of a fine turned, elegant, and bell-like form, with trenches round them, are royal sepulchres. 4. Large oblong barrows, with or without trenches, are those of the

Arch-Druids. In several of these have been found the Celts wherewith the *Misseltoe* was cut."

But might not the same people, as occasion served, vary considerably the shape, &c. of their sepulchral monuments? In the same cairn we find the remains of the funeral rites of different nations. The one on Cathkin hills, already described, may be mentioned as an example. An antiquary would not hesitate to say, that the brass ornaments were of Roman workmanship: and that the ring of schistus, and the rudely formed urns were Celtic. The great stone on the top, and the coffin of large flags at the bottom, would lead some to suppose, that it was raised by the Danes or Saxons: but the small stones, of which it is chiefly composed, would lead others to imagine, that it was raised by the Celts. The surest way is, to suspend our positive assertions on so dark a subject, till the more advanced study of antiquity, divested of groundless theories, throws greater light on the ancient customs of our country. Of one thing we are sure, that these monuments carry back our views to very remote periods, when barbarism, idolatry, and superstition marked the character of our forefathers. Serious reflections, when we are discovering the abodes of the dead, and raking up the ashes of the men of former times, have a tendency to abstract our thoughts from the world;

world: to foothe the mind amidft the hurry of bufinefs: to beget fentiments of gratitude for our fuperior advantages: and to improve thefe for anfwer-
ing the important ends for which they are given
us. Thus the living may reap advantage from the
dead.*

* When mentioning the abodes of the dead, it would be highly improper to omit the following remarkable phenomenon. Upon digging a grave, on the 12th of November 1792, in the church-yard of Rutherglen, a *Scull*, retaining a very great quantity of hair, was dug up. The hair, when ftretched out, was nearly a yard in length. It was very ftrong, of a reddifh colour, and adhered pretty firmly to the fcull. As I had not an opportunity of examining it, I can fay nothing about the ftate of the fcalp. The quantity of hair was faid to be fo great, that three or four perfons could, with difficulty, wear it. The grave was in a dry foil, and had not been opened for, at leaft, 30 years. The fcull was little more than two feet below the furface of the ground. It is extremely probable, that this hair muft have grown, after the perfon to whom it belonged was interred. That hair grows, after death, is well known. Sometimes the growth, after burial, is amazing. Of this we have fome well attefted facts.

THE
NATURAL HISTORY
OF
RUTHERGLEN AND KILBRIDE.

───────

CHAP. V.

CONTAINING AN ACCOUNT OF INDIGENOUS ANIMALS, PLANTS, AND FOSSILS.

ANIMALS.

AMONGST the Quadrupeds may be mentioned the *Fox*. He finds convenient coverts in the shady, and rugged banks of Calder, between Torrance and Crofsbasket. In these haunts also the *Badger* and *Polecat* find a safe retreat. A *Mole* of a beautiful white colour was lately catched at Rawhead. That the *Bison*, now a native of India and South America, was once in this place, appears probable, from one of their horns that was lately found in a peat-mofs in the neighbourhood of Torrance,

where

where it is preserved. This curious production of nature is not entire. Confiderable pieces have been broken off from both ends. The circumference of the larger end is 18 inches: of the smaller, 6¼. The length, in a straight line, is 3 feet; but when measured alongst the inside of the curvature it is 4¼. Probably more than a foot has been broken off. It is composed of five or six *lamellæ*, which may be separated from one another.

This part of the country does not abound with a great variety of Fowls. Of the *Hawk* are several species, but none of them uncommon. The *Owls* frequenting this place are the *Otus*, *Ulula*, and *Flammea*. The first of these is not nearly so numerous as the two last. In one that was lately shot, in the banks at Calderwood, were seven feathers in each ear. A hen of the Ulula kind, with some of of her young, was, in 1789, killed near Torrance. She had the following peculiarity, that the extremities of her talons were broken off, and the ends much rounded: a precaution dictated by instinct for the safety of her eggs, during incubation. The *Wood-Lark* sometimes, although not frequently, visits both Rutherglen and Kilbride. The *Pheasant*, a few years ago introduced into Hamilton wood, is no stranger in the banks of Clyde, at Rosebank, and Farme. Several places in both parishes are frequented by the *Bull-finch*; and most other kinds of finging birds in Scotland. At Caftelmilk is a tame *Thrufh*, or *Mavis*, of a fnowy whitenefs. It was hatched in the wood adjoining to the caftle, and has never changed its colour.* *Fieldfares*, *Snowflights*, and *Woodcocks* are amongft the number of migratory birds that vifit this country. The moors in Kilbride abound with moor-fowl of different kinds. But, fince the late game acts, their number here, as well as in moft other places of the country, is greatly decreafed. The commonalty being, by thefe laws, forbid fhooting, even on their own lands, are at no pains to preferve the nefts, either of moor-fowl or partridges. Do not mankind frequently, by being too fevere, totally fubvert the fcheme they intended to promote?

The Clyde abounds with a confiderable variety of Fifhes; as the *Salmon*, *Pike*, *Trout*, *Flounder*, *Perch*, *Braze*, (Roach *Anglis*) and *Eel*. The Cart and Calder contain Trout; but in no great plenty.

Amongst the teftaceous order of Vermes are the *Turbo perverfus*, *T. bidens*, and *T. mufcorum*. They are found in the banks adjoining to Calderwood. The *Mytilus exiguus* of Lifter, is a native of feveral places in Kilbride: and the *Patella fluviatalis*

---

* Dr. Borlafe (Hift. of Cornwall, p. 247.) mentions, as a great rarity, a white Thrufh that was obferved in Cornwall, in the year 1724.

viatalis (Lacuſtris *Lin.*) is very common in almoſt all the rivulets, in both pariſhes. In Clyde are conſiderable quantities of the *Anatinus* of *Lin.* or horſe muſcle, as it is here called. Small pearls have ſometimes been obtained from them.

The Moths in this country are not very numerous, or uncommon. The *Phalaena priſmicornis, ſpirilinquis,* &c. of Hill, is ſometimes found in Rutherglen. The *Phalaena pavonis,* or peacock-eyed moth, is a native of the moors in Kilbride. It's caterpillar, which is extremely beautiful, feeds on heath, among the branches of which it takes up its abode, during its chryſalis ſtate.

Of uncommon Inſects, in theſe pariſhes, may be mentioned the *Polype.* It is a freſh-water inſect, of the genus of Hydra, in the claſs of Vermes, and order of Zoophyta. When cut in any direction, or number of pieces, each of the ſeparated parts very ſoon becomes a perfect animal. Leeuwenhoek was among the firſt who diſcovered theſe curious animalculi. Their oeconomy and properties were afterwards accurately deſcribed by M. Trembley

The ſpecies that prevails here is the *Hydra viridis, tentaculis ſubdenis brevioribus.* (Linn. Syſt. Nat. gen. 349.). The green polype, with ſhort arms, ſometimes to the number of ten. They are

of

of a fine green colour; and, when in a state of contraction, especially out of water, apparently of a gelatinous, unorganized substance, of about the bigness of a pin-head. They catch their prey with their arms, which they extend, or contract, and move in different directions, at pleasure. They are found adhering to grass, &c. in small ponds and ditches, particularly at Shawfield-bank, and Lime-kilns. I have found them in almost all the parishes in the vicinity of Glasgow.

This was the species that M. Trembley first discovered, and of which he could obtain too few specimens to enable him to ascertain what was their food, or how they caught it. He soon, however, found the *Hydra grisea, tentaculis subseptenis longioribus.* This species, of which M. Trembley found two varieties, is rare in this neighbourhood. It has, however, been discovered in some few places in this part of the country, especially in a piece of water, near Dugaldstoun, in the parish of New Kilpatrick. None of these with the very long arms, extending to 6 or 8 inches, which M. Trembley describes, are found in Britain, so far as I know.

Of the Leech (*Hirudo*) there are, in this place, some species that are exceedingly rare. Amongst these the *Hirudo complanata*, of Linn. seems to be one. The colour is generally a dusky brown, and the *viscera* beautifully pinnated. The back is ornamented with four rows of *papillae*, or small protuberances, of a white colour. These on the two middle rows are larger than the rest; and lie in two black lines, that extend from the head to the tail of the animal. The *papillae* are placed on every third ring, or annular division, of which there are about 60 in whole. These curious insects are found adhering to the bottom of stones, in a pond at Castelmilk, and in the rivulet that runs alongst the west boundary of Rutherglen.

Along with them is found another species, which is not, as far as I know, described by any author. It is *subcomplanata*, of a whitish colour, and, when stretched out, is above an inch in length. It is *bioculata*, and has a large blackish spot a little above the eyes. Its body consists of about 70 rings. Soon after it is taken out of the water it projects from its mouth a tube, or proboscis, of about ¼ of an inch in length, but retracts it when put again into water.

The manner in which the animal produces its young is very singular. About the month of June, a number of whitish eggs, commonly about a dozen, are discovered, seemingly in a gelatinous substance, that adheres to the belly of the mother. In a few days they elongate, and become smaller at the one

end

end than at the other. Soon after that, they are seen to move at the small end; whilst they adhere firmly, by the broad end, to the belly of the parent, till they are of sufficient strength to provide for themselves, when they quit their hold, and fix on any substance that may be near them. But they do not all arrive at perfection at the same time. A day or two commonly intervenes between each. The gelatinous-like substance, in which the *ova* are included, is quite limpid, like the white of an egg, and adheres pretty closely to the animal. I examined several of the Leeches, but could not discern any perforation through which the *ova* might come.

The parent takes great care of her young, when come to life. She expands the sides of her belly over them, when she transports herself from one place to another, which she does very slowly. When at rest she fixes herself both at head and tail, making a small curve with her body. In this position she moves herself, at the same instant, both by a lateral and longitudinal motion, and thus gently agitates her appending burden. To see this little animal in motion, whilst a dozen, or more, of her offspring are sprawling on her belly, naturally leads the contemplative mind, to adore the great Author of nature, whose wisdom, goodness and power are conspicuous in every part of his works.

This species of the Hirudo adheres to the bottom of stones, in ditches, ponds, and rivulets. It would appear that they delighted in very cold water. The only food I ever observed them take was the *Patella fluviatalis*. They lie in wait, close to their prey, till an opportunity offers, when they push their head below the shell, and instantly kill the animal, which they afterwards totally devour.

Along with the above-mentioned is found another species of the Leech, and which, I believe, is likewise a *nondescript*. The colour is a deep brown, inclining to red. When at full stretch it is about two inches in length, and $\frac{1}{7}$ in thickness. The skin is very sleek. It has four eyes, and does not seem to be furnished with a proboscis. Although it generally moves by means of contracting itself into a circle, yet it sometimes swims freely in the water, like the medicinal leech, but is extremely quick in all its motions. If another leech chances to fix upon its body, it twists itself with the greatest agility, into knots, or small circumgirations, through which it forces its way, and obliges the other to quit its hold. The rings of which the skin is composed are very fine. It appears to have no spots, when viewed externally; but when seen through, between the eye and the light, two rows of whitish spots, of a round form, lying in two transparent lines near the edge, make their appearance. Each line

line contains about 20 spots. Of this species I could find no more than one specimen.

MANY places in this country, especially the ditches in the Green of Rutherglen, abound with what seems, by its motion, to belong to the genus of *Limax*: but whether it is named, and described by Linnæus, I am not certain. It is nearly half an inch in length, and one-eighth in breadth. The head is ornamented with two short protuberances, resembling ears, and which probably serve in place of feelers. It moves in the water with a slow, but uniform motion. The colour is generally black; but in some varieties it is gray, or white. It is found commonly adhering to grass, &c. in muddy water. The parts of this creature, when cut, regenerate themselves like the Polype. One, on which a Gentleman in the University of Glasgow lately made an experiment, exhibited a singular phenomenon. A section was made in the middle of the creature, in a direction from the head to the tail; but a small piece at the tail was left uncut. Each part soon became an entire animal, only they were joined together near the tail. Sometimes they would move peaceably in the same direction; at other times they attempted to go in a different direction, as if they were influenced by contrary volitions. The struggle, however, was neither long, nor violent; for the one, generally without much reluctance,

reluctance, yielded to the other. My knowledge of the œconomy of this curious creature is not, as yet, so extensive as enables me to describe its food, &c. &c.

THE narrow limits within which I confined myself, in the commencement of this publication, will not allow me to give draughts of these insects, and of some other things, that require to be illustrated by plates.

VEGETABLES.

IN Kilbride, both soil and climate are unfavourable for the luxuriant production of exotic plants. Fruit trees very seldom do well: and a flower of any delicacy is hardly to be found. Small fruit comes to much greater perfection than the large. This is ascribed to the cold schistus, or till, that lies at no great depth from the surface; and which greatly injures the roots of large fruit trees, whilst the roots of Currant and Gooseberry bushes, not striking so deep, suffer less hurt. Besides, the trees are much injured by various species of *Lichens*, which almost wholly cover their bark. This, probably, is owing chiefly to the coldness and stiffness of the soil. The disease of the root greatly hurts the bark, by depriving it of that solidity, and
smoothness,

smoothnefs, which are conducive to the health of the plant. The natural confequence is, that the very minute feeds, of the extremely prolific genus of Lichens, lodge in the blemifhes of the bark. In thefe convenient apartments, replete with proper nourifhment, they grow with amazing luxuriancy. That the fertility of the lichen is owing more to the foil than to the climate, appears from this, that fome trees and fhrubs, of the fame fpecies with thofe that are covered with it, and which are exposed to the fame climate, but which happen to grow in a better foil, are greatly exempted.

In Rutherglen greater encouragement, both from foil and climate, is given for the cultivation of exotics. The gardens and orchards at Farme, Hamilton-Farm, Hanging-fhaw, and Rofebank are in a tolerable condition.

To enumerate all the indigenous plants of thefe parifhes, would render this part of the fubject unneceffarily prolix. I fhall therefore content myfelf with giving the following Lift of fuch as are not very frequently met with in this country.

A

A LIST

OF

SCARCE INDIGENOUS PLANTS,

IN

RUTHERGLEN AND KILBRIDE.

Adoxa	moschatellina	Tuberous Moschatel. *Banks of Calder.*
Æthusa	meum	Bawd-money. *Kittochside, Crossbill in Kilbride.*
Agrimonia	eupatoria	Agrimony. *Crossbasket, Farme.*
Aira	caryophylea	Silver Hair Grass. *Scotstoun.*
A.	coespitosa	Turfy do. *Whitemoss.*
A.	flexuosa	Mountain do. *Maxwelltoun.*
Allium	ursinum	Ramsons, or Wild Garlic.* *Maudslanhole.*
Anemone	nemorosa	Wood Anemone. *Banks of Clyde and Calder.*
Anthericum	ossifragum	Bastard Asphodel. *Peat-mosses, K.*
Anthyllis	vulneraria	Kidney Vetch. *Quarry near Philipshill, and pastures between Kittochside & Carmunnock moor.*
Arenaria	rubra	Purple-flower'd Chickweed. *Stonelaw.*

Arum

---

* Cows eat this plant so plentifully, in the beginning of Summer, that the milk partakes of the taste and smell of garlic.

Arum	*maculatum*	Wake-Robin. *Under a hedge at Castelmilk.*
Asperula	*odorata*	Woodroof. *Banks of Calder.*
Asplenium	*scolopendrium*	Harts-Tongue. *Fissures of rocks near Calderwood.*
A.	*trichomanoides*	Common Maidenhair. *Banks of Calder.*
A.	*ruta muraria*	Wall Rue. *Walls at Calderwood.*
A.	*adiantum nigrum*	Black Maidenhair. *Browncastle.*
Boletus	*igniarius*	Touch-Wood Boletus. *On decayed wood, Kilbride.*
B.	*auriformis*	Earlike Boletus. *Castelmilk, R.*
B.	*lateralis*	Lateral Boletus. *Woodside.*
Bromus	*sterilis*	Barren Brome-Grass. *In the hedge between Rutherglen and Farme.*
B.	*giganteus*	Tall Brome-Grass. *do.*
Byssus	*aurea*	Saffron Rock Byssus. *On stones in Pollskin-glen.*
B.	*candida*	White Cobweb Byssus. *Ruth.*
B.	*botryoides*	Green Cluster Byssus. *Bank at Crossbasket.*
Campanula	*rotundifolia*	Round-leav'd Bell-flower.* *Blawart, Scotis.*
C.	*latifolia*	Giant Throatwort. *Banks at Calderwood, and in a hedge between Hamilton-Farm & Clyde.*
Cardamine	*hirsuta*	Hairy Ladies-Smock. *Gillburn-synke.*
Carex	*montana*	Vernal Carex. *Moors, Kilbride.*

* I mention this plant not because it is rare, but because it has given a proper name to some places in Scotland; as Blawart-hill in the parish of Renfrew.

Carex	vulpina	Great rough Carex. *Banks of Cl.*
Chara	vulgaris	Common Chara. *Ditches at Rogertoun, Limekilns, and Hamilton-Farm.*
Cheiranthus	cheiri	Wall Flower. *Ruins of Mains.*
Chenopodium	bonus henricus	All-good. *South-side of the church-yard next the main street, Ruth.*
Chrysosplenium	oppositifolium	Common Golden Saxifrage. *Banks of Calder, &c.*
C.	alternifolium	Alternate-leav'd Golden Saxifrage. *Mauchlan-hole, and banks at Castlmilk.*
Circæa	lutetiana	Enchanter's Night-shade. *Gillburnsynke.*
C.	alpina	Mountain Night-shade. *Mauchlan-hole.*
Conferva	rivularis	River Conferva. *Kittoch at the Piel.*
C.	fontinalis	Spring Conferva. *Polliskin-glen, Cart.*
C.	gelatinosa	Frog-Spawn Conferva. *In the Cart a little above Rawhead.*
Convolvulus	sepium	Great Bindweed. *Hedges near Farme.*
Cratægus	oxyacantha	Hawthorn. *Banks of Cl. & Cald.*
Cucubalus	behen	Bladder Campion. *Kittochside.*
Daucus	carota	Wild Carrot.* *Scotstoun, Rosebank.*

Drosera

* Although this useful plant grows abundantly in Rutherglen, Cambuslang, Blantyre and some other neighbouring parishes; yet I could not find, in all the parish of Kilbride, more than a specimen or two. The scarcity is probably owing to the exposed situation of the place.

Drosera	*rotundifolia*	Round-leav'd Sundew.*	*Peat-mosses, Kilbride.*
Empetrum	*nigrum*	Crow-Berries.	*Moors, Kilbride.*
Equisetum	*sylvaticum*	Wood Horse-tail.	*Crossbasket.*
Erica	*vulgaris alba*	White-flowering Heath.	*Herstocks*
E.	*cinerea*	Fine-leav'd Heath.	*Banks of Calder, Moors.*
E.	*tetralix*	Cross-leav'd Heath.	*do. do.*
Erysimum	*barbarea*	Winter Cresses.	*Castelmilk, and banks of Calder below Calderw.*
E.	*alliaria*	Sauce-alone.	*Rocks at Calderw.*
Festuca	*decumbens*	Decumbent Fescu-Grass.	*West quarry, Rutherglen.*
Filago	*germanica*	Common Cudweed.	*Stonelaw.*
F.	*montana*	Least Cudweed.	*Gallostat.*
Fontinalis	*antipyretica*	Great Water-moss.	*Calder, Cart.*
F.	*minor*	Less Water-moss.	*Gillburnsynke.*
Gentiana	*campestris*	Gentian.	*Ardochrig.*
Glecoma	*hederacea*	Ground-Ivy.	*Banks near Torr.*

Gnaphalium

---

* Dr. Borlase (Hist. Cornw. p. 230.) says, " that this plant is extremely hurtful to sheep that feed upon it, and of which they eat greedily, wherever they find it. Its hurtful qualities are thought to be owing to an insect, or worm, which, feeding on this herb, lays its eggs on the leaf, and fixes them there by some poisonous gum; the eggs are swallowed with the flower and leaf, and, eluding the menstrua of the stomach, get into the chyle and blood: they are detained in the capillary vessels of the liver, where, meeting with the requisite degree of heat and moisture, they fecundate; the animalcules grow, and there make holes in which several of them lodge together, and feed upon the liver, till it can no longer perform the functions of its station, and the sheep dies. In Cornwall sheep-feeders take all possible care that the sheep may not come near it."

Gnaphalium	*dioicum*	Mountain Cudweed. *Bank of Cald. near Pateshall, Rawhead.*
Helvella	*mitra (fortaffe)*	Curled Helvella.*
Hieracium	*murorum*	Wall Hawkweed. *At a wall near Limekilns.*
Hydnum	*repandum*	Yellow smooth Hydnum. *Woods near Torrance.*
Hypericum	*quadrangulum*	St. Peter's Wort. *Banks of Crofsbafket.*
H.	*perforatum*	St. John's Wort. *Banks of Clyde and Calder.*
H.	*humifufum*	Trailing St. John's Wort. *do.*
H.	*hirfutum*	Hairy do. *do.*
H.	*pulchrum*	Elegant do. *Crofsbafket.*
Hypnum	*bryoides*	Little pinnated Hypnum. *In a clump of firs near Stonelaw.*
H.	*undulatum*	Waved Hypnum. *Pollifkin-glen.*
Jasione	*montana*	Sheep's Scabious. *Way fide near Galloflat, Hamilton-Farm.*
Ilex	*aquifolium*	Holly-Tree. *Banks of Calder.*
		Imperatoria

---

* Of this plant I found several specimens, in a wood near Caftelmilk, in the month of October 1792. The ftalk was about an inch in height, and ⅛ in thicknefs. It was cylindrical and folid, and grew from a thick tuberculated, or bulbous-like root, without fibres. The *pileus* was entire, but greatly deflexed on two fides, whilft the other fides were raifed up in two regular arches. The margin all round bended upwards with a beautiful curve. The colour was a bright white; but faded a little in the dry ftate. The fubftance was wax-like, brittle and foft to the touch. Neither the ftalk, nor *pileus*, was ornamented with furrows, gills or pores; but, when viewed through a magnifying glafs, feemed to be covered with a kind of down. All the specimens were growing feparately.

Imperatoria	ostruthium	Masterwort. *In an old wall at Langland-house, and waste ground near Jackton.*
Lichen	scriptus, geographicus, &c. &c. &c.	This numerous genus of plants grows very plentifully in Kilbride.
Ligustrum	vulgare	Privet. *Bank of Calder a little above Torrance.*
Lychnis	dioica	Wild Campion. *Banks of Clyde and Calder.*
L.	flos cuculi	Meadow Pink. *Avenues at Torr.*
Lycopodium	clavatum	Common Club-Moss. *Moors, K.*
L.	selago	Fir Club-Moss. *do.*
Lysimachia	nemorum	Yellow Pimpernell of the woods. *Mauchlan-hole.*
Lythrum	salicaria	Willow Herb, or Loosestrife. *Clinkert-hill.*
Marchantia	polymorpha	Great star-headed Marchantia. *Pateshall.*
Melampyrum	pratense	Meadow Cow-wheat. *Mauchl.*
Menyanthes	trifoliata	Trefoil. *Meadows near Mains.*
Mercurialis	perennis	Dog's Mercury.* *Banks of Clyde and Calder.*
Myriophyllum	spicatum	Spiked Water Millfoil. *In ponds at Galloflat, Farme & Torrance.*
Ononis	arvensis	Restharrow. *Way-side at Shawfield-bank.*
Osmunda	spicant	Rough Spleen-wort. *Polliskin-glen*
Parietaria		

* A whole family, in the parish of Cambuslang, was, a few years ago, poisoned nearly to death, by drinking an infusion of this plant, which, by mistake, had been gathered in place of the *Teucrium Scorodonia*, or Wood Sage.

Parietaria	officinalis	Pellitory of the wall. *In an old dyke, on the road-side, between Rutherglen and the Farme.*
Paris	quadrifolia	Herb Paris. *Banks a little above Calderwood.*
Peziza	cyathoides	Smooth scarlet Peziza. do.
Phalaris	arundinacea	Reed-grass. *Clyde.*
Phallus	impudicus	Stinking Morel. *In a belt of Firs above Calderwood.*
Pilularia	globulifera	Pepper-Grass. *In the pond at Galloflat.*
Pimpinella	saxifraga	Burnet Saxifrage. *Pastures near Kittochside.*
Pinguicula	vulgaris	Butterwort. *Rawhead Moor.*
Plantago	lanceolata β multacapita.*	
P.	maritima	Sea Plantain. *On the way-side, near the entry of the avenue into Whitemoss.*
Polygonum	bistorta	The greater Bistort, or Snakeweed. *In the east end of Shawfield-bank; in waste ground near Kilbride, and in a bank at Castelmilk in great abundance.*
P.	convolvulus	Black Bindweed. *In corn-fields, Rutherglen.*

Polygonum

---

* I have taken the liberty to give this name to a variety of Ribwort, which, in 1790, I found growing at Stonelaw; and a specimen of which I transplanted into Major John Spens' garden at Rutherglen, where it grows in great perfection. Every stalk bears about 12 or 15 spikes, which are *sessile*, and adhere to the base of the main spike. They are, however, well shaped, and bear seed: but whether the seeds will produce the same variety is yet uncertain.

RUTHERGLEN AND KILBRIDE.

Polygonum	*hydropiper*	Water-Pepper. *Stonelaw.*
P.	*amphibium*	Perennial Arsmart. *Shawfield-bank.*
Polypodium	*vulgare*	Common Polypody. *Banks of Calder.*
P.	*lonchitis*	Rough P. *In fissures of rocks below Calderwood.*
P.	*phegopteris*	Soft pale-stalked P. *Near the Cascade at Mauchlan-hole.*
P.	*cristatum*	Crested P. *Polliskin-glen.*
P.	*aculeatum*	Prickly P. *Crossbasket.*
P.	*fragile*	Fine-leav'd brittle P. *Gillburnsynke*
P.	*dryopteris*	Small-branch'd P. *Polliskin-glen.*
P.	*filix mas*	} Male and Female Fern. *Banks and way-sides.*
P.	*filix femina*	
Potomogeton	*natans*	Broad-leav'd Pondweed. *Peat-mosses, Kilbride.*
P.	*perfoliatum*	Perfoliated P. *Clyde.*
P.	*crispum*	Curled P. *do.*
P.	*compressum*	Flat-stalk'd P. *Pond at Castelmilk*
P.	*gramineum*	Grass-leav'd P. *Clyde.*
Prunus	*padus*	Bird-Cherry. *Gillburnsynke, and the bank from that to Crossbasket.*
Ranunculus	*hederaceus*	Ivy-leav'd Water Crowfoot. *In spouty ground at Whitemoss, Crosshill, Braehead, &c.*
R.	*aquatilis*	Various-leav'd Water Crowfoot. *In Clyde, Calder, Cart, and in a rivulet between Nook and Bossfield.*
Reseda	*luteola*	Dyers-weed, or Strawaald. *East-quarry, Rutherglen.*
Rubus	*idaeus*	Raspberry-Bush. *Calderwood, Crossbasket, Torrance.*

Sambucus

Sambucus	ebulus	Dwarf Elder, or Dane-wort. On the road-side between Kittochside and Carmunnock.
Sanicula	europea	Sanicle. Woodside.
Scabiosa	succisa	Devil's Bit. East-quarry, Law-moor.
Scirpus	setaceous	The least Rush. Clinkert-hill.
Scrophularia	nodosa	Fig-wort. Banks of Clyde.
Scuttellaria	minor	Little Scull-cap. Rosebank.
Sedum	villosum	Marsh Stonecrop. Highflat, Rigfoot.
Senecio	viscosus	Viscid Groundsel. Rawhead.
Solanum	dulcamara	Common Woody Night-shade. In hedges near Farme.
Sorbus	aucuparia	Quicken-Tree, or Mountain Ash. The Rown, or Roan-Tree (Scotis.) Banks of Calder.
Spergula	nodosa	Knotted Spurry. Clinkert-hill.
Stellaria	nemorum	Broad-leav'd Stichwort. Banks of Clyde, and under a hedge near Drumlaw.
S.	Holostea	Greater Stichwort. Woodside.
S.	graminea	Lesser do. Farme, Rosebank.
Symphytum	officinale	Comfrey. Under a hedge at Castelmilk.
Teucrium	scorodonia	Wood Sage. Banks of Clyde, Kittoch, Calder.
Thymus	serpyllum	Mother of Thyme. Drumlaw, Rogertoun.
Trifolium	mel. officinalis	Melilot. On the road-side between Rutherglen and Farme.
Triglochin	palustre	Arrow-headed Grass. Ditches and peat-mosses near Crosshill, Kilbride.

Trollius

Trollius	europeus	Lucken-Gowan. (*Scotis*) Globe-Flower. (*Anglis*) Mauchlanhole, and meadows in the higher parts of Kilbride.
Tussilago	petasites	Common Butter-bur. *In the artificial bank at Hamilton-Farm.*
Vaccinium	myrtillus	Blae-berries (*Scotis*) Billberries (*Anglis.*) *Banks of Calder, and moors in Kilbride.*
V.	oxycoccos	Common Cranberry, or Mossberry. *Peat-mosses, Kilbride.*
Valantia	cruciata	Crosswort. *Banks of Clyde.*
Valeriana	officinalis	Valerian. *Rutherglen-Green, Polliskin-glen.*
V.	locusta	Corn-Sallad, or Lamb's Lettuce. *Calderwood.*
Verbascum	thapsus	Broad-leav'd Mullein, Shepherd's Club (*Scotis.*) *In old walls at Calderwood.*
Veronica	hederifolia	Ivy-leav'd Speedwell, or small Henbit. *In gardens near R.*
Viburnum	opulus	Marsh Viburnum, or Gelder-Rose. *Polliskin-glen, Gillburnsyke.*

FOSSILS.

FOSSILS, comprehending according to Mineralogists, all unorganized bodies under the surface of the earth, are divided into Native, and Adventitious. The former include those bodies that were never organized: the latter such as once belonged to the animal or vegetable kingdom, and which retain some of their organized properties, but have now lost their organization.

Native fossils, or minerals, comprehend Earths, Inflammables, Salts, Metals. Under some one or other of these divisions, Adventitious fossils, when chemically considered, are also included: but from the remains of their once organized structure, they are generally arranged in a class by themselves.

The native earths comprehend the Argillaceous, Calcareous, Siliceous, Ponderous, and Magnesian. These earths are seldom, in a state of nature, found without mixture: but the kind that predominates fixes, in general, the character.

Of all the Earths, in Rutherglen and Kilbride, the Argillaceous is found in greatest plenty. Soft clay, or potter's clay, abounds in many places, but on where, perhaps, in so fine a state as at Shawfield, where it is used for making bricks. The small quantity of sand in its composition, renders it not the most proper for that manufacture. This clay, for many yards in depth, is disposed in layers, or thin strata, from $\frac{1}{12}$ to $\frac{1}{4}$ of an inch in thickness; and which, owing to a small quantity of mud between them, are easily separable from one another. In the clay are great numbers of small concretions, vulgarly

vulgarly called *Cam-stones*, from half an inch, to an inch and a half in diameter. They lie in a horizontal position: all of them are oblate, and generally of an oblong figure, but some of them are pretty round; and not unfrequently three or four adhere to each other; in which case their figure is extremely irregular; but commonly they are shaped like buttons, and are composed of horizontal layers. They are not so hard but they may be scraped with a knife. When put into the fire they burst in pieces with a great explosion. They readily absorb water, but do not, with it, fall down into clay. Nitrous acid acts upon them very powerfully, and decomposes them into an impalpable powder; the solution, however, by the addition of the vitriolic acid, deposites a considerable quantity of Selenite: the clay in which they are imbedded is not affected by the acid. They become harder, and of a black colour, by torrefaction; but are not attracted by the magnet. They are easily reduced, by the blowpipe, to a black glass. In several specimens which I have examined, I could observe no *nucleus* round which they might have been formed. It is evident from certain inequalities on their surfaces, that they did not acquire their shape by attrition, but must have been concreted, probably by means of calcar, in the place where now found. They break with rough surfaces, and are harsh to the touch.

A bluish coloured pipe-clay is found near Lime-kilns. It was for some time used in the pipe-manufacture at Glasgow; but, owing to the expence of carriage, it is now neglected.

INDURATED clays abound in both parishes. The most plentiful is the *Schistus* or *Till*.* It generally splits into lamellæ, and is of a grayish or blackish colour. It contains the following varieties: 1. Till, of an uniform and compact texture; smooth to the touch, and, by exposure to the air, falls down into a soft clay. It is of a blackish gray colour, and retains vegetable impressions, afterwards to be described. 2. Fire-clay, found between strata of coal, at Torrance and Stonelaw. It readily breaks, in various directions, into small pieces of no determined shape: the surfaces are uneven, and harsh to the touch: it is of a dusky colour, and does not readily fall down into clay. It is full of streaks and blotches, which seem to be the remains of grasses and reeds; but their original characters are so much effaced, as not to be easily distinguished. 3. Till, replete with Shells, Entrochi, and other spoils of the ocean. It is of a grayish colour, and, by ex-

posure

---

* Schistus, and Till, are words indiscriminately used to denote the same argillaceous, hard, fissile substance. The word Till is, indeed, sometimes vulgarly used to denote a stiff clay, although in a soft state.

posure to the air, is readily decomposed. It is found above iron-stone, lime and coal. 4. Inflammable schistus. This kind is hard and black; burns, for a short time, with a clear flame, and is reduced to hard and white ashes. Found in the neighbourhood of coal. 5. Till, hard, black and slaty: is not decomposed by the air, nor kindled into a flame by heat. Found in various situations. 6. The most uncommon variety of till, in this country, is one that, by the miners, is called *Maggy*. It is incumbent on a coarse iron-stone, or doggar, at Mauchlanhole, and Torrance; and is generally found in the shape of cones, as pl. XX. fig. 8. These cones are of a dirty black colour, and are composed of concentric lamellæ, of various thickness, and which may be separated from one another, exhibiting surfaces adorned with small, but irregular undulations. The apices of the cones, which are of various dimensions, rest upon the stone, and the bases are lost in the surrounding till. They are softest at the base; but gradually increase in hardness towards the apex. The whole, however, is, in general, very hard. This curious fossil contains, along with clay, a considerable proportion of iron and lime, and, perhaps, some other substance which co-operates in the formation of its peculiar figure.

Most of the schistus contains a quantity of Mica, and a little sand, but not much Allum.

The Rough-hill, and the adjacent banks, are compofed of indurated clay, which breaks in all directions, and ferves as a cement to a vaft number of fmall ftones which it envelopes. Thefe ftones, although argillaceous, are confiderably harder than the cementitious matter; and moft of them readily fplit into thin pieces. They are all rounded by attrition; lie in all directions, as if thrown together in the greateft diforder; and are of different colours and confiftencies. This rock exhibits an excellent fpecimen of what may be called an argillaceous Breccia.

The chief component part of the *Ofmund ftone*, found at Burnhoufe, Rawhead, and feveral places in Kilbride, feems to be clay. This remarkable ftone, which is univerfally known all over the country, is of various colours; as gray, brown, whitifh, &c. It is generally fo foft, when lately quarried, that it may be cut with a chifel; but afterwards becomes much harder. It breaks in all directions; the furfaces are unequal, and harfh to the touch. It readily abforbs water, and, if recently heated in the fire, the abforption is attended with a hiffing noife. The acids do not affect it: nor are the brownifh coloured kinds deftitute of iron, in its calciform ftate. The ofmund ftands a very great heat, without being rent or melted; for which reafon it is ufed for ovens, furnaces, &c. where a ftrong

and

and conftant heat is neceffary. But when ufed for paving ovens, care muft be taken to have it all of the fame kind: for if one ftone is more denfe than another, the bread will be unequally fired. For want of this precaution feveral ovens have been rendered ufelefs, and the ftone held in difrepute. In fome fpecimens a great variety of fmall ftones of different fubftances, colours and fhapes are clofely cemented together. The greateft part of the ofmund, when burnt, affumes a darker colour, and and lofes three per Cent. of its weight, but afterwards regains it, by abforbing moifture from the atmofphere. Some of it is confiderably porous, and almoft femivitrified: in this cafe it has, when ftruck, a ftrong and clear found: the pores, in fome fpecimens, are pretty large.

The ofmund is found in large maffes in the form of rocks, and in fome places it has the appearance of ftratification. In many places, as at Kilmalcom, it is found below whin-ftone, with hardly any other kind of fubftance intervening. The pores and crevices are, in fome fpecimens, filled with filiceous, and in others, with calcareous fpar, and fometimes with Zeolite. A white Steatites, afterwards to be mentioned, is lodged in the crevices of this ftone: and, in the parifh of Eaglefham, a great quantity of the ponderous fpar is interfperfed in it. Not unfrequently thefe two fubftances are beautifully
intermixed:

intermixed: and, in many specimens, large fragments of osmund are imbedded, or insulated in the barytes. It is probable that the osmund is a volcanic production.

A small specimen of what appears to be a vitreous volcanic production, is all of the kind I have met with in this country. It was found in the Eldrig not far from a rock of osmund. The colour is a dull green. When broken the fractures were glossy, conchoidal and smooth, but contained a great number of minute specks, shaped like the point of a dart. It is not transparent, and does not emit fire with steel. In appearance it pretty much resembles what is vulgarly called bastard Jasper, found plentifully in a hill called Dumfuen, in the Island of Arran.

ZEOLITE* is found, although sparingly, in Kilbride. The most rare is a variety in which the fibres are of a white colour, extremely fine, having the appearance of cotton wool, and lying loosely across each other, without any regular order. It is found in the pores, or bladder-holes of whin-stone. The compact crystallized Zeolite, in which the fibres diverge from a point, is found in different kinds of stones. The colour is commonly white, but metallic

* This name is given to this curious fossil on account of its property of forming a jelly with acids.

tallic mixtures give it various tinges. It is found at Blackburnmill, Browncastle, and the Piel.

STEATITES,* or Soap clays, are arranged, by some authors, among argillaceous fossils; by others among magnesian earths. The finest, perhaps, in Britain is found a little above Rawhead. It is considerably heavy; greasy to the touch; free from sand and metallic mixtures; and of a beautiful white colour. When tried by Mr. Young, in the Delf Manufacture at Glasgow, it produced Porcelain, equal, if not superior in fineness, to ware made of the best materials in Europe. It makes an excellent paste for Crayons, and may be wrought up with the most delicate colours. It is found in small quantities in the crevices, and pores of an osmund rock. This valuable fossil, upon proper search, may, probably, be found in considerable plenty.

OF the *Calcareous* class of earths, Kilbride contains a very great quantity. Limestone bears the greatest proportion of any other kind. It is found at Jackton, Hermyres, Limekilns, &c. &c. The strata are generally from 3 to 7 feet in thickness: they lie below different substances, as mould, clay and till. In some places their surfaces, when uncovered, are entire and smooth; in others, as at

K k Hermyres,

* So called because it resembles *Suet*.

Hermyres, they are rent into wide perpendicular fissures, almost the whole depth of the stratum. These rents, which observe no regular direction, are extremely rough in their surfaces, and gradually diminish in their wideness, as they descend into the stone, and are commonly found near the extremity of the stratum. The roughness is occasioned by shells, and other marine productions, with which the stone is replete. There is something in the construction, or composition, of these *exuviæ*, that withstands the corroding substance that acts upon the limestone, and wastes it away. Owing to this, these once organized remains of the ocean preserve their shape, whilst the matter in which they were originally imbedded, and to which they now but slightly adhere, is worn away. The stone, at the upper edge of these fissures, is not unfrequently branched out, like irregularly shaped horns, of about half a yard in length, and two or three inches in thickness.

The original cause of these fractures in limestone is not, perhaps, easy to ascertain. Similar effects have been produced by a transition from heat to cold; from a state of fluidity, by a solvent, to a state of dryness, by evaporation; or by some powerful pressure from beneath, by which a stratum has been raised from a horizontal, to an oblique or circular direction.

Two strata, or, in the language of workmen, two *posts* of limestone are found in most of the quarries in Kilbride. They are divided from one another by a stratum of till, about 3 feet in thickness. Below the under post is commonly a stratum of coarse limestone-flag, not worth burning. It is chiefly composed of sand and clay, combined with a little lime.

Limestone strata are found at various depths: from 1 to 50 feet. When they are deeper than 24, or 30, the working of the stone is reckoned unprofitable.

Besides the regular strata, a great number of detached pieces, called *Stammerers*, are, in many places of the parish, found imbedded in clay. They are from an inch, to 3 or 4 feet in thickness; but of no regular shape. The most of them are, by attrition, rounded on the corners. They are not all of the same texture, quality or colour. Many of them differ considerably from any stratum of limestone, as yet discovered in the parish. Some of them, being very good, are carefully preserved by the workmen; whilst others are so bad that they are not worth collecting.

Of all the varieties of limestone in the parish, the grayish coloured is by far the most common.

A stratum of a white colour, and close fine texture is wrought at Jackton. Limestone, containing a considerable proportion of iron, which gives it a red colour, is found in the lands of East-Milton. It is little valued. All the varieties contain extraneous fossils, which, in some places, are so numerous, that, except a little cement by which they are combined, they compose the whole substance of the stone. Some kinds admit of a polish, equal almost to the finest marble. Their beauty is set off to advantage, by the shells, entrochi, madrepores, &c. with which they are replete.

Lime from Kilbride is in high repute both for manure and building. It generally takes a strong band: and some of it, especially what is produced at Hermyres, has this peculiar quality, that, when properly mixed, and wrought warm, as the workmen express themselves, it very readily takes a firm band in water. For this reason it is used in building bridges.

No lime that comes to Glasgow, if we except the Netherwood lime, belonging to Mr. Glasford, is in so great estimation for house-plaster, as lime from Kilbride. But care must be taken in preparing it. If wrought new, that is, soon after *slacking*, it frequently rises in blisters. These are produced by what the workmen call *particles* in the plaster.

These

These particles, when examined, are found to be either small pieces of cinders, or coal, that have got among the plaster; or small fragments of shells, corralloides, &c. which have not been thoroughly decomposed during the slacking of the lime. There seems to be something in the construction, or composition of these crystallized substances, that prevents them from falling down into powder, so readily as the rest of the stone. Afterwards, however, they swell, by absorbing moisture from the air, and thereby occasion the blisters above-mentioned. This is entirely prevented by properly *souring* the lime before it is wrought into plaster.*

Besides a tendency to rise in blisters, the lime from Hermyres has been found to lose its hardness and consistency, and to fall down into powder, after it had been for some time on the wall. A considerable quantity of moisture seems necessary to make this uncommon lime retain its solidity. Owing to this quality, however, it may in some cases be preferable to most other kinds of lime. Its peculiarities are probably owing to a considerable quantity of selenite and manganese, that appear to be in the stone.

The

---

* Lime is, by workmen, said to be *soured*, when, after being slacked, it is for a considerable time kept wet. During this stage of the preparation, all the parts of the stone that were not so readily slacked as the rest, have time to be decomposed, and thoroughly incorporated in the mass.

The only calcareous ſtratum in Rutherglen, is one that runs through a great part of the pariſh, and is a continuation of what, in this country, is called Cambuſlang Marble. It is from a few inches, to two feet in thickneſs; and lies in a ſtratum of till, above the main coal. The ground is a darkiſh gray, ornamented with white bivalve ſhells; but ſometimes it is reddiſh. Both varieties take a good poliſh, and are uſed in the Marble Manufacture at Glaſgow. Pieces of this marble, and alſo of metallic limeſtone in Kilbride, are ſometimes found in the earth, in a ſtate of decompoſition.

SPATUM (ſpar) forms a beautiful claſs of calcareous ſubſtances. The moſt plentiful is the *rhomboidal;* ſo called, becauſe it breaks into fragments of a rhomboidal ſhape. It is commonly found in limeſtone ſtrata; and frequently in iron-ſtone, and ſometimes in whin. It is moſtly ſemitranſparent; but ſome of it is opaque, and of a reddiſh colour. Of the *pyramidal* ſpar the quarry at Philipshill affords a few ſpecimens. In the fiſſures of a limeſtone ſtratum, near Jackton, is a conſiderable quantity of the *priſmatic* ſpar. The cryſtals are hexahedral, and truncated: they adhere to a ſparry incruſtation formed on the ſtone; they are of different lengths, commonly about half an inch; and lie in all directions. In one ſpecimen they adhere to the inſide of a petrified bivalve-ſhell. Similar cryſtallizations are

are found in Lochrig quarry, near Stewarton, county of Ayr.

Fibrous, or striated calcareous spar, is found a little above Kittochside. It is of a chalky appearance, and the stratum, or vein which it composes, is about an inch in thickness. The fibres are prismatic crystals, probably of six sides; are arranged like basaltic columns: they are pretty fine; in close, but not inseparable contact with each other; and make an oblique angle with the horizon, or particular direction in which the stratum, or vein lies. Specimens of this curious fossil are frequently found in till and stone marle, in the immediate neighbourhood of whin-stone rocks; and sometimes in fissures of the rocks themselves. The colour is often tinged with carnation, and not unfrequently with a faint blue. It is commonly of a silky, or silvery appearance, resembling some kinds of Gypsum.

Calcareous *Incrustations* are found chiefly on limestone, sometimes on freestone, but seldom on roots or branches of trees.

Stalactites, *Isicles*, or *Dropstones*, are found in the cavities of limestone, and large masses of petrifactions at Gillburnsynke. Their texture is chiefly lamellar, and their colour whitish, except when particles of iron communicate a reddish or yellowish tinge.

tinge. Their shape is generally that of a perforated cone, or tube; but they are sometimes solid and variously branched.

STALAGMITES are formed in the bottom of cavities, chiefly where the dropstone is found. They are commonly of a roundish, or mammillary shape, and their colour, by reason of earthy and metallic mixtures, is not always the same.

To calcareous earths belong *Recent Petrifactions*, of which there is a confiderable variety in Kilbride. They confift of different *genera* of vegetables, as the Hypnum, Bryum, Marchantia, &c. belonging to the Cryptogamia clafs, which are petrified by water containing calcareous particles, and a certain proportion of fixed air. It is obfervable, that moffes are more fufceptible of a thorough petrifaction, than any other kind of plants. The reafon, by fome, is fuppofed to be, " That moffes, &c. being deftitute " of *congenial falt*, readily admit into their pores " adventitious ones, whilft the gramineous plants, " being already furnifhed with it, will admit of no " heterogeneous acceffion."* If this peculiarity is not owing to the particular conftruction, or texture of thefe plants, the true caufe is, perhaps, yet to be difcovered.

THESE

* Wallis' Hiftory of Northumberland.

XII

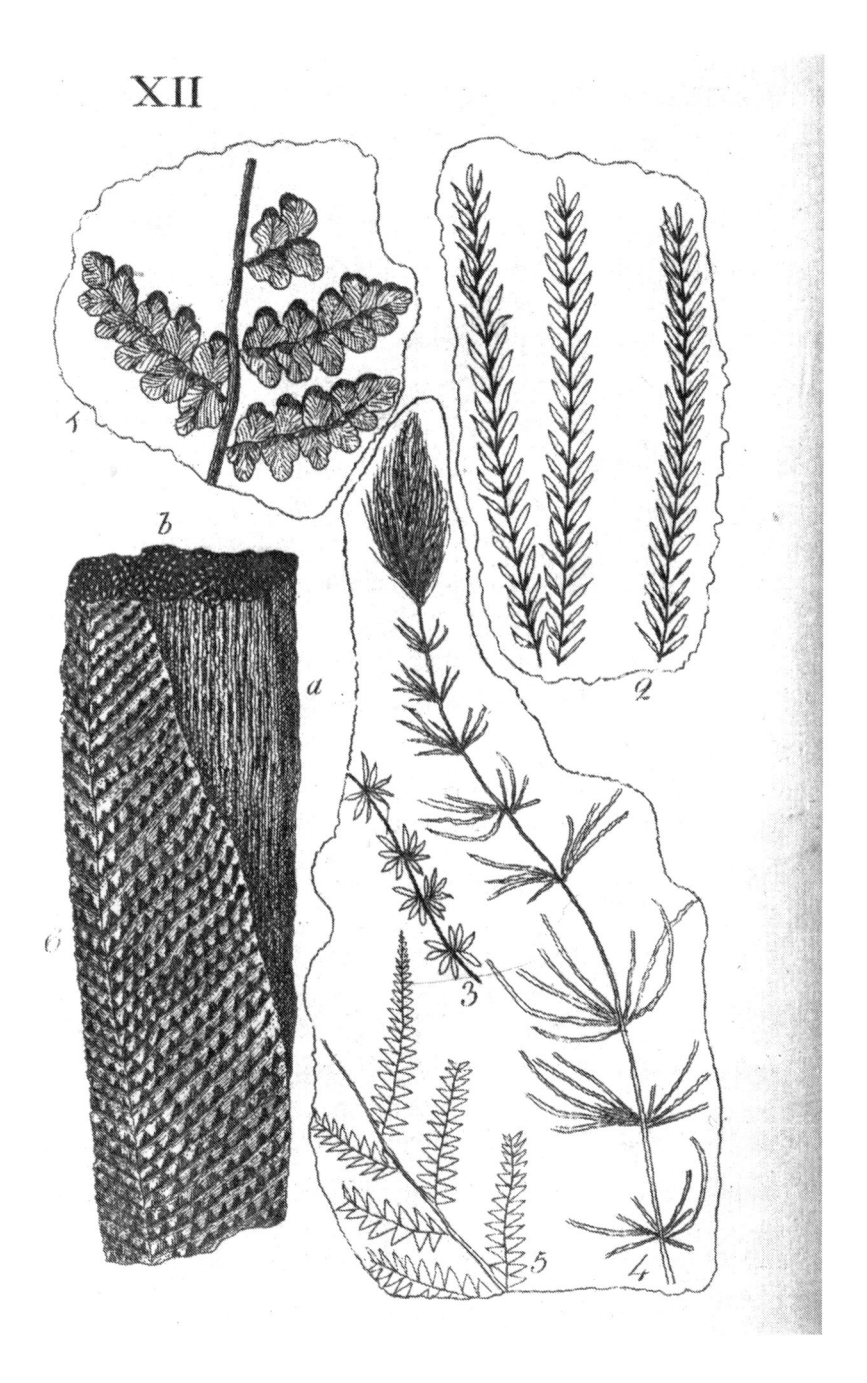

XIII

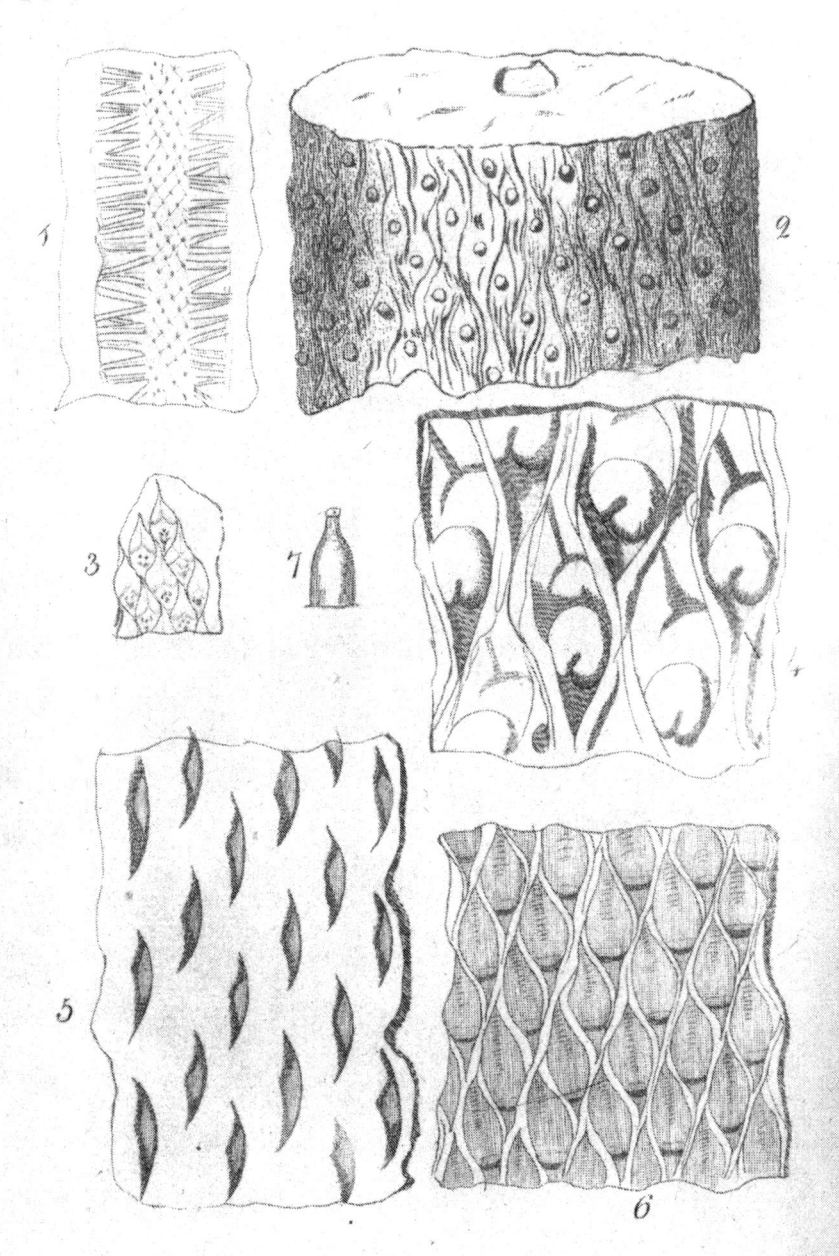

XIV

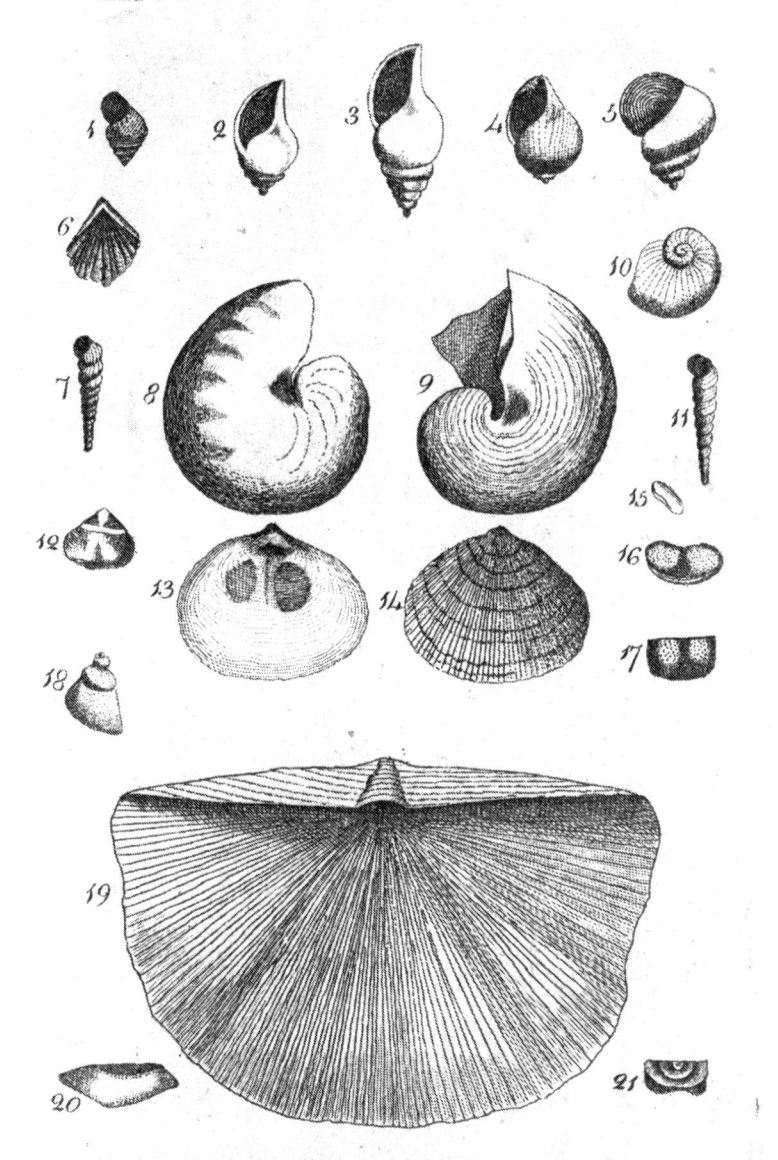

XV

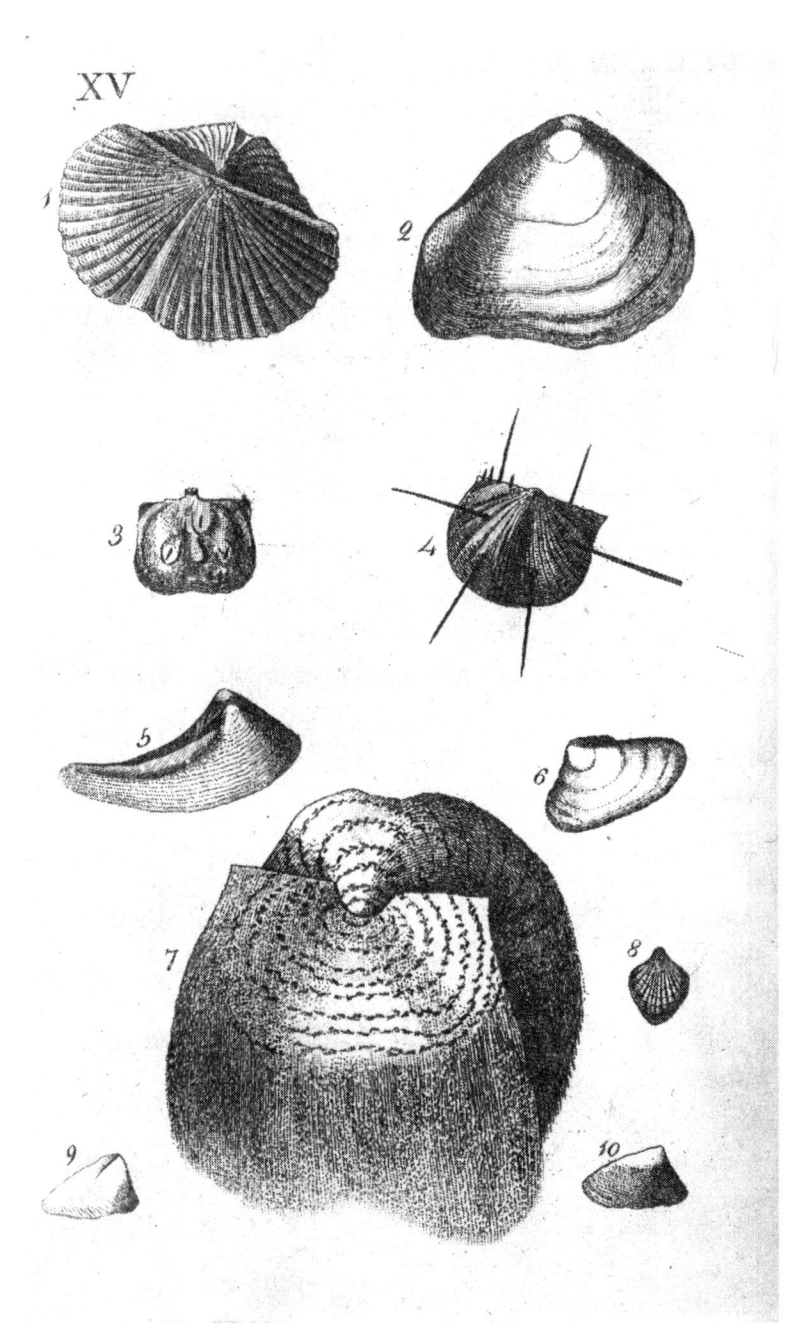

XVI

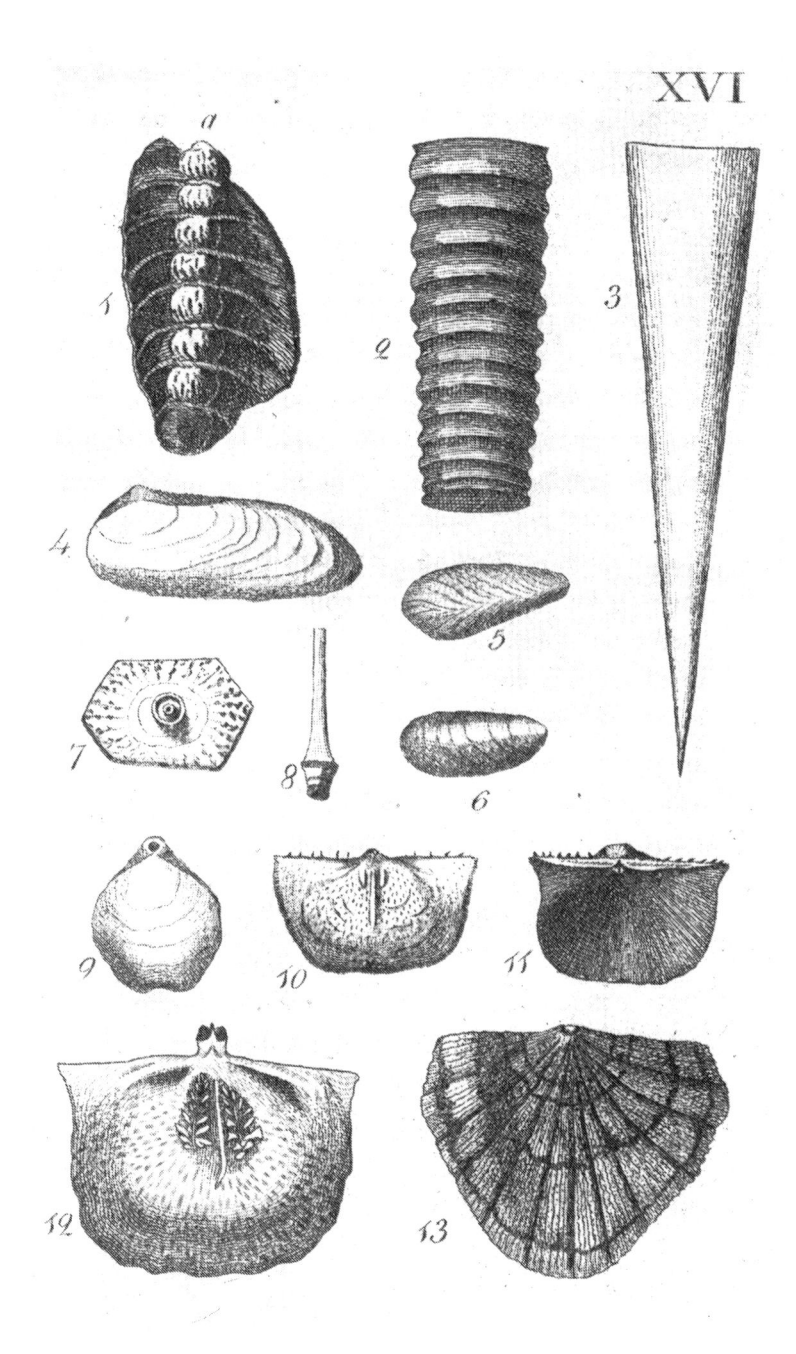

These petrifactions are chiefly found at Gill-burnsynke, Mauchlanhole, and Pateshall; on the banks of Calder; and on the south bank of Kittoch, a little below Burnbrae. They were, in 1787, in great perfection at Pateshall.* A large space was covered with moss, which, on the surface, retained a beautiful verdure, but about an inch or two below, exhibited the various degrees of petrifaction, from the slightest adhesion of the calcareous matter, till the vegetable was thoroughly replete with it. The whole was, at the depth of about 6 inches, a mass of stoney hardness. The stem and branches of the same plant, although in perfect vegetation near the top, could be traced a considerable way downward. The petrifaction is not of that kind which consists of an incrustation only, but the whole of the plant is replete with the petrifying substance. Whilst this curious operation of nature was going on, and inviting the diligent investigators of the works of God, to this pleasant, though retired spot; the impending bank gave way, and buried the petrifactions under huge masses of stone, with the earth and shrubs that were above the rock. Instead of affording an agreeable retirement, where many of the genuine beauties of nature were to be seen, the place now exhibits a scene of wild desolation.

------

* The property of *John Millar* of Millheugh, Esq; Professor of Law, Univers. Glasgow.

Sixty or seventy years will, perhaps, be insufficient for producing a group of petrified mosses, equal to the former. From every appearance it is evident, that Gillburnsynke, a considerable number of years ago, underwent a fate in some respects similar. On the face of the rock over which the petrifying water runs, and which is about 30 feet high, large masses of petrifactions had, in a long series of years, been formed. But the weight had, at length, accumulated to such a degree, that they brought away part of the rock to which they adhered, and fell into the glen below, where they now lie. This operation of nature is, on the face of the rock, again going forwards, and large pieces of petrified mosses are now making their appearance.

The existence of the Sulphate of Lime, is evident from specimens of beautifully radiated crystals of *Selenite*, that are sparingly found in Lawrieston quarry.* They consist of about 20 or 30 radii, diverging from a center containing a small piece of pyrites, like a pin-head. These radii are transparent, of different lengths, commonly about $\frac{1}{4}$ of an inch; and the thickness of a horse-hair in breadth. They are as broad and gross at the extremity as at any other part. These radiated, and superficial crystallizations, are formed on the surfaces of a blackish

---

* The property of Sir William Maxwell of Calderwood, Bart.

blackish coloured till, of pyritaceous clay, incumbent on limestone.

The *Barytes*, or *ponderous spar*, has, in small quantities, been found in a quarry near Nook. Probably a vast quantity of that *matrix metalli* exists in the Eldrig, and the neighbouring hills. It makes its appearance in great plenty, and in various forms and situations, in an adjacent glen. Some specimens are semitransparent; others opaque. Its hexahedral crystals, in the form of thin plates, are likewise found here: they are sometimes confusedly arranged in the shape of a crest, or cock's comb, from the bigness of a hazel nut, to several inches in diameter. The spar is, in some few specimens, ornamented with rock-crystals. Some of them are hexahedral prisms, terminated at each end by a pyramid of the same number of sides. In some the pyramids are joined base to base: others consist of a single pyramid only. Some of them are nearly an inch in length, and ¼ in thickness; and others are not much larger than the point of a pin, and appear on the surface of the spar like minute granulations. All of them make a deep scratch on glass. Considerable numbers are enveloped in the barytes, and lie in all directions: and in some specimens, pieces of the barytes are enveloped in clusters of crystals. Not unfrequently a congeries of barytical crystals is found united with a broad plate of rock cryftal; an irregular ftratum of which runs through part of the rock. Detached, and fharply angulated, pieces of ofmund ftone are frequently found wholly inclofed in the barytes: and pieces of the barytes, in like manner, inclofed or infulated in the ofmund. Thefe varieties lay a foundation upon which a theorift might build not a few conjectures.

SILICEOUS fubftances are not unfrequent in Rutherglen and Kilbride. Quartzy nodules, or *chuckie-ftones*, as they are vulgarly called, are very common, and are of various colours. The Quartz is alfo found in fmall veins running through whin-ftone, and fometimes micaceous fchiftus.

WHIN-STONE affords, in this country, a confiderable variety of the *faxa filicea*. The Scottifh term *whin* is frequently, in common language, made ufe of to exprefs any thing that is hard, fharp and prickly. According to this meaning the whin-ftone fignifies one, the fragments of which have fharp and prickly corners. The word taken in this peculiar fenfe, is equally fignificant with any name, as yet given to this clafs of ftones, from the Greek, German, or Englifh languages.

THE whin-ftone is various in its hardnefs, colour, &c. in proportion to the filex, and extraneous mixtures, which it contains. The kind that moftly
prevails

prevails in Kilbride, is what is commonly called rotten whin, becaufe, when expofed to the weather, it cracks and falls down into fmall pieces, and is reduced to clay, or mud. Of this kind many hills in Scotland are compofed. They generally, however, contain great numbers of roundifh pieces of hard whin-ftone that refift the action of heat, air and water. They are generally inclofed within concentric lamellæ of rotten whin, that are eafily decompofed. Thefe balls contain a great quantity of quartz, feld fpar, and fchorl, and freely emit fire with fteel, which the reft of the rock very fparingly does. They are from 1, to 6 or 8 feet in diameter. No ftones in the country afford better materials for making roads: but owing to their great hardnefs, they are commonly neglected; whilft the more eafily procured rotten whin is preferred, and thereby the roads are greatly hurt.

To this clafs of ftones may be added the *Bafaltes*, of which the eftate of Cathkin,* a little above Rutherglen, affords a beautiful fpecimen. A Colonnade, confifting of 164 pillars were, by workmen procuring materials for a turnpike road, brought into view. They are about 30 feet high, and a foot and a half in diameter. They are moftly five-fided, but the fides are not equal. A thin *diffepimentum*, fome parts of which are ochreous, and

others

* The property of Walter Ewing McLae of Cathkin, Efq;

others argillaceous, separates them from one another. Not a few specimens of it are very hard, approaching to a vitreous and metallic texture; whilst others are loose, and friable between the fingers. It is generally of a reddish colour, and becomes darker and magnetic by torrefaction. Some of it is porous, having some of the cavities filled with a sooty-like substance, among which are found transparent rock-crystals, of hexahedral pyramids. In the columns, the transverse subdivisions are very imperfect: in some instances they exhibit a convex, and a corresponding concave surface. The basaltic stone is considerably brittle; does not emit fire with steel; is not acted upon by acids; and is generally of a darkish gray colour. It affects the magnetic needle; a proof that it is not destitute of iron. After being heated in the fire it becomes darker in the colour; and grows so hard as to strike fire with steel. The flame of a blow-pipe readily melts it into a black glass. The columns, some of which are a little curved, incline to the south, at an angle of about 75 degrees. In the west side of the rock, the pillars gradually coalesce into one another, as their bases, till they become a solid mass.*

CATHKIN hills are not altogether destitute of *Petrosilex* and *Rock Crystal*. The finest *Jasper* I have met with is of their production. The ground of
which

* To this account I have subjoined a view of this curious rock.

A View of the BASALTIC ROCK *at Calthkin,*
near Rutherglen.

which is a faint yellow, is beautifully striped and blotched with a blood red. The fractures present surfaces of a fine polish.

GRIT, *Cos arenarea, sand-stone,* or *free-stone,* is, in great abundance, in those parts of both parishes where coal is found. This useful fossil admits of several varieties, according to the colour, shape and size of the particles of sand, and the cement by which they are combined. The colour, in general, is white, grayish, or inclining to brown. The stone, in the west quarry of Rutherglen, is beautifully blotched with red spots, of various diameters. Their colour proceeds from small nodules of argillaceous iron-ore which are imbedded in the stone, and are so soft as to be scraped with the nail. They commonly contain particles of mica. These nodules must have been interspersed in the sand, before it was hardened into stone; and strongly indicate, that a considerable quantity of this kind of ore exists in Cathkin hills, near the bottom of which the quarry lies. The east quarry of Rutherglen contains a white free-stone, of an excellent quality. It is, in Glasgow, highly valued for building.

ARGILLACEOUS grit, having the sand combined by means of a clayey cement, is very plenty in Kilbride. It lies in strata, and readily splits into flags, or thin layers. From a stratum of this kind, in the Gill* near Bogton, excellent grind-stones have been taken. When the cement is siliceous the stone is generally very hard, and difficult to cut. Some of this kind is found above coal; and often composes a great part of the dykes, or troubles, which derange the regular strata. It is commonly white; and emits fire copiously with steel. To the siliceous class belongs a stratum of mill-stone grit, at Polliskin-glen, above Torrance, from which mill-stones have been procured. With the cement is combined a small quantity of iron, which, after the stone has been long exposed to the air, makes its appearance in the form of ochre. Grit, of which the cement is mostly calcar, abounds in the neighbourhood of Limekilns, and Edwardshall. It contains fragments of shells, entrochi, and other marine productions. It splits in thin layers, and is used for hearth-stones, dykes, &c.

Along with the free-stone, may be mentioned the *Breccia quartzosa*, detached pieces of which are found both in Rutherglen and Kilbride.

Inflammable substances are found in great abundance, within the bounds under our review. Coal (*Lithanthrax*) is, in Rutherglen, of the very best quality. It is commonly divided into soft and hard.

---

* A name commonly given to a deep narrow glen, with a small rivulet in the bottom.

hard. Both kinds are free, and are easily broken into fragments of right angles, and clear surfaces. They burn with a bright flame; have no sulphureous smell; and leave a very small quantity of white and light ashes. None of the varieties cake in the fire. A splint, or cannel coal, of a hard compact texture is found in the main coal at Stonelaw; and in a thin stratum in Freeland, and Murrays. It takes a fine polish; is highly inflammable; and, when burnt, leaves a hard calx. It is specifically lighter than the other varieties. The coal in Kilbride, if we except the splint coal, is not nearly so good as in Rutherglen. It is not sulphureous, nor of the caking kind; but contains a great proportion of sand and clay; and is kindled with difficulty.

Coal has been found no where, perhaps, in more uncommon situations than in Kilbride. Some of the *Ludi Helmontii*, afterwards to be described, contain good coal. But this is not the only uncommon situation in which that useful fossil has been found. A miner, in 1790, digging for iron-stone in the Basket mines, struck down a piece of schistus, in which was inclosed a small, but complete bed of coal. It was about an inch in thickness; 11 in length; and 8 in breadth, at the broadest. It gradually diminished to a sharp edge, when it was lost in the schistus. The coal was of an excellent quality; broke into quadrangular fragments, having smooth

smooth and glossy surfaces; it contained no sulphur, and burnt with a bright flame. It had every appearance of having been produced in the very spot where found.

Here an opportunity is afforded of investigating the theories that have been given of the origin of coal. But more facts are, perhaps, yet necessary to enable any person to form a true theory, concerning this part of the mineral kingdom.

The purest of all the inflammables, in this country, is *Petroleum*. This bituminous substance oozes from the fissures of a rock of argillaceous grit, in the banks of Calder, a little below the Blackcraig. This fossil is likewise found near Gillburnsynke, in a free-stone rock that may be called a Bituminous grit; it is of a black colour; burns in the fire with a bright flame, till the pitch is consumed, when the colour becomes a darkish gray; and then the stone easily crumbles down between the fingers into pure sand. Petroleum, as shall afterwards be taken notice of, is also found in some varieties of the *Ludus Helmontii*. This pitchy substance is of a black colour; readily adheres to the fingers; grows hard by exposure to the air, but never so hard as jet; it is electrical; may be melted and cast into moulds; and burns with a clear flame. Bitumen, of similar qualities, oozes from the fissures of a limestone

stratum

ftratum, in the neighbourhood of Hawk-head, near Paifley. It is alfo, at Stewarton, found in a lime-ftone quarry, belonging to William Cunningham of Lainfhaw, Efq; It is ufed, with fuccefs, by the people in the neighbourhood, as a plaifter for cuts and feftered wounds. In Kilbride it has, fometimes, been ufed to befmear the naves of cart-wheels: which purpofe it anfwers better than any artificial mixture.

WHETHER bitumens are, *fua origine*, minerals: or whether they derive their origin from bodies once organized, is not fully afcertained.

THIS part of the country is not altogether defti-tute of *Sulphur*. Nodules and cryftals of Pyrites are fparingly found among coal, till, iron-ftone and lime-ftone. None of it is collected for ufe.

PEAT (*Geanthrax*) is in fo great plenty in Kil-bride, that it occupies a confiderable number of acres. This ufeful fuel varies in its quality, even in the fame peat-mofs.* Peats dug near the furface are light, foft and yellowifh: they readily confume in the fire, and leave a fmall quantity of a very light, and whitifh coloured afh. But thofe that are dug near the bottom are hard and heavy: their colour,

---

* This word is defcriptive of the origin of peat, which is chiefly decayed moffes, as the Sphagnum, Polytrichum, &c. &c.

colour, when first exposed to the air, is a faint yellow: but, owing to the absorption of pure air, in less than five minutes, becomes extremely black: they burn a long time without being consumed, and their ashes are heavy, and of a reddish colour.

Peat-mosses, in this parish, are generally incumbent on clay; are about 10 or 12 feet in depth; and almost wholly free from stones and other heterogeneous substances. They abound, however, with trees of different species and dimensions. Most of the trees are broken off, a little above the roots; many of which remain in the ground, in their natural position. From this it appears, that they grew on the spot where now found. Some of them retain the marks of burning, in their lower end. Similar circumstances have been observed with trees, in several places of Scotland. A few years ago, a root of a tree, with part of the trunk, was dug out of a peat-moss near Renfrew. In the trunk, a little above the root, was found sticking an iron hatchet of a very uncommon shape. Whether this antique instrument is yet preserved I could not learn.

The slightest inspection makes it evident, that peat-mosses, if we except the trees found in them, are chiefly composed of vegetable substances, similar to these that grow on their surface. The stems of plants, at present in a living state at the top, may be be traced downward, in the mofs, to the depth of some feet. As the under part decays, the upper part fhoots forth, feemingly with greater vigour. Such a peculiarity is common to not a few of the moffes, even in a ftate of petrifaction, where the under part is converted into ftone.

One of the moft uncommon productions of peat-moffes in Kilbride, is a foffil *Boletus*, probably of a fpecies not now a native of Scotland. Two fpecimens only are all that have been difcovered. One was in fragments, the other entire; and was, by a herd-boy, picked up, and kept feveral years, from the belief that it was a horfe-hoof, to which, both in fhape and fize, it bears a near refemblance. To this circumftance alone it owes its prefervation. The pores are vifible to the eye; they are round, regular, and penetrate the whole thicknefs of the plant, except about ¼ of an inch at the top. They are pervious and free from all obftructions, except at the extremities; but when thefe are cleared away, the light fhines freely through them. This is the more extraordinary when we confider, that no fewer than 5184 pores are contained in the fpace of a fquare inch. The colour is a dark brown. This curious and rare foffil, probably the only one of the kind hitherto difcovered, was found near the Eldrig, in a peat-mofs belonging to Mr. John Park of Raw-head, from whom I had it in a prefent. It muft
have

have originally been produced on the trees, over the ruins of which the mofs was afterwards formed.

Of *Metallic* fubftances, in Rutherglen and Kilbride, Iron is by far the moft common. It abounds in great plenty where there is coal. A few fpecimens of the *Hæmatites*, were lately found in Rawhead moor; but no veins of it have yet appeared. The moft plentiful ore is the argillaceous, or ironftone. It lies in regular ftrata; or in detached pieces.

That which lies in regular ftrata is not all of the fame quality. The fineft, with refpect to texture, compofes a ftratum near Edwardshall. The colour is bluifh: the furface, when broken, is of a flinty appearance; extremely fmooth, without any palpable, or vifible particles; and, when fcratched with the nail, fhews a trace uncommonly white. The kind that chiefly prevails is of a darkifh gray, or brown colour; and the furfaces are harfh to the touch. Some ftrata are calcareous: of thefe are two kinds; one contains the exuviæ of the ancient ocean; the other not. A ftratum at Mauchlanhole is, when expofed fome time to the air, very regularly fubdivided into fmall tetrahedral prifms; which, in fome fpecimens, fall down into coarfe powder. The extraction of the metal, from almoft all the varieties, is attended with profit.

Besides

Besides the regular strata, there is great abundance of ferrugenous nodules, or iron-stone balls, as the workmen call them. They are of various shapes, dimensions and qualities: and the situations in which they are found, are not nearly the same. With regard to their shape, they may be divided into two kinds: such as have regular, and such as have irregular shapes.

To the former belongs that curious fossil called *Ludus Helmontii, Septarium,* or *Waxen veins.* It is of a spherical shape, more or less oblate, or depressed. " Paracelsus, who had the cubic pyritæ
" in great esteem, for dissolving the stone, called
" these bodies, from their resembling a die in shape,
" by the general name Ludus; and Van Helmont
" afterwards mistaking the bodies here described,
" for those Ludus's of Paracelsus, gave them in the
" same cases, and called them by the same name,
" hence the Latin name of Ludus Helmontii. The
" English one is acquired from the resemblance of
" the *Tali,* in some species, but of the *Septa* in
" many more, to yellow wax in colour.*

These very singular stones are found chiefly in Kilbride. The strata of schistus, in which they are imbedded, begin to appear near Calderwood, and extend more than a mile towards Crofsbasket.

Above

---
* Hill's History of Fossils, p. 502.

Above and below them are several alternate strata of iron-stone and schistus. They lie in a regular direction, making a kind of interrupted stratum; one stone being several inches, and often a foot or two separated, by the schistus, from another. They universally lie on their depressed sides. In one stratum of till there are two rows, at a few feet distance from each other; and keeping the same direction. The iron-stone of which they are composed, is of an excellent quality; yielding about 50 per cent. of iron.

What renders them a striking example of the curious and admirable workmanship of Nature, is their internal structure. They are beautifully subdivided by *Septa*, generally filled with calcareous rhomboidal spar, or pyrites. Not a few of them contain, along with the spar, a considerable quantity of Petroleum, which sometimes fills the whole of the spaces between the tali. In some specimens, if a section is made perpendicularly, the one half of the stone is wholly subdivided with pitch, and the other with spar. Specimens of this variety are extremely rare. Besides, there is another variety, equally, if not more uncommon. Instead of petroleum the Ludus Helmontii contains coal: this, however, does not subdivide the tali, by way of septa, but runs chiefly in a horizontal direction. The coal is of a good quality; it breaks easily into quadrangular

quadrangular fragments, and smooth glossy surfaces; it burns with a bright flame; is not liquified by heat; is reduced to a soft white ash, and has not the smallest appearance of ever having been charred. The stones in which the coal is inclosed, are found in the same stratum with the rest, and are generally pretty large. The diameter of one, from which I obtained specimens of coal, was nearly 4 feet.

Ludi Helmontii are sparingly found at Stonelaw, in a stratum of till above coal. They are chiefly of the variety, in which the tali are inclosed with calcareous spar. The surfaces of some specimens are beautifully reticulated by the sparry septa, which are prominent above the tali, about $\frac{1}{7}$ of an inch. In a variety, of which the above-mentioned is, probably, an example, the solid part of the stone, beyond the septa, is easily separated from the part which is subdivided by the septa. In this respect they resemble some kinds of Geodes. The separation is occasioned by a small quantity of ochre. Of this kind I found, in August 1792, several specimens in the parish of Kirkintilloch.

Many of the Ludi Helmontii have in their center an elliptical *Nucleus*, round which they were, perhaps, originally formed. Its dimensions bear a considerable proportion to the dimensions of the stone. The *nuclei* are not so thick as broad. They are generally

rally of a dirty white colour, refembling burnt limeftone; and are partly cryftallized. They readily effervefce with acids; and greedily abforb water; after which a certain proportion of them falls down into powder. They are infeparable from the reft of the ftone, and from them all the fepta feem to proceed. In fome fpecimens they feem to be compofed of concentric lamellæ.

It appears, from various circumftances, that the feptaria were formed in the ftratum of fchiftus, in which they are imbedded. Various opinions have been given concerning the original caufe of their peculiar conftruction: but it is more than probable, that our knowledge of the manner in which thefe, and many other foffils in the bowels of the earth, were formed, is too fcanty, to enable us to decide pofitively about many things concerning them.

Several varieties of *Ætites*, or *Eagle-ftones*, another kind of iron-ftone balls, are found in this country. Thefe foffils are of a round, or elliptical form; and confift of a *nucleus*, commonly argillaceous, furrounded with a covering of iron-ftone. The name Ætites is given them from a report that Eagles put them in their nefts, to facilitate the hatching of their eggs. Superftition, which is ever inventive, taught for a certainty, that, being worn by pregnant women, they had great influence in rendering

rendering labour, in childbirth, eafy and fafe. They are divided, according to the ftate of the *nucleus*, into male, female, or neuter. Superftition afcribed, even to this fanciful divifion, certain extraordinary powers, over, not only the chick *in ovo*, but alfo the human fpecies.

Nodules of iron-ftone, irregularly fhaped, are to be met with almoft every where. In fome places they are found in regular ftrata, in others not. Some contain fea-fhells, and are calcareous; others are deftitute of fhells, and are not affected by acids. They are known by different names, as Kidney-ftone, Button-ftone, &c. from their bearing a general refemblance to thefe bodies. Very few of them received their fhape by attrition. They commonly contain the beft of iron-ftone.

Fragments of an argillaceous iron-ore, of a blood-red colour, are found at Stonelaw, and fome other places in Rutherglen. This variety is ufually called *Keel*; and is fometimes ufed as a cryon for drawing.

That Lead exifts in Kilbride, is evident from fome fmall pieces of the *galena communis*, that lately were picked up at the Eldrig. No vein of the metal could, however, be difcovered.

BOTH Rutherglen and Kilbride abound with excellent WATER. Copious and permanent springs are found at Mains, Rawhead, Clochern, &c. &c. One of the most remarkable rises a little below Crofshill: it produces a run that would fill a pipe of a two inch bore. It is called *St. Mungo's*, from its having been confecrated to that famous ecclefiaftic. But the virtue of the confecration gradually diminifhed, as ignorance and fuperftition decreafed.

HARD, or mineral water is chiefly found, where coal, iron and lime prevail. Calcareous and chalybeate fprings muft, therefore, abound in both parifhes. A few Hepatic, or fulphureous fprings make their appearance in the banks of Calder, a little above Calderwood. But the moft celebrated in the parifh, is in the lands of Long Calderwood, the property of Doctor John Hunter in London. The exiftence of the hepatic gas is evident by the colour, tafte and fmell of the water; and by its difcolouring filver, when put into it. Many applications, in the way of medicine, have, with fuccefs, been made to this water. At Shawfield there is a fpring of the fame kind; although neither fo copious nor ftrong.

THE village of Kilbride is plentifully fupplied with water, there being no fewer than 26 pit-wells, fome of which are pretty deep. The method of
procuring

procuring the water is none of the beft: it is raifed by means of a long pole, having a hook, or *cleek* faftened at the lower end, and on which the pitcher, or *ftowp* is fufpended. This method, as the wells are always open above, is attended with danger, as well as difficulty. There is one pump-well in the village, but, like all the reft of the wells, is private property.

The town of Rutherglen is furnifhed with a confiderable number of pump-wells, built of ftone, at the public expence. Thefe, with private wells in clofes and gardens, afford a copious fupply of water.

Before I proceed to defcribe the extraneous foffils, it will not be improper to give fome account of the fubterraneous geography of thefe parifhes.

The general fucceffion of the ftrata, in Rutherglen, as far as the parifh has been explored, will appear from the following Table.

A Table of the Strata at Stonelaw.

	Feet.	In.
Earth and clay,	12	0
Free-stone, *white, argillaceous,*	20	0
Till, *with plies,**	18	6
Till, *with vegetable impressions,*	16	0
Doggar, *coarse iron-stone,*	0	6
Coal, *soft,*	4	6
Till, *with plies,*	6	0
Free-stone, *extremely hard,*	24	0
Coal, *soft,*	1	0
Till, *with some seams of iron-stone,*	62	0
Coal, *soft,*	5	0
Till,	20	0
Marble, *full of bivalve shells,*	1	6
Till,	8	0
Free-stone, *white, very hard,*	2	8
Till, *with iron-stone,*	32	0
Coal, *soft,*	6	0
Till, *with a stratum of free-stone,*	47	6
Doggar,	0	8
Coal, *soft,*	3	0
Till, *with vegetable impressions,*	10	0
Free-stone,	6	0
Till, *with bivalve shells,*	14	0
Iron-stone, *two strata,*	0	10
Coal, *hard, good for Iron-works, Forges, &c.*	3	6
Till,	3	0
Coal, *soft,*	1	6
Till, thin seams of coal, free-stone and iron-stone, penetrated by boring,	84	0
	413	8

* *Plies,* a word used to denote very thin strata of free-stone, separated from each other by a little clay or mica.

This arrangement is not invariably the same. The stratum of marble, for example, is, in some places, no more than an inch or two in thickness, and in others it is entirely lost. The thickness of the seams of free-stone varies considerably. The coal itself is, in this respect, liable to exceptions. The strata are frequently deranged by troubles, or dykes, of which three large ones run in a direction east and west, and at pretty regular distances from each other. They are intersected by smaller ones, running generally from south to north. The derangement is so great at one place in Stoneslaw, that the hard coal, at the depth of about 50 fathoms, on the north of the dyke, is, in the space of a few yards, raised to near the surface. Owing to these troubles, the dip of the metals is various, from one foot in 6, to one in 18. The strata rise to day at one o'clock.

The general succession of strata in the space intervening between Cathkin hills on the north, and Rawhead hills on the south of Kilbride, is argillaceous free-stone, schistus, iron-stone and coal. Among these substances, however, there is no small disorder, with respect to arrangement, position and qualities.

No where in the parish are they displayed to better advantage, and are, perhaps, no where more regular

regular than in the Blackcraig. The face of this craig is about 140 feet perpendicular, and exhibits more than 40 diſtinct ſtrata, in regular ſucceſſion. Of theſe about 17 are iron-ſtone; the reſt are free-ſtone and till. The appearance, eſpecially to a perſon who takes pleaſure in contemplating the works of the Almighty, is ſo beautiful and grand, that a Gentleman, ſtruck with the ſight, gave the following account of it in the Glaſgow Mercury, May 1785. When addreſſing the inhabitants of Clydeſdale, reſpecting their manufactures, and mentioning the many local advantages they enjoyed, he ſays, " That at a place called the Blackcraig, " near Calderwood, may be counted 17 ſeams of " iron-ſtone lying one above another, a ſight, I " verily believe is not to be found any where elſe " in the world." The Gentleman who gave this account is a careful obſerver of the works of nature, and has travelled the greateſt part of Europe.

The general arrangement of the ſtrata, in different parts of the pariſh, will be ſeen from the following Tables.

RUTHERGLEN AND KILBRIDE.

A TABLE *of the* STRATA, *penetrated by boring near the Mains of Kilbride.*

	Feet.	In.
Earth,	2	0
Free-stone, *argillaceous*,	1	0
Daugh, *a soft and black substance, chiefly of clay, mica, and what resembles coal-dust*,	0	6
Free-stone, *brownish*,	12	0
Do. *white*,	3	0
Plies,	3	0
Daugh,	0	6
Plies,	2	0
Free-stone,	4	2
Till,	58	10
Iron-stone,	0	6
Till,	5	9
Whin-stone,	0	7
	93	10

HERE the search was left off, owing to an opinion that coal, at least in this country, is never got below whin-stone.

A TABLE *of the* STRATA *near Torrance.*

	Feet.	In.
Earth,	8	0
Free-stone, *whitish*,	6	0
Till,	1	4
Free-stone,	2	9
Till,		

	Feet.	In.
Till, soft and black, called the coal crop,	3	3
Till, hard,	10	0
Doggar, or Cathead band,	0	8
Till,	5	0
Coal,	1	6
Till,	4	0
Coal, called jaunt coal,	1	8
Fire-clay,	3	6
Coal, called smithie coal, because used for smith's forges,	1	2
Mill-stone grit, argillaceous, fine grained,	1	2
Till,	5	0
Plies,	3	6
Till, with iron-stone,	9	6
Coal,	0	6
Till,	1	4
	67	10

Strata in the Murrays.

	Feet.	In.
Earth and clay,	43	0
Till,	2	9
Plies, gray,	1	5
Free-stone, with vegetable impressions,	0	10
Till, black and hard,	2	1
Coal,	0	2
Free-stone,	2	0
Till,	0	10½
Free-stone, with 3 black stripes or seams,	5	2
Till,	4	8
Free-stone,	2	7

Till,

		Feet.	In.
Till, *very hard*,	-	1	3
Iron-ftone,	-	0	3
Free-ftone,	-	10	1
Till, *inflammable*,	-	0	5
Do. *not inflammable*,	-	2	0
Coal,	-	3	4
Till, *called the pavement*,	-	3	0
Coal,	-	0	7
Free-ftone, *with vegetable impreffions*,	-	2	5
Plies,	-	2	0
Till, *black*,	-	4	3
Plies,	-	0	10
Till,	-	0	5
Plies,	-	1	0
Free-ftone, *white*,	-	5	8
Till,	-	2	0
Free-ftone, *white*,	-	4	7
Plies,	-	1	8
Coal,	-	0	7
Till,	-	1	4
Free-ftone, *white*,	-	4	6
Plies,	-	1	2
Till, *hard, inflammable, with a large portion of iron*,	-	0	2
Coal,	-	0	10
Till, *pavement*,	-	2	1
		121	11¼

A few yards north of the pit in which the laft mentioned metals were dug through, is found a thick dyke of hard argillaceous free-ftone, fouth of which

which the strata are altered, as appears by the following Table.

	Feet.	In.
Earth,	18	0
Till,	2	0
Doggar, *coarse iron-stone,*	0	4
Till,	2	0
Free-stone,	9	0
Till, *with sea-shells, entrochi, &c.*	24	0
Splint-coal,	0	8
Iron-stone,	0	4
Daugh,	0	2
Till,	5	10
	62	4

A TABLE *of the* STRATA, *as they appear in the Gill, near Bogton.*

	Feet.	In.
Earth,	12	0
Free-stone,	7	0
Plies,	2	4
Coal,	0	3
Till,	2	0
Free-stone, white, of a fine close texture,	6	0
Do. very hard, called the whin-stone band,	2	0
Do. called the mill-stone band, excellent grind-stones are made of this,	8	0
	3	6
	8	4
	4	0
	6	0

RUTHERGLEN AND KILBRIDE. 293

	Feet.	In.
Iron-stone,	0	4
Till,	2	0
Iron-stone,	0	5
Till,	1	6
Iron-stone,	0	5
Till,	3	0
Iron-stone,	0	5
Till,	2	7
Iron-stone,	0	5
Till,	3	2
Iron-stone,	0	4
Till,	2	6
Iron-stone,	0	5
Till,	4	0
Iron-stone balls, *from 4 feet to a few inches in breadth, and from 6 to 2 inches in thickness: they are not the septaria: and lie in a flying stratum*,	0	6
Till,	6	0
Iron-stone, *coarse*,	1	0
Till,	3	0
Lime-stone, *good*,	4	0
Do. *coarse, with a mixture of iron*,	2	0
Chert, *or rock flint*,	0	4
Fire clay,	2	0
Sclutt, *soft, and coarse till*,	10	0
Lime-stone, *coarse, with sea-shells*	1	0
Free-stone, *calcareous, with shells*,	2	0
Earth and clay,	2	6
Till,	1	6
Lime-stone, *good*,	1	8
Do. *coarse, called the causeway bed*,	0	6
Do. *thickness not known.*		
	120	6

LIME-STONE

Lime-stone abounds in many parts of the parish; and so far as has been explored, is incumbent on alternate strata of till and iron-stone, but not on coal. The lime-stone is full of marine productions. The strata generally dip to the north-east.

It may in general be observed, that here, as well as in most places in Britain and Ireland, coal is found attended with strata, formed of matter deposited by water, as till, free-stone, &c.

Coal, in many places of Scotland, is found immediately below a thick stratum of lime-stone, containing the exuviæ of the inhabitants of the Antediluvian ocean. Examples of this we have at Hurlet, Loudoun, New-Kilpatrick, &c.

CHAP.

CHAP. VI.

OF EXTRANEOUS FOSSILS.

CONTAINING AN ACCOUNT OF VEGETABLE IMPRESSIONS, PE-
TRIFIED WOOD, SHELLS, ENTROCHI, CORALLOIDES AND
FISHES TEETH.

EXTRANEOUS, or Adventitious Fossils are such as originally were organized bodies. They are arranged into two classes. The one comprehends the fossil remains of animals and vegetables, that were natives of the land: the other, those of the sea. Both are subdivided into subordinate Orders, Genera, Species and Varieties, founded on characters established in Zoology and Botany. The parishes of Rutherglen and Kilbride contain a greater variety, in both classes, than, perhaps, any other bounds of equal extent in the world.

PETRIFIED PRODUCTIONS OF THE LAND.

THE most extensive order of terrene productions consists of *Vegetable Impressions*. They are chiefly found in argillaceous strata, above coal, in Rutherglen. Many thousands of them are contained in a
solid

solid foot of till; and make their appearance on the surfaces of the lamellæ, into which it may be subdivided. They are also found in strata of sand-stone; and likewise in pieces of iron-stone, interspersed in the till. They are thrown together in the utmost disorder; only they lie flat, in a horizontal direction. From several circumstances it appears, that they did not grow where now found; but were carried by water from their native soil, and deposited among sand or mud, now converted into stone or till.

Such a vast quantity of mud, containing many millions of vegetables, must have been collected in a deep and large bay, where the smallest particle of argilla, or mica, had sufficient time to subside. The depth of water, in which they were suspended, must have been very great. Any calculations, instituted upon phenomena, coming within the reach of our experience, may be very erroneous. In our enquiries into such subjects, great allowances must be made for the different states of the earth, at different periods. We cannot, perhaps, form an adequate idea of the state of the upper strata of the earth, soon after it emerged out of the chaotic waters, or the universal deluge. A local inundation might, for ought we know, have then produced effects, of which the recent phenomena of the world can give us no examples. We should, therefore, proceed

with

X

XI

with great caution, in drawing comparisons between the ancient and present state of the globe: and the theories we presume to make of the formation of the earth, and many of its pristine phenomena, should be proposed with the utmost diffidence.

The vegetable impressions, found in Rutherglen and Kilbride, are mostly of plants belonging to the *Cryptogamia* class; the order of *Filices;* and genera which are the indigena of woods, glens and marshes. The specimens are mostly in fragments. Some of the species are not now natives of Europe: and others have never, any where in the world, been discovered in a recent state. Their characters will best appear by the annexed plates, in which the natural size of the impressions is, in general, preserved.

Fig. 1. pl. X. seems to be an *Arundo*, or *Bamboo* of India. Fig. 2. is distorted and swollen, owing to a wound, at *a*, which it had received in a recent state. Some specimens of the Bamboo, found in free-stone, at the east quarry of Rutherglen, retain their original shape: but most of them are a little depressed. Some are of a brownish colour. Whether fig. 3. is a variety of the above is uncertain; the striæ are exceedingly minute and regular. Fig 4. appears to be an *Equisetum*, of which fig. 5. is a joint, with the leaves spread out. That fig. 6.

is a plant of the same genus does not admit of a doubt. Fig. 7. and 8. may be roots of plants, or mutilated skeletons of some of the Ferns. I never heard of them being discovered any where but at Stonelaw. Whether fig. 1. pl. XI. is of the Bamboo kind is not certain: if it is, the diameter must have been very large. It is sometimes found on coal, in which case the surface is extremely smooth. The characters of fig. 2. are not so perfect, as to ascertain the particular genus to which it belongs. Fig. 3. is probably a fragment of what Lhwyd (*Lithoph. Brit. No.* 186.) calls *Lithopteris fœmina Glocestrensis, Trichomanis pinnulis longioribus.* This variety is very rare. Fig. 4. is, by Lhwyd, called *Lithosmunda minor; sive Osmunda mineralis pinnulis brevioribus, densius dispositis.* Some of the single leaves, or pinnulæ, many of which are found separately, are two inches in length, and of a proportionable breadth. Fig. 5. from its habit, seems to be the *Osmunda spicant.* That fig. 1. pl. XII. is an *Asplenium* is highly probable. Fig. 2. is a plant, probably yet unknown, in a recent state. Fig. 3. seems to be what Lhwyd calls *Rubeola.* It bears a distant resemblance to the *Asperula odorata.* The *Equisetum,* fig. 4. is very distinct: it seems, however, to be different from fig. 4. pl. X. That fig. 5. pl. XII. belongs to the Ferns, is very probable. Certainty with respect to some of the species of these impressions cannot be obtained, till we are better acquainted with exotic plants, of the Cryptogamia

gamia clafs. The varieties above-mentioned are not equally plenty. Fig. 4. 6. 7. pl. X. and all the figures in pl. XII. are fcarce.

The ftrata of coal, in both parifhes, frequently retain many fragments of branches of trees, in a charred ftate. They lie blended together in the utmoft confufion; and many of them retain diftinct traces of the concentric lamellæ which originally compofed the ligneous part of the wood. Many of the fpecimens are replete with pyrites. Thefe once organized remains afford a ftrong proof, that vegetable fubftances were originally concerned in the formation of coal. This circumftance alone, however, is not conclufive; for feveral fpecimens of charred wood have been found in free-ftone, where there was no appearance of coal accompanying the wood. I have found fome fpecimens of charred wood, retaining its original ftructure, imbedded in whin-ftone, as in the rock of Dumbarton. Examples of this are very rare.

Exotic Pines exhibit another clafs of impreffions. They may be divided into two kinds: fuch as are fuperficial only; and fuch as retain, at leaft in part, the original fhape of the tree. The varieties they contain, however, are not numerous. Fig. 4. pl. XIII. is on a level furface, in an argillaceous free-ftone. The fpecimen was, in 1789, found in the bed of Calder

Calder water, near Torrance. Other specimens of chequered impressions, found at the same place, are considerably larger than in this draught. Fig. 6. is on till found, *ann.* 1790, in the iron-stone mines, in the lands of Basket.* It is on a concave surface, with a convex one corresponding to it. The original bark, between the two surfaces, is converted into a coally substance. Fig. 1. is perhaps of the same species, but of a much younger plant. The configurations are on a level surface, and are amongst the smallest I have seen. What renders the specimen a great curiosity is the remains of the leaves, lying on each side, as had they been pressed down by a superincumbent weight. Specimens with this peculiarity are extremely rare: two or three are all I have seen, and I know not if they have been discovered any where else. The impressions are on inflammable till, found above coal, at Stonelaw, *ann.* 1792. The till contains great numbers of bivalve shells, of the kind delineated fig. 4. pl. XVI. On the same piece of till is the impression fig. 3. pl. XIII. It is of a larger plant than the other, and the denticulations occasioned by the bases of the leaves are distinctly seen. Of this kind several specimens, on iron-stone, coal, till and free-stone, are found in many places of Scotland. The surfaces are sometimes level, but more frequently concave.

One

---

* The property of Capt. Thomas Peter of Crossbasket.

One specimen of the impression fig. 5. is all of the kind I have discovered. It is of a level surface, on iron-stone, found *ann.* 1788, near Mauchlan-hole. Specimens of figured stones, having rows of holes, in an oblique direction, are not unfrequent in Kilbride. The holes are not of the same depth nor wideness. Each of them commonly contains a small column, mostly of the shape and size of the draught fig. 7. These pillars are generally hollow, and regularly punctured on the top. They adhere to the stone at their bases, and are from $\frac{1}{4}$ to $\frac{1}{8}$ of an inch in length. In some specimens the surface of the stone, between the rows of holes, is ornamented with the rugosities, &c. of the external surface of the vegetable, from which the impression was made. These curious stones are of excellent iron-stone: they are turned out along with coal, and are mostly found in the bed of Calder water, near Torrance. Externally they are of an irregular and rugged shape, having no appearance of any organized figure; but when broken, the impressions are found in the middle of them.

The most common impression of what is supposed to be the Pine, is the kind delineated fig. 2. The specimens are chiefly on free-stone, and sometimes on coal, or till. They are ornamented with small protuberances, running obliquely round the trunk or branch. The more perfect specimens are

likewise

likewise adorned with small furrows, among the protuberances, as in the figure. This particular structure is not uncommon with many species of plants. When on free-stone the original shape of the branch is preserved entire; only the internal structure of the ligneous part is destroyed, the whole being converted into a solid mass of stone; excepting what is thought to have been the pith, which is distinguishable, and often separable from the rest. It is seldom found in the middle. The specimens are of various sizes, from 2 feet, to 2 inches in diameter; and sometimes 8, or 10 feet in length. They are seldom or never branched; and lie chiefly in a slanting, but sometimes in a horizontal direction. Not unfrequently they penetrate the thickness of the rock, and spread themselves alongst the upper surface of a stratum of coal, or other substance that may be below it. Of this we have some beautiful examples in *Glen-Garvel*, in the parish of Kilsyth. These impressions abound in coal countries; and are, in many places, not improperly known by the name of *Coal-Stalk*. This term, however, is, in Campsie, Baldernock and some other places, ascribed to a recent vegetable root, that penetrates a considerable way in the earth; and, in some few instances, even through the crevices of the free-stone itself. The shrub to which it belonged must have been cut down, when clearing the ground for cultivation. That this root, therefore, springs out of

the

the coal, and vegetates on the top, is unqueftionably a vulgar error.

Among the coal, near Torrance, is found a very curious fpecies of an exotic plant. Inftead of the protuberances, mentioned above, it is covered with oblique rows of fpines, about half an inch in length, and ⅛ in thicknefs, at the bafe: they are drawn out to a fharp point, and lie flat on the ftone. Moft of them are fractured; owing apparently to fome violent preffure: the fractures, in fome inftances, are near the bafe, in others near the point. The fpecimens are of excellent iron-ftone, and moftly retain evident marks of the pith; but are totally deftitute of the internal ftructure of the wood. They are frequently branched, the branches going off at an angle, confiderably acute: and are not oppofite; but whether fparfe or alternate, is not known. The fpecimens are commonly no longer than 5, or 6 inches; and are from 3, to 1 in diameter: thofe retaining the fpines entire are very rare.

Of all the varieties of petrified wood, in thefe bounds, the moft perfect is one found among the coal at Stonelaw. Moft of the fpecimens are of the fize of the draught fig. 6. pl. XII. The bark, which is regularly denticulated by a kind of fharp pointed papillæ, appears to have been cut, or broken afunder, on the one fide; and to have contracted itfelf

itfelf backward, as we fometimes fee examples in the bark of living plants. Owing to this difruption the fibrous, or vafcular ftructure of the ligneous part is exhibited. When viewed on the fide, at *a*, it appears to be ftriated: but when viewed on the end, at *b*, a great number of pores are feen. Thefe pores are filled with white Selenite, which is fet off to advantage by their being inclofed in a very black, ftoney fubftance, containing a confiderable proportion of lime. From the ftructure this petrifaction would appear to belong to the Cane, rather than to the Pine. None of the fpecimens are branched, or jointed: they are not found in great plenty.

Impressions of the bark of what feems to have been the Oak, Elm, &c. are fometimes, though fparingly, found in free ftone.

PETRIFIED PRODUCTIONS OF THE SEA.

The exuviæ of the once animated inhabitants of the ocean, far furpafs, in variety and number, the petrified remains of vegetables. They are arranged into four claffes, namely, *Shells*, *Entrochi*, *Coralloides* and *Fifhes Teeth*. The figures referred to for the illuftration of thefe claffes, exhibit the natural fize of the fpecimens, from which they were drawn, unlefs otherwife mentioned.

SHELLS.

SHELLS.

Order I. Univalves.

A species of the *Patella*, or *Limpet*, is found among till, incumbent on lime-stone, in many of the quarries in Kilbride. The specimens sometimes adhere to small stones and fragments of shells. They are generally small, few of them being larger than the draught, fig. 10. pl. XV. The native shell is, for the most part, entire: it is of a bluish colour inclining to black. The apex is placed a little to one side: it is not perforated, but all the casts, where the shell is worn off, have a small slit, apparently occasioned by a thin prominent ridge, on the inside of the apex of the shell, fig. 9. Good specimens are found in Magpie-hill quarry, parish of Stewarton. Limpets are but rarely found fossil in Britain.

Orthoceratites, the *Tubuli concamerati* of Klein; or, according to Da Costa (*Conchol.* p. 156.) the " Orthoceros, simple straight conical shells, or nowise turbinated; and gradually tapering from a broad end to a sharp-pointed top, like a strait horn, whence their name. They are chambered from bottom to top, and have a siphunculus, or pipe of communication, from chamber to chamber." Two species

species are found in Kilbride: the sulcated, *superficie sulcata*, fig. 2. pl. XVI. and the smooth, *superficie lævi*, fig. 3. They are generally in casts. Both kinds, wholly covered with the original shell, are found at Thornlie-bank in the parish of Pollock, formerly the Eastwood. They lie in a horizontal position, in a thick stratum of till. The shell of the smooth kind is of a horny appearance, and a dirty white colour. The sulcated is finely striated in the same direction with the *sulci*. The shells of both species are very thin, and extremely well polished on the inside. Specimens retaining the shell, are, in the fossil kingdom, very rare. The greatest number of the specimens are bruised, apparently by some violent pressure, when in a recent state: the bruises are commonly near the bottom, though in some specimens they are almost at the point. The Septa are thin, convex and polished, like the recent Lituus. In some specimens the pipe is thick and rugose. Perhaps this peculiarity is common to a certain part of the pipe in every specimen. Of this peculiar structure I have two examples from Hermyres.* They are corroded on that side, which, in other specimens, is usually bruised. By this means the internal structure of the chambers, &c. is exposed to view. The pipe is swelled out to an uncommon size, is very thick and rugose, and has the appearance of a string of beads, fig. 1. The pipe,

* The property of John Boyes, Esq;

pipe, as at *a*, adheres to one side of the shell, and is perforated in the center. Da Costa (*Conch.* p. 156.) mentions a similar specimen, a draught of which he takes from Breynius *de polythalamiis.* The longest specimen of the Orthoceratites I have met with is 5¼ inches: it was mutilated at both ends; the diameter of the thickest was an inch, of the other ¼. Some fragments are nearly 3 inches in diameter.

This part of the country affords but few specimens of the *Cornua Ammonis*, the *Nautilites*, of Lhwyd; and the *Serpent stones* of the vulgar. Two varieties are all I have met with in Kilbride. The spires of the one are smooth and round, without any depression or *sulci;* the specimen is about 6 inches broad. The other, which is nearly of the same size, is likewise smooth, but the sides are flat, and are destitute of *sulci.* Both kinds were found at Hermyres.

Two species of the *Cochleæ Helices*, are all that have been discovered in this place. Casts of the one, having 5 round spires, are found in lime-stone, at Limekilns. The other is never found without the shell, which is of a horny appearance, and consists of 5 spires of a triangular shape, and which are always replete with till. 1 never found specimens of this variety imbedded in stone. The largest are not above 1¼ inch broad, and some of them are

very

very small. They are found at a quarry at Lickprivick, and in many other places in the west of Scotland.

The shell, fig. 8. pl. XIV. seems to be a chambered *Nautilus*: it is thin and deeply umbilicated. The specimens frequently retain the shell, which is thin, polished, and of a horny appearance. They are found, though sparingly, at Lawrieston, &c. One that was found at Thornlie-bank is almost wholly inclosed in the valve of a bivalve shell.

The shell, fig. 9. is probably a *Nautilus*; it is of a globose form, and beautifully adorned with fine prominent threads, giving it a kind of striated appearance, and is not chambered. The specimens, for the most part, retain the shell, which is of a whitish colour, pretty thick, and very well polished within. Some are an inch in diameter, others not nearly so big. They are found at Lawrieston.

The varieties of the *Turbo*, fig. 1, 5. are not numerous in a fossil state. Of the *Terebra*, or *Turbo clavicula longissima*, are two species. One is striated transversely, fig. 7. the other, fig. 11. is striated spirally, and is found in a recent state on all the shores of Europe. The till in which they are enveloped lies between the two strata of limestone at Stuartfield and Lawrieston. Many specimens

mens are no thicker than a fine thread, and about $\frac{1}{12}$ of an inch in length. By a microscope they are found to be equally perfect, and to contain the same number of spires, with the largest specimens. *Quære*, if they are young shells, how come they to have as many spires as the oldest in the species?

THE *Buccinum*, fig. 2, 3, 4. does not afford, in Kilbride, many species. Fig. 4. is of a white colour, and transversely striated.

THE *Trochus* is not plenty. The species which Da Costa calls *Buccinum Heterostrophon*, or other handed whelk, in which the spires take a direction from the left to the right hand, instead of from the right to the left, like other shells, is sometimes, but not frequently, found, fig. 18. Specimens are met with at Limekilns and Stuartfield quarries. Along with them the species, fig. 10. is sometimes found. It bears a near resemblance to the *Umbilicaris*.

THE *Serpula planorbis* may be ranked among the univalves. I have not met with more specimens than two or three, adhering to fragments of shells.

ORDER

Order II. Bivalves.

Divifion Firft. *Shells having both valves equal.*

The *Cockle*, fig. 2. pl. XV. is not frequently found in Kilbride. I picked up fome fpecimens near the Blackcraig. Some found at Thornlie-bank are fo perfect that they appear to be living. They are imbedded in Schiftus along with Orthoceratites, Buccini, Entrochi, &c.

Of the *Multarticulate Cockle*, fig. 5, 6. exhibit two fpecies. The hinge, which is obfervable in the cafts only, confifts of about 12 teeth on each valve. Both kinds are found at Lickprivick, Shields and Lawriefton. The beft fpecimens I have feen were lodged in till, on the banks of the Water of Aven, near Netherfield, in the parifh of Avendale. Some are fo perfect that feveral perfons, fuppofing them to be living, have attempted to open them. The fhell, in both fpecies, is white, and commonly in a high ftate of prefervation. The fpecies, fig. 5. is finely ftriated.

Two fpecies of the *Mufcle* are found in Kilbride, fig. 5, 6. pl. XVI. Specimens of the former are in cafts, and are very rare. Numberlefs fpecimens of the latter are imbedded in till incumbent on iron-
stone

stone at Mauchlan-hole; and sometimes in the iron-stone itself. They are mostly in single valves, and lie flat in a horizontal position. Whole specimens are found, but rarely, at Lawrieston.

The marble in Rutherglen, already mentioned, abounds with a vast quantity of the Muscle, delineated fig. 4. Some entire specimens are enveloped in the till, containing impressions of the Pine, formerly described. The shells are commonly entire, and were, probably, produced in fresh water.

The most uncommon shells in this division are three kinds of what may be called *Microscopic*. They are, with difficulty perceived, by the naked eye, to be shells. The specimens, when viewed by the microscope, appear to be very perfect: but I have sometimes met with detached valves. None are so numerous as that represented fig. 15. pl. XIV. The shell is of a pure white colour, and retains an extremely fine polish. The figure is greatly magnified. The species, fig. 20. is commonly five or six times larger than the former. The specimens are not nearly so numerous: they are white, and retain a good polish. Some of them exhibit marks of bruises which appear to have been given them in a recent state. The scarcest and most curious is the one delineated fig. 16. Different views of it are given fig. 17, 21. The shell is of a brown colour,

and

and ornamented with minute indentings. The dots in fig. 17. exhibit the natural fize of the fhell.

These very uncommon, and, as far as I know, hitherto undefcribed fhells are found at Lawriefton and Stuartfield. I have not been able, even after a diligent fearch, to find them any where elfe, except in a lime-ftone quarry about 15 miles weft from Newcaftle-upon-Tyne, near the fpot where the Roman Wall is interfected by Watling-Street. What I found there was only the variety, fig. 20. and the fpecimens were very rare. From Kilbride, however, I have made a collection of thefe extremely fmall objects of nature, that might furnifh abundance of fpecimens for all the Mufeums in Europe. They are beft exhibited by putting them, in feparate apartments, in a fmall picture frame, with a glafs before them. By this means a magnifying glafs can with eafe be applied to them.

Divifion Second. *Shells having unequal valves.*

The *Anomia* contains the greateft number of genera, in this divifion. Fabius Columna, an accurate naturalift, was the firft who introduced this name into the fyftem of foffil fhells. Finding that many fpecies were not defcribed by writers on Conchology, he called them *Conchæ rariores Anomiæ*. This name,

name, ever since, has been adopted as the *nomen proprium* of that numerous family of shells. I shall divide them into three kinds. 1. *Læves.* 2. *Striatæ.* 3. *Echinatæ.*

First. *Anominæ læves.* The species which to appearance is the most simple, is the one delineated fig. 9. pl. XVI. Both valves are convex. Great abundance of bruised ones and fragments are found at Lawrieston. The Floors quarry, near Johnston-Bridge, contains good specimens of this shell. In some the beaks are not perforated. Along with it is found, but not frequently, a species in which the beak is very seldom perforated. The shell is broader than the other; whiter in the colour; not of so horny an appearance, and is destitute of the shallow groove in the under valve.

In the species, fig. 12. pl. XIV. the beak is never perforated, and the hinge is on a straight line. Most perfect specimens of this shell are plentifully found in a lime quarry, on the east bank of Aven, a little below Strathaven. Elsewhere, as far as I know, they are very scarce.

Second. *Anomiæ striatæ.* To this family belongs the genus represented fig. 6. It is found in great plenty in several places of Kilbride, but the specimens are mostly bruised, as in the figure. They

They are, in moſt places, found in the ſame imperfect ſtate. Some entire ones, however, are found in the Floors quarry, already mentioned.

The ſhell, fig. 1. pl. XV. is very beautiful. The ſpecimens from Lawrieſton, and ſome other places of Kilbride, are in fragments, or greatly bruiſed. The hinge is exactly in the middle of the ſtraight line below the beak. It conſiſts of two teeth in the under valve, which are inſerted into two correſponding furrows in the upper. The ſtraight line below the beak is not multarticulated. Specimens, in great perfection, are found at Thornlie-bank: ſome of them retain the marks of bruiſes received in a living ſtate.

The ſpecies, fig. 14. pl. XIV. is found in a quarry at Philipshill, and very plentifully in the lands of Treehorn, near Beith. The one valve is only a little ſmaller than the other. The ſpecimens are thin; of a white colour; and finely ſtriated. The valves are ſometimes detached. Fig. 13. ſhows the inſide of one of them.

Third. *Anomiæ Echinatæ*. By theſe are underſtood unequal valved foſſil ſhells that are furniſhed with ſpines.

The ſmalleſt and moſt numerous in Kilbride is the

the species delineated fig. 4. pl. XV. The under valve is convex, having the contour greatly curved over the upper valve, which is almost level, or a little concave; the whole making a thick semiglobose shell. The spines are few, and regularly placed, and are all on the under valve. They are long and slightly flexible. Their appearance is that of wires of Mother of Pearl, retaining the most finished polish. They consist of two parts. An external covering composed of a great number of concentric lamellæ, extremely thin, and shining like white mica; they constitute about the half of the thickness of the spine. Within that is a white, solid, opaque substance, which composes the other part. The lamellæ seem to be an elongation of the several coats, or lamellæ of the shell, to which the spines adhere, or rather out of which they seem to grow. They were not, therefore, moved by articulations, or cartilages, like the spines of the recent Echini. Many of the fragments are greatly bruised and flattened, which injuries they must have received when recent. They are placed on the under valve in such a manner, as to assist the animal in suspending itself on the surface of the water: they might also be helpful in procuring food, and warding off danger. The specimen from which the figure was taken is very singular. It lies horizontally in a piece of till, in which it was originally deposited. The spines are stretched out as in the figure. The

peculiar

peculiar conftruction of the infide of the upper valve is exhibited fig. 3.

A species larger than the former is found in all the lime-ftone quarries in the parifh. The fpecimens are commonly about the bignefs of an hen's egg. The beautiful conftruction of the infide of the upper valve is delineated fig. 12. pl. XVI. The fpecimen from which the draught was taken was found at Limekilns.

The largeft of all the foffil fhells in Kilbride is a fpecies belonging to this genus. The fpecimens are 5 or 6 inches in length, and of a correfponding breadth and thicknefs. They are generally imbedded in lime ftone. The colour is whitifh, and fometimes faintly tinged with red. By workmen they are called lime-ftone oyfters. I have feen beautiful fpecimens of this fhell in a quarry near Bathgate.

To this divifion belongs a genus, the fpecimens of which may be called *Conchæ pilofæ*, rather than *Echinatæ*. Both valves are entirely covered with very fmall fpines refembling fine hair. They are of the fame colour and confiftency with the fpines above defcribed, and are placed in rows nearly concentric with the beak. The draught, fig. 7. pl. XV. is partly covered with them, and partly not. They are

are so numerous that a shell of the size of the figure contains upwards of 10000. Their true length, from any specimens I have seen, cannot be ascertained: they do not seem, however, to have reached far beyond the contour of the shell. They lie so closely together that the surface of the shell is entirely concealed from view. The insides of the valves are ornamented with short papillæ, placed in rows like the spines. The specimens of the shells are of different diameters. Some are not above half an inch in length, and others are as large as the figure. They are very sparingly found among till in lime-stone quarries.

PECTEN. Of this family the most delicate and beautiful shell is delineated, fig. 11. pl. XVI. The under valve is very convex; the upper very concave; and both are so thin that they are frequently taken for a single valve: and both are finely striated. In some specimens they can be easily separated from one another without injury; in which case the internal structure is fully exposed to view. They are furnished with very small papillæ, and other configurations, as in fig. 10. This beautiful and rare fossil is found among the till that separates the two lime-stone posts at Lawrieston.

FIG. 13. represents a species that is but rarely found in this country. Some specimens are of an elliptical shape.

THE

THE largest of the pectens, in these bounds, is delineated fig. 19. pl. XIV. Some specimens are larger than the draught; but others are no bigger than a farthing. They are found, but sparingly, at Philipshill quarry. I have seen good specimens in a lime-stone quarry at Darnley.

A very small and beautiful pecten is delineated fig. 8. pl. XV. Specimens of this kind are very rare: the one from which the figure was taken was found at Limekilns.

Fossil *Echini*, or the *Echinatæ* of Hill, are very scarce in this country. I have not observed more species than one, and the specimens were always in fragments; a draught of one is given fig. 7. pl. XVI. Along with them are found, in most of the quarries in Kilbride, a few of the *Aculei Echinorum*, fig. 8. Some of the fragments are a little larger than the figures; but most of them are less. Good specimens of both are found at Craiginglen, parish of Campsie.

ENTROCHI.

THE *Entrochi* comprehend a class of fossils, the recent characters of which are not well known. They have obtained various names, as *Screw-stones*;
Fairy

Fairy-beads, of the vulgar in England; *Witch-beads*, of the vulgar in Scotland; by workmen in Kilbride they are more properly called *Limestone-beads*. They are frequently called *St. Cuthbert's beads*, from a vulgar opinion that they were made by that holy man; or because they were used in the Rosaries, worn by the devotees of that Saint.* It is not in England only that they have obtained a name from a Romish ecclesiastic: on the continent they have been known by the name of *Nummuli Sancti Bonifacii*. Linnæus considering this fossil as the remains of an animal, which he ranks under the *Zoophyta*, calls it *Isis Entrocha stirpe testacea tereti, articulis orbiculatis perforatis, ramis verticillatis dichotomis.*† The name Entrochi was, more than two centuries ago, given them by Geo. Agricola. The propriety of the name appears from their construction; for they consist of a great number of beads, or whirls connected with one another by means of futures, or minute striæ. These beads, when found separately, are called *Trochitæ*. They are composed of calcareous rhomboidal spar, of a lamellated texture, but the lamellæ diverge from the center of the entrochi

---

* St. Cuthbert was the eighth Bishop of Landisferne, about the latter end of the 7th century, and highly famed, in legendary records, for his piety and austerity, when living; and, for miracles performed by his body, when dead.

† Syst. Nat. p. 1288.

entrochi in an oblique direction. By Hill (Hist. of Fossils, p. 653.) it is called an obliquely arranged, tabulated spar. It readily dissolves in acids, leaving a little clay, or selenite. At first they were supposed to be *Lapides sui generis*, originally produced in the earth. This theory was too gross to be long retained by careful observers of nature. It was soon believed that they were productions of the ancient ocean: but whether they belonged to animals or vegetables, was uncertain. They are now generally thought to be Vertebra of the Encrinus, Medusa, or some such animal. Their true history, however, is far from being well known.

The entrochi are commonly of a whitish gray colour; but in general they partake of the same tinge with the substance in which they are inclosed. From several specimens it would appear that their constituent parts were a Medulla, a Cortex, and what may be called the main body, that lies between, and resembles the ligneous part of a plant. Examples of this are given in fig. 8, 10. pl. XVII. *a, a* is part of the cortex adhering to the main body. The specimens from which I took the figures had, probably, been partly decomposed, prior to the time when they became fossil. These component parts seem originally to have possessed different degrees of solidity, by which some of them were able to resist, for a longer time than others, the action of the corroding matter, to which they were exposed.

The

The proportion which the medulla bears to the diameter, is not alike in every specimen: nor are the medullæ uniformly of the same shape. Some of them are oblong, as in fig. 1. In this variety they change their direction in the same bead, for if, on the one side, the medulla lies in the direction as at *a*, it will take, on the other, the direction, as at *b*. If the medulla is pervious, which it does not appear to be, the contortion must be exceedingly quick, since the space in which it is made, does not sometimes exceed the eighth part of an inch. In some few specimens the medulla is triangular, or quadrangular, as in fig. 2, 3. and sometimes hexangular, but this is extremely rare. In some it is pentangular, fig. 4. but in far the greatest number of specimens, it is round, as in fig. 5. Brachia adhering to specimens of the pentagonal kind, have sometimes an oblong, or triagonal medulla. This part of their structure, therefore, is an improper mark on which to fix their classification.

Next to the medulla is the main body; draughts of which are given fig. 6, 7, 9. Its proportionable thickness is different, in different specimens: in general, however, it is about $\frac{1}{4}$ of the diameter. At the divisions between the beads, it projects farther than in any other part, as at *a*, fig. 6. This prominency enters a corresponding cavity in the cortex. It frequently has two thin plates, one on each side,

running

running the whole length, an example of which is given at *a*, fig. 7.

The cortex is sometimes found detached from the other parts, as in fig. 13. The concave surface, which, in the figure, is expofed to view, and is full of ridges and furrows, is wholly covered with ſtriæ, or futures, anſwerable to correſponding ones in the main body.

The ſtriæ, with which this claſs of foſſils is always ornamented, are moſtly bifurcated, and very diſtinct. They are ſeldom viſible in fractures, newly made. It is hardly poſſible to diſlocate the beads from one another, without violence to their ſtructure: and the fractures are ſeldom horizontal, but extremely irregular. But as vaſt numbers of the beads are found ſeparately, without any injury in the moſt minute ſtriæ, and as it is impoſſible to make ſuch a ſeparation, in their preſent ſtate, it follows that theſe diſlocations were made, prior to the time when the entrochi became foſſil. They muſt alſo have been made with very great eaſe, ſince the fineſt and moſt tender of the beads were in no danger of being broken, or the extremely minute ſutures injured in any reſpect. Many of theſe diſlocations appear to have been made by a preſſure acting equally upon the entrochi, at the ſame time, as fig. 2, 3, pl. XVIII. This curious foſſil ſeems to have been frangible, in

a

a recent state; and capable to receive compressions and fractures, of which living shells are susceptible, fig. 6.

Specimens of entrochi are of all intermediate sizes, from the thickness of a small pin, to an inch in diameter: and some specimens are five inches long. They are all in fragments, lying confusedly in every direction, and imbedded in various substances, as lime-stone, free-stone, till and clay. The peculiarities of the whirls or beads are considerable. In the specimen, fig. 15. pl. XVII. they are equally thick, without any convexity or depression in the middle. In fig. 20. they are likewise equally thick, but rise to a sharp ridge in the middle: in specimens of this kind the striæ are remarkably fine. In the specimen, fig. 11. they are regularly thicker and thinner, and more or less prominent in proportion to their thickness. The round and pentagonal medullæ belong indiscriminately to this variety. Sometimes the whirls are concave, fig. 14. at other times convex, fig. 12. In these varieties the oblong medulla is very frequent. The species, fig. 5. pl. XVIII. is pentangular, with a round medulla. The surface of some varieties, as fig. 19, 22. pl. XVII. is rough, owing to small papillæ. In some specimens the whirls are extremely thin, fig. 21. The specimen from which the draught was taken, is $\frac{1}{4}$ of an inch in circumference, and contains 35 beads in the space of half an inch; a circumſtance never, perhaps, before met with, in an entrochi of ſuch a diameter: the medulla is pentagonal. Some ſpecimens are curved, and uniformly ſerrated on the concave ſide, fig. 8. pl. XVIII. They are always thicker at one end than at the other, and diminiſh gradually to a point: the medulla is round. From a fragment, fig. 7. it is probable, that the brachia of the common round entrochi terminated in this variety. Some appear to have been wounded in a recent ſtate, fig. 11 this is indicated by an unuſual ſwelling, which, in every caſe, exhibits a large and deep puncture, probably the cauſe of the ſwelling.

The *Brachia*, which are not uniform in their direction, lay a foundation for ſeveral varieties. Many of them make acute angles with the ſtem, fig. 17. pl. XVII. others, right, fig. 18. The greateſt number are ſparſe; but ſome few are oppoſite, fig. 18. They penetrate deeper than the cortex, but do not extend to the medulla. Some of them, as in fig. 15. are inſerted in one of the beads only; but others extend over a conſiderable number, fig. 16. The place of their inſertion, at *a*, is large and hollow. Some ſpecimens are found having one end convex, exactly correſponding to the cavity in the ſtem where it was inſerted, and from which it ſeems to have been torn. I never obſerved any marks of brachia on the ſpecimens

that

XVII

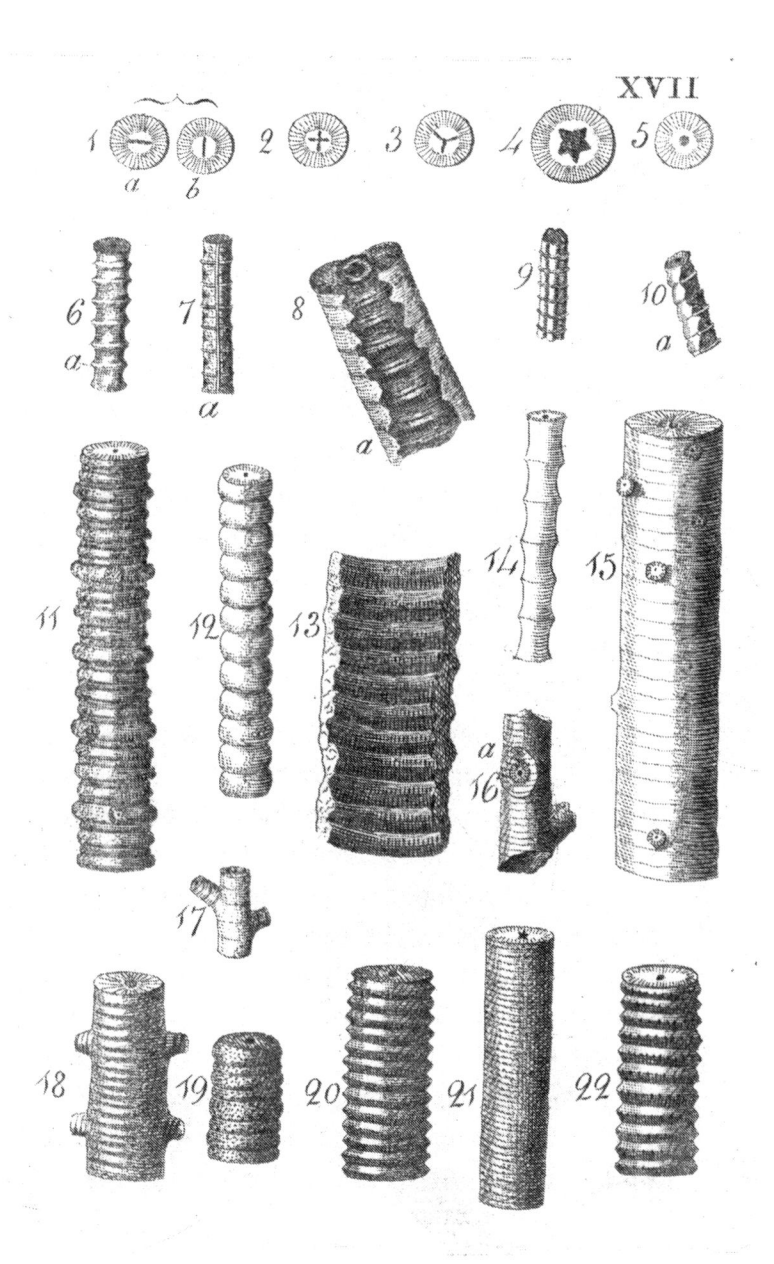

XVIII

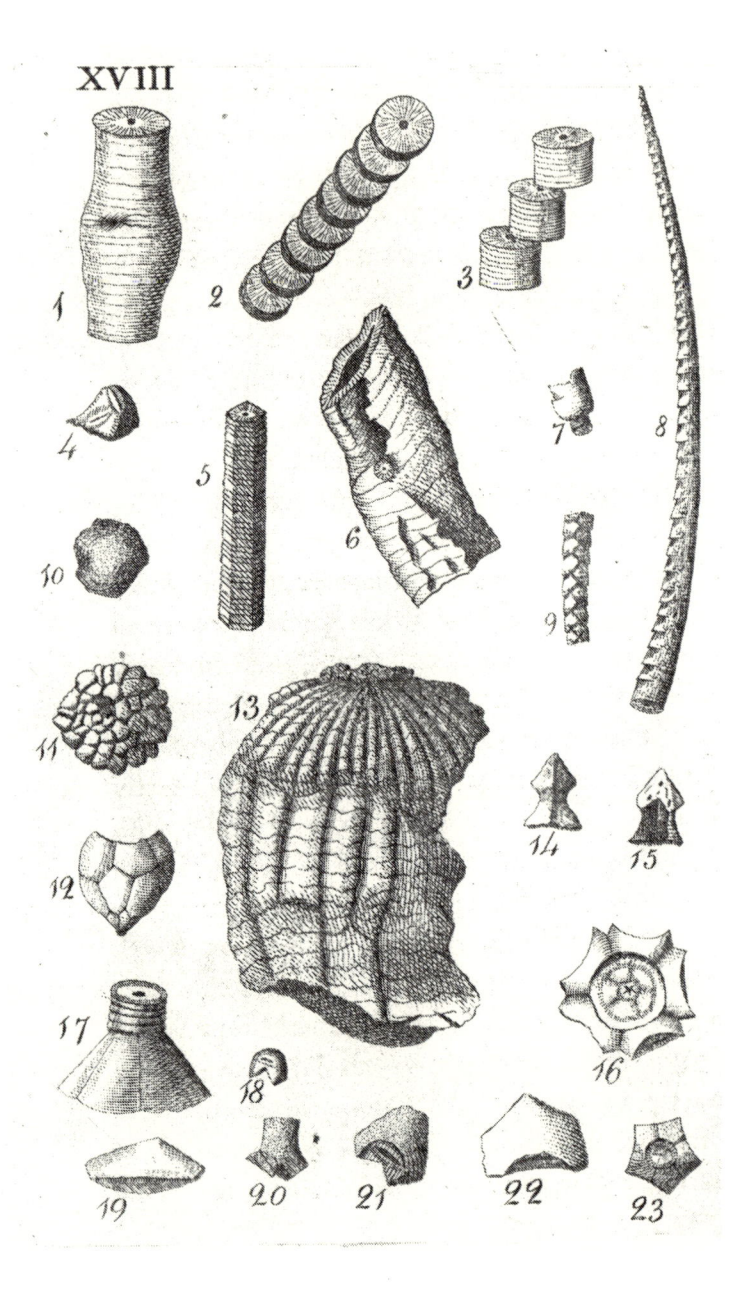

that are curved and ferrated. Fig. 13. pl. XVIII. reprefents a fragment of the *Encrinus*, the fuppofed head of the entrochi. The fpecimen from which it was taken was found, along with entrochi, fhells, &c. in till incumbent on lime-ftone at Hermyres; and is the only one of the kind I ever faw. The pieces of which it is compofed are joined to one another by means of futures. Many of the quarries contain fragments of a different kind: one of which is delineated fig. 12. It is made up of five-fided pieces, that are fmooth on both fides, and about $\frac{1}{10}$ of an inch in thicknefs: they are concave within, anfwerable to the convexity without. Great numbers of thefe pieces are found feparately, but feldom conjoined. Two or three whole fpecimens were all I could find: they are open at top, and commonly full of till. The bafis is made up of 5 pieces, of a different fhape from the reft; very much refembling the Calex in vegetables. Thefe pieces are fo exactly fitted in the lower end as to form a circle, with radii, and a medulla, correfponding to the ftem of an entrochi, as in fig. 23. The upper edges of the pieces at the top are furnifhed with ftriæ, which muft have correfponded with other pieces of a fimilar conftruction, probably the fragments reprefented fig. 14. This fragment, which is always found feparately, is raifed up like a ridge, on the one fide, but hollowed out into a groove, on the other, as in fig. 15. Draughts of detached bafes are given fig. 16, 17.

THE

The specimen, fig. 11. is compofed of fmall pieces, of different fizes. This variety is very fcarce; two fpecimens were all I could find. They are greatly crufhed, and have the fame appearance on both fides. Originally they were, perhaps, fhaped like a ball. Having no remains of entrochi adhering to them, it is uncertain whether they belonged to that genus or not. Several fragments, or fingle pieces of confiderably large dimenfions, fig. 10. are fometimes found.

Fig. 9. is a draught of a fragment of what Lhwyd (*Lithoph. Brit. No.* 1106.) calls *Aftropodium multijugum, five Loricatum cinereum feptentrionalium. Encrinus cinereus Lachmundi.* He fpeaks of it as a very rare foffil, that was firft difcovered in England, by William Nicolfon, Archdeacon of Carlifle, who found them along with entrochi in lime quarries in Wales. It is a fragment of what Whitehurft calls *lilium capidium.* It confifts of fmall pieces connected by means of ftriated articulations, as in fig. 18. which exhibits one of the fingle pieces. Specimens are found in many of the lime quarries in Kilbride.

Fig. 4, 19, 20, 21, 22. are the delineations of fragments which commonly go under the name of *Aftropodia.* They feem to be parts of the Encrinus, &c. Some of them, as fig. 20, 21. are finely granulated.

granulated. All the varieties are found, with shells, &c. in most of the lime quarries.

CORALLOIDES.

Coralloides, or Corals in a fossil state, belonged originally to that class of submarine plants commonly called *Lithophyta*. The parish of Kilbride affords several varieties. The *Junci Lapidei* are not scarce at Philipshill, fig. 12. pl. XIX. They are generally imbedded in lime-stone or till, and lie parallel to one another. Sometimes a mass of them containing many thousands, or rather millions, is found in some quarries. Sometimes they are separable, but frequently not. They consist of perpendicular lamellæ, intersected horizontally, at small distances, which give them a radiated structure. Few specimens are thicker than a goose-quill. Whether fig. 13. is a distinct species, or only a variety, I shall not determine. The specimens are generally flat and branched: some of them retain what seems to be the remains of a cortex, as in the figure. Some specimens of the *Astroitæ* are found in a field near Crosshill: some of the radiations are about half an inch in diameter. The varieties, fig. 9, 10, 11. are beautiful on account of their denticulations, &c. They are very rare. The *Fungites*, fig.

fig. 6. pl. XX. affords a confiderable number of fpecimens of various dimenfions, from a quarter of an inch, to two inches in diameter. Internally they are of a radiated ftructure, arifing from the regular interfection of perpendicular and horizontal lamellæ, of which they are moftly compofed. They vary in colour according to the colour of the fubftance in which they are enveloped; generally the lamellæ are white, and the reft blackifh. In their original ftate they adhered to ftones, and other hard bodies in the bottom of the fea: for which reafon the bafis, or broad end, where the adhefion took place, retains the impreffion of the fhape of the body on which it grew. The only inftance I have met with of the adhefion, in a petrified ftate, is on the fragment of a fhell, fig. 5. This peculiarity, as it confirms, without a doubt, the manner of their growth, adds no fmall value to the fpecimen from which the figure was taken.

The *Millepore* is a very beautiful genus of the coralloides. It abounds in moft of the lime quarries, not only in Kilbride, but in the weft of Scotland. The fpecimens are in fragments, and commonly branched. They are from the thicknefs of a fine hair, to that of a large quill. Some fpecimens continue to adhere to the fhells, &c. on which they were originally formed, as fig. 1. The pores are round, and of different diameters in the fame fpecimen,

XIX

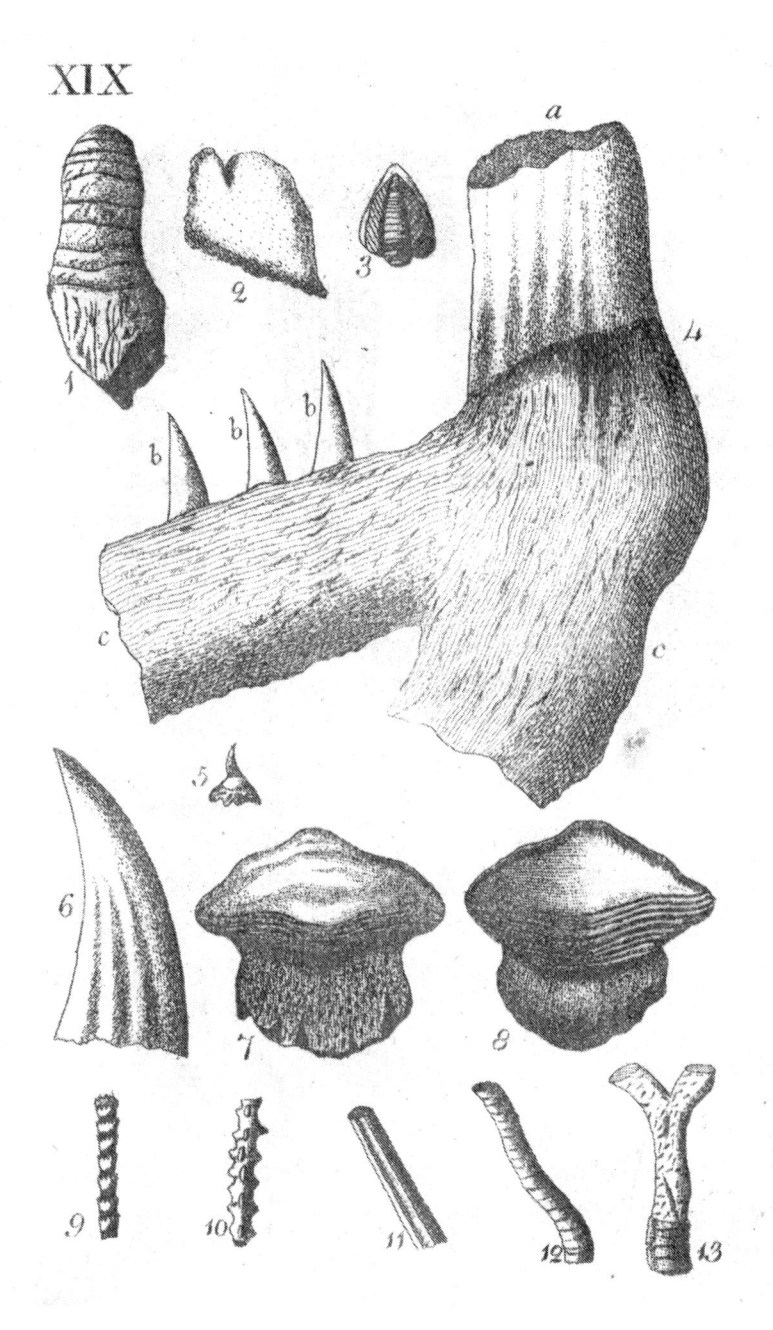

XX

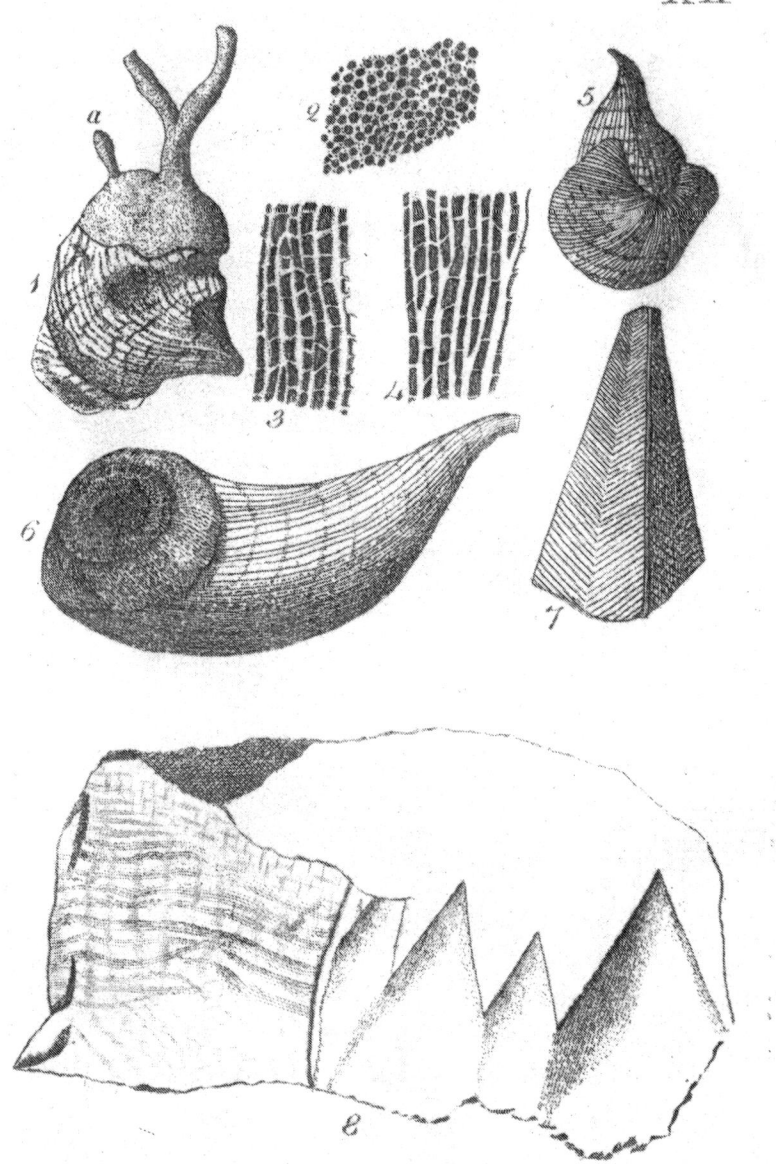

men, fig. 2. which is greatly magnified. The extremities of the branches were originally round, as at *a*. The millepore is frequently spread on the surfaces of shells, entrochi, &c. like the *Seratula pumila*.

The *Eschara*, *Retepori*, or *Fan coral*, is another beautiful genus of Coralloides which abounds in Kilbride. It is found, with shells, &c. among till incumbent on lime-stone; and the specimens are generally lying flat, some of them covering a space of several inches square. They are commonly punctured on one side, as in fig. 3. and smooth on the other, as in fig. 4. Some specimens are very fine and close in the reticulations. Along with them is found a kind in which the whole surface is rough like a rasp or file. It spreads itself on shells, entrochi, &c.

FISHES TEETH.

Of these this part of the country affords but a small variety. The *Plectronites*, fig. 5. pl. XIX. is seldom larger than the figure: some specimens are partly worn away at the point. The Incisores, fig. 7, 8. are found along with the former in some quarries in Kilbride, and at Lochrig quarry* in the parish

* The property of Capt. M. Stewart of Lochrig.

parish of Stewarton. The specimens are seldom larger than the figure, but some of them less. The figures represent both sides. The edge is very sharp, and minutely striated or cut. The colour is generally white: in one specimen, however, it is bluish: the enamel is commonly in high perfection. The root is a dull grayish colour. It is a beautiful and scarce fossil. The teeth delineated fig. 4. are very singular. The fragment of the great tooth, broken off at *a*, shows a texture extremely compact. The enamel on it, and also on the smaller ones, *b b b* is of a brownish colour, and perfectly entire. Whether the substance *c c* is the root of the tooth, or part of the jaw-bone, I shall not determine: it is of a whitish colour, and not very compact. This curious fossil was found among schistus, in the quarry at Philipshill. The fragment fig. 6. is of the same kind of tooth: it is grooved like the other, and is of the same colour and texture. It was found in the till above coal, at Stonelaw. The tooth fig. 1. is probably a molares; specimens are found at the quarry at Philipshill so often mentioned already.* It preserves little or no enamel, and is not very compact. Fig. 2. is the delineation of a fragment of a crustaceous animal; it retains a fine gloss. The specimen fig. 3. is supposed to be the petrified palate of a fish. The class to which the curious fossil, fig. 7. pl. XX. originally belonged, is not, so far as

* The property of John Reid of Kittochside, Esq.

I know, determined. The specimens are in casts of iron-stone, sometimes found inclosed in iron-stone like a *nucleus;* at other times found among till along with marine shells, &c. Specimens are very rare.

I shall conclude the chapter with a few observations concerning the petrified exuviæ of the ancient ocean.

1. These once organized bodies are imbedded in various substances, as till, lime-stone, argillaceous free-stone, iron-stone and soft clay. It has been generally thought, that none of them existed in siliceous substances, or were ever petrified into that kind of earth. Some late discoveries, however, put a negative on that opinion. Several specimens of a siliceous substance, containing great abundance of shells, entrochi, &c. were lately found in the lands of Bogstoun,* in the neighbourhood of Beith. The shells, which are inseparably united with the stone, are white, of a fine texture, and not of a sparry, but flinty appearance and fracture: the rest of the stone is blackish. Both strike fire copiously with steel. Specimens of a similar nature are found in a quarry at Bathgate.

2. Bivalve

* The property of Robert Montgomery of Bogstoun, Esq.

2. Bivalve shells, with both valves entire as when in life, are found imbedded in the same stratum, along with univalves, entrochi, &c.

3. By far the greatest number of specimens retain the shells, and many of them preserve evident marks of violent contusions, which they must have received in a living or recent state: and not a few of them had been worn by attrition, seemingly on the sea-shore.

4. Fossil shells, supposed to have been *pelagia*, as the orthoceratites, &c. are found along with shells that are believed to be *littorales*, as the limpet.

5. These remains of the ancient ocean become highly interesting, when we consider them as furnishing us with an undeniable proof, that the earth, in some remote period, underwent a very great change. It is certain that these bodies are not *lapides sui generis*, produced from the *semina* of shell-fish, &c. carried out of the sea, up into the air, by vapours, whirlwinds, &c. and afterwards falling down in rain, were deposited in the earth, where they arrived to the state in which we now find them. This was the belief of some naturalists of no small note. (Lithoph. Brit. p. 134.) It is evident, on the slightest attention, that these bodies possessed

possessed organization and life, in the same manner that shell-fish and other marine productions do at present. It is almost certain, that most of them lived and died in the places where now found; and that these places were once covered with sea. From this view of them some plausible theories of the earth have been formed; and a multiplicity of arguments drawn to illustrate the causes by which the great revolutions of the earth were brought about. Facts, however, are daily occurring which stand in opposition to most of these theories, and prove them to have been too hastily made. The more enquiries, unbiassed by theories, we make, and the greater number of facts that are undisguisedly related, the more able, surely, will mankind be to discover the phenomena by which the globe of the earth was thrown into its present state. I can say for my own part, that the more attentively I enquire into this subject, and the greater number of theories I consult, the more clearly I perceive the truth of the sacred theory given by Moses.

6. The serious contemplation of these natural objects affords a great source of pleasure to an inquisitive mind. They exhibit, in clear characters, the wisdom and goodness of the Deity. They lead back our ideas to the most remote ages of time, when these, now petrified, substances answered, by their various functions, some important purpose in

the scale of animated existence. It must afford rational pleasure to reflect upon the means by which these exuviæ have, for thousands of years, been preserved, without being totally destroyed: how some fragments as thin as paper, and equally fine with the hairs of our head, still retain their original shape and most minute configurations. A mind led into a train of thinking upon these curious parts of the natural kingdom of God, must enjoy more solid satisfaction, than can be procured from some of the more noisy pursuits in life. These objects, although heedlessly trodden under foot by the rustic and unthinking clown, are far from being useless in medicine, and some of the sciences: they open to the lovers of Natural History an extensive field for the most rational contemplation; and they raise the mind to grand and elevated conceptions of the *Great Creator* and *Preserver* of all things.

THE END.

Index

Agriculture, Kilbride, 180
Agriculture, Rutherglen, 112
Antiquities, Kilbride, 159
Antiquities, Rutherglen, 123ff
Bankhead, 110
Basaltic Rock at Rutherglen, A View, opposite 270
Basket, 153
Blacklaw, 165
Calderwood, 154, 168
Castlehill, 148
Castlemilk antiquities, opposite 160
Castlemilk, 133, 158
Castlemilk, opposite 158
Cathkin Hills, 270
Church of Kilbride, 209
Church, Rutherglen, 80
Church, Rutherglen, details, opposite 80
Coal-works, 120
Contents, vii
Cotton Spinning, 202
Craig-Mulloch, 209
Cross, Rutherglen, 80
Crossbasket, 145, 153
Crosshill, 132
Cummins, 151
Customs of the Burgh of Rutherglen, 45
Drumlaw, 132
Dunlop, Thugirt stone, 88
East Kilbride, 141
Eldrig, 145
Ellwand-Stock, 45, 46
Errata, viii
Fairs, Kilbride, 204
Fairs, Rutherglen, 34

Farme, 109, 134
Farmer Society, 198
Farm-houses, 194
Flakefield
Fossils, 249, 295ff
Four cakes, 94
Funerals, 205
Galloflat, 110
Gill, near Bogton, a table of Strata, 292
Green, Rutherglen, 110
Hamilton Farme, 110
Hammermen, Rutherglen, 77
Herlaw, 213
Hunter, Drs John and William, 175
Indigenous Plants, A List of Scarce, 240
Iron-stone, 203
Irvine, Water of, 146
Kilbarchan, Clochodrig Stone, 88
Kilbride operatives, 201
Kilbride, Parish, 141
Kilbride, village, 147
Kirktounholm. 147
Kittochside Mill, 199
Kittochside, 147
Knocklegoil, 211
Ladles, 45, 46
Lawknow, 215
Lickprivick, 163
Limekilns, 147
Limestone Quarry, 202
Lindsays, 153
Mains of Kilbride, 150, 213
Mains of Kilbride, a Table of Strata, 289
Market-hill, 168
Masons, Rutherglen, 77
Maxwells of Calderwood, 175
Mill of Drips, 199
Mill, Rutherglen Town, 117

Mills, 199
Ministers of Rutherglen, 90
Monk, General J George, 53
Mount Cameron, 165
Muckmiddins, 69
Murrays, a Table of Strata, 290
Names of Most remarkable Places in Kilbride, 178
Names of Places in Rutherglen, A Table, 136
Natural History, 215
Nerston, 213
Parochial Register of Births, Kilbride, 142
Parochial Register of Births, Rutherglen, 122
Piel, 164
Places in Kilbride, Names of Most remarkable, 178
Places in Rutherglen, A Table, 136
Plants, A List of Scarce Indigenous, 240
Preface, iii
Price of labour, Rutherglen, 64
Printfields, Rutherglen,, 118
Provosts, Rutherglen, 104
Public Taxes, 47
Reid of Castlehill, John, 197
Rosebank, 110
Rough-hill, 148
Rutherglen , history of, 1 ff
Rutherglen Bridge, 117
Rutherglen, charters, 5
Rutherglen, Coat of Arms, x
Rutherglen, Commissioners to the Parliament of Scotland, 102
Rutherglen, Constitution, 57
Rutherglen, Magistrates, qualifications for, 63
Rutherglen, Parish, 107
Schools, Rutherglen, 69
Scotstoun, 110
Servants' Wages, 193
Shawfield, 108
Stipend, 91
Stonelaw, 110

Stonelaw, a Table of Strata, 286
Strata at Stonelaw, a Table, 286
Strata in the Gill, near Bogton, 292
Strata in the Murrays, 290
Strata near the Mains of Kilbride, a Table, 289
Strata near Torrance, a Table, 289
Stuart, Alexander, of Torrance, 152
Stuarts of Castlemilk, 156
Stuarts of Torrance, 175
Surnames of Male Heads of Families in Kilbride, A Table, 174
Surnames of Male Heads of Families in Rutherglen, A Table, 137
Three Auld Wives' Lift, 85
Torrance Estate, View, opposite 162
Torrance, 142, 156, 161, 168
Torrance, a Table of Strata, 289
Town-House, Rutherglen, 80
Trades and Manufactures in the parish of Kilbride, 201
Tradesmen, Rutherglen, 118
Trees, 195
Trone, 49
Tumuli, 210
Urn found at Cathkin, opposite 215
Value of money, comparative, 66
Vegetables, 238
Weavers, Rutherglen, 77
West Kilbride, 143
White Cart Water, 146
Wrights, Rutherglen, 77

Printed in the United Kingdom by
Lightning Source UK Ltd., Milton Keynes
138296UK00001B/124/A